Erik Burger

Flexible Views for View-based Model-driven Development

The Karlsruhe Series on Software Design and Quality
Volume 15

Chair Software Design and Quality
Faculty of Computer Science
Karlsruhe Institute of Technology

and

Software Engineering Division
Research Center for Information Technology (FZI), Karlsruhe

Editor: Prof. Dr. Ralf Reussner

Flexible Views for View-based Model-driven Development

by
Erik Burger

KIT Scientific Publishing

Dissertation, Karlsruher Institut für Technologie (KIT)
Fakultät für Informatik
Tag der mündlichen Prüfung: 17. Juli 2014
Referenten: Prof. Dr. Ralf H. Reussner
Prof. Dr. Colin Atkinson (Universität Mannheim)

Impressum

KIT Scientific Publishing

Karlsruher Institut für Technologie (KIT)
KIT Scientific Publishing
Straße am Forum 2
D-76131 Karlsruhe

KIT Scientific Publishing is a registered trademark of Karlsruhe Institute of Technology. Reprint using the book cover is not allowed.

www.ksp.kit.edu

Print on Demand 2014

ISSN 1867-0067
ISBN 978-3-7315-0276-0
DOI: 10.5445/KSP/1000043437

Flexible Views for View-based Model-driven Development

zur Erlangung des akademischen Grades eines

Doktors der Ingenieurwissenschaften

der Fakultät für Informatik
des Karlsruher Instituts für Technologie

genehmigte
Dissertation

von

Erik Burger

aus Mosbach (Baden)

Tag der mündlichen Prüfung: 17. Juli 2014
Erster Gutachter: Prof. Dr. Ralf H. Reussner
Zweiter Gutachter: Prof. Dr. Colin Atkinson (Universität Mannheim)

Abstract

Modern software development faces growing size and complexity of the systems that are being developed. To cope with this complexity, several languages and modelling formalisms are used during the development of a system in order to describe it from various view points and at multiple levels of abstraction. These languages and modeling formalisms are specific to the domain of the system under development, to the paradigms that are followed, and to the developer tools being used. For example, in a component-based process, the software architecture may be defined using a component meta-model, while class diagrams are used for the object-oriented design of the system; performance and reliability models express the extra-functional properties; program code in a general-purpose programming language defines the execution semantics, and is used for the implementation of the system. Although all these artefacts follow different concepts and formalisms, they express the same system from various view points and can thus be understood as *views* on the system under development. The entirety of these views can be identified as a complete definition of the system. Although the usage of multiple formalisms offers the advantage that different developers can describe the system from different view points, and in languages and models that are specially designed for this purpose, it introduces the problem of fragmentation of information across heterogeneous artefacts in different formats, concepts, and languages. With increasing complexity of the systems, this makes navigation through the system description difficult for developers and other roles in the development process. Furthermore, since the concepts and formalisms are managed independently, they can share semantic overlaps, so that a piece of information about the system under development can be expressed in several ways and contexts. For example, while a component model may be used to express the prescriptive software architecture of a system, the implementation in a general-purpose programming language also determines an implicit architecture of the system, which leads to redundancies in the system descriptions. The independent evolution of these artefacts can lead to inconsistencies, which cannot be identified automatically if the semantic correspondances between the artefacts are not modelled explicitly.

View-based software development processes offer two fundamental principles of adressing this problem: While *synthetic approaches* integrate the information of heterogeneous models to form a complete system description, *projective approaches* introduce a common formalism in which all view points of the system can be represented, and generate the views from this central model. While the pure synthetic approach suffers from a quadratic increase of interdependencies between the view types, which become very numerous with a growing number of formalisms that have to be supported, the projective approach faces the problem of providing a common formalism that is able to cover all the view points of the development process, while at the same time providing compatibility to existing formalisms.

The VITRUVIUS approach for view-based software development is based on model-driven technologies and combines the advantages of the projective and synthetic approach, while aiming to reduce the disadvantages. It is based on the concept of *Orthographic Software Modeling* and its core idea that all information about the system under development is represented in a single underlying model (SUM). This concept is refined in the VITRUVIUS approach by constructing metamodels for SUMs as virtual, modular entities that are composed of existing metamodels, and concepts for the semantic correspondances between them. The contribution of this dissertation is an approach for view-based engineering with VITRUVIUS. To that end, this thesis contains a conceptual foundation and a development process for the single underlying model. The development process presented in this dissertation contains a method for the systematic construction of such a modular SUM metamodel for specific development scenarios.

The view types, which are used for retrieval and modification of information in a SUM, hide the modular structure and offer a uniform way of access that makes modifications to the structure of the SUM metamodel possible without having to change the view type structure. The focus of this work and the main contribution is the declarative definition of these view types. This thesis contains the definition of the *flexible views* concept and the supporting *ModelJoin* language. Flexible views offer a compact definition of views at the metamodel and at the instance level, together with information about the editability of elements in the views.

The modular nature of the SUM and the decoupling of view definitions and the underlying model is also beneficial for the evolution of the modular SUM metamodel and the view type definitions, since the impact of changes can be describe in a fine-granular way for sub-metamodels, correpondences, transformations, and existing instances. One contribution of this dissertation is a change metamodel for the description of changes at the metamodel level as well as at the instance level. Based on this metamodel, we have developed a change impact analysis method for changes to Ecore-based metamodels. The method is agnostic of the way in which the change is applied to the metamodel, since it uses a state-based differencing approach to determine deltas between two metamodels, which serve as the basis for a rule-based analysis of change severity.

The view-based VITRUVIUS approach and the flexible view type concept have been validated using a two-step approach: The completeness of the flexible view definition method is demonstrated by showing that the elements of the Ecore metamodel are covered, as well as all possible change operations that can be applied to these elements. The concept of flexible views has been realised in the *ModelJoin* language, for which a prototypical implementation based on EMF, Xtext and QVT-O has been created. In the second step, the VITRUVIUS approach as a whole was validated using case studies in the field of model-driven software development, which combine several established standards in the field of component-based development, such as the Palladio Component Model, UML, and the Java programming language, as well as in the field of automotive and embedded software, using the standards SysML, EAST-ADL, and MATLAB/Simulink.

Kurzfassung

Moderne Software-Systeme weisen eine hohe Komplexität und eine umfangreiche Größe auf. Daher werden in der Entwicklung solcher Systeme mehrere Sprachen und Modelle verwendet, um unterschiedliche Gesichtspunkte und Abstraktionsebenen der Systeme zu beschreiben. Diese Sprachen und Formalismen unterscheiden sich je nach der Domäne des zu entwickelnden Systems, dem jeweiligen Entwicklungsparadigma, sowie den eingesetzten Entwicklungswerkzeugen. Zum Beispiel werden in komponentenbasierten Entwicklungsprozessen Komponentenmodelle zur Beschreibung der Software-Architektur verwendet, Klassendiagramme für den objektorientiertem Entwurf, Performance- und Zuverlässigkeitsmodelle für nichtfunktionale Eigenschaften, und schließlich Programmcode für die Beschreibung der Ausführungssemantik der Software. Obwohl all diesen Artefakten unterschiedliche Konzepte und Formalismen zugrunde liegen, beschreiben sie dasselbe System aus unterschiedlichen Blickwinkeln, und können daher als *Sichten* auf das Software-System verstanden werden. Die Gesamtheit dieser Sichten stellt dabei die vollständige Definition des Systems dar. Während die Aufteilung in unterschiedliche Sichten eine Arbeitsteilung durch verschiedene Entwicklerrollen erlaubt und diesen Entwicklerrollen spezialisierte Sprachen und Modelle für den jeweiligen Entwicklungsschritt bietet, kommt es durch diese Aufteilung jedoch auch zur Fragmentierung der Information über das System in mehrere Entwicklungsartefakte, die in verschiedenen Formaten, Konzepten und Sprachen verfasst sind. Bei steigender Komplexität des Systems erschwert dies die Navigation durch die Entwicklungsartefakte für die Entwickler und andere Rollen im Entwicklungsprozess. Da die unterschiedlichen Konzepte und Formalismen unabhängig voneinander verwaltet werden, ist es möglich, dass sie semantische Überlappungen aufweisen. Eigenschaften des zu entwickelnden Systems können somit auf mehrere Arten und in verschiedenen Kontexten ausgedrückt werden. Während ein Komponentenmodell beispielsweise dazu verwendet werden kann, eine präskriptive Architektur für ein System zu definieren, wird auch durch die Implementierung in Programmcode eine implizite Architektur des Systems definiert. Die unabhängige Weiterentwicklung dieser Artefakte kann zu Inkonsistenzen führen, die nicht automatisch erkannt werden, wenn die semantischen Beziehungen zwischen unterschiedlichen Artefakten nicht explizit modelliert sind.

In sichtenbasierten Software-Entwicklungsprozessen wird dieses Problem auf zwei grundlegende Arten angegangen: Bei *synthetischen Ansätzen* werden die Informationen aus heterogenen Modellen integriert, um eine vollständige Definition des Systems zu erstellen. Bei *projektiven Ansätzen* hingegen wird ein gemeinsamer Formalismus eingeführt, der alle Blickwinkel auf das System abdeckt, und von dem aus Sichten auf das zentrale Modell erstellt werden können. Bei rein synthetischen Ansätzen ergibt sich das Problem, dass die Anzahl der Konsistenzbeziehungen quadratisch mit der Anzahl der Sichten wächst und mit einer steigenden Anzahl von Formalismen somit sehr groß werden kann. Bei projektiven Ansätzen hingegen muss jeweils ein gemeinsamer Formalismus gefunden werden, der alle Schritte des Entwicklungsprozesses abbildet und dennoch die Kompatibilität zu bestehenden Formalismen wahrt.

Der VITRUVIUS-Ansatz zur sichtbasierten Software-Entwicklung basiert auf modellgetriebenen Techniken und kombiniert die jeweiligen Vorteile des projektiven und synthetischen Ansatzes, während die Nachteile der beiden Ansätze vermieden werden sollen. Der Ansatz baut dabei auf der Idee des *Orthographic Software Modelling* (OSM) auf, dass alle Gesichtspunkte eines Software-Systems in einem einzelnen Modell (Single Underlying Model, SUM) ausgedrückt werden, auf das ausschließlich durch benutzerspezifische, automatisch generierte Sichten zugegriffen wird. Da bisherige

Implementierungen des OSM-Ansatzes nicht beschreiben, wie ein solches allumfassendes Modell für Software erstellt werden kann, wird im Rahmen des VITRUVIUS-Ansatzes ein Verfahren entwickelt, mit dem das SUM-Metamodell als modulare Kombination bestehender Metamodelle erzeugt wird, dessen Instanzen automatisch synchronisiert werden. Ein Beitrag dieser Dissertation ist ein Konzept für die sichtbasierte Entwicklung mit VITRUVIUS. Dazu werden die Grundlagen des Konzeptes definiert und ein Entwicklungsprozess für die systematische Konstruktion eines modulare SUM-Metamodells für spezifische Entwicklungsszenarien vorgestellt.

Die Sichten auf das SUM-Metamodell werden durch *Sichttypen* beschrieben und werden für das Extrahieren und Modifizeren von Informationen in einem SUM verwendet. Die Sichttypen kapseln die modulare Struktur des SUM-Metamodells und bieten eine einheitliche Zugriffsmethode auf das SUM, die es ermöglicht, die innere Struktur des SUM-Metamodells zu ändern, ohne die Zugriffsmethode verändern zu müssen. Der Fokus dieser Dissertation liegt auf einer Methode zur deklarativen Beschreibung dieser Sichttypen, welche den Hauptbeitrag der Arbeit bildet. In dieser Arbeit wird das Konzept der *flexiblen Sichttypen (flexible view types)* vorgestellt, das in der textuellen Beschreibungssprache *ModelJoin* realisiert wurde. Flexible Sichttypen bieten eine kompakte Definitionsmethode für die Eigenschaften von Sichten auf Metamodell-Ebene und Instanz-Ebene, sowie Informationen über die Editierbarkeit der Elemente in den Sichten. Die Herausforderungen bestehen dabei darin, die benutzerspezifischen Informationsbedürfnisse so zu erfassen, dass von der Komplexität der zugrundeliegenden Modell-zu-Modell-Transformationen abstrahiert wird.

Aus dem modularen Aufbau des SUMs und der Entkopplung der Sicht-Definitionen von dem zugrundeliegenden Modell ergeben sich Vorteile für die Evolution des modularen SUM-Metamodells und der Sichttyp-Definitionen, da die Auswirkungen von Änderungen auf feingranulare Weise für die einzelnen Elemente (Teil-Metamodelle, Korrespondenzbeziehungen, Transformationen, bestehende Instanzen) beschrieben werden können.

Die automatische Genierung von Metamodellen, Transformationen und Instanzen vermeidet Inkonsistenzen zwischen diesen Artefakten im Fall von Änderungen. Ein weiterer Beitrag dieser Dissertation ist ein Änderungs-Metamodell für die Beschreibung von Änderungen sowohl auf Metamodell-Ebene als auch auf Instanzebene. Basierend auf diesem Metamodell wurde eine Methode zur Änderungs-Auswirkungs-Analyse (change impact analysis) für Ecore-basierte Metamodelle entwickelt. Diese Analysemethode ist unabhängig von der Weise, in der diese Metamodelle verändert werden, da sie auf einer zustandsbasierten Differenzberechnung zwischen zwei Metamodellversionen basiert, die als Grundlage für eine regelbasierte Analyse des Schweregrads der Änderung dient.

Der sichtenbasierte VITRUVIUS-Ansatz und das Konzept der flexiblen Sichttypen wird durch einen zweistufigen Ansatz validiert. Die Vollständigkeit des Konzepts der flexiblen Sichttypen wird durch eine Abdeckungsanalyse für die Elemente des Ecore-Metamodells gezeigt, bei der alle möglichen Änderungsoperationen, die auf Ecore-Elementen ausgeführt werden können, berücksichtigt werden. Weiterhin existiert eine protoypische Implementierung des Konzepts und der *ModelJoin*-Beschreibungssprache, die mit den modellgetriebenen Technologien EMF, Xtext und QVT-O umgesetzt wurde. Im zweiten Schritt wird der VITRUVIUS-Ansatz als ganzes durch Fallbeispiele validiert, die verschiedene modellgetriebene Software-Entwicklungsszenarien und etablierte Standards abdecken. Hierbei wird ein Szenario aus der komponentenbasierten Entwicklung gewählt, das das Palladio-Komponentenmodell, UML und die Programmiersprache Java verwendet, sowie ein Szenario aus der Entwicklung eingebetteter Systeme im Automobilbereich, in dem die Standards SysML, EAST-ADL und MATLAB/Simulink zum Einsatz kommen.

Contents

List of Figures

List of Tables

Listings

1. Introduction

1.1. Motivation

Most of today's software delopment processes make use of models and model-based technologies to cope with the complexity of larger systems by expressing features of the system at a higher level of abstraction. With the extensive use of models in complex systems, these models can themselves grow large and become too complex to be understood by a single developer. Furthermore, with the use of several metamodels, information is spread across instances of metamodels, which are often heterogeneous. Thus, inconsistencies can occur, which lead to drift and erosion between the models and the implementation of the system. To lower the complexity for the developer, partial views on the system restrict the amount of information that is presented to the developer and structure the displaying and manipulation of information. Pre-defined views are however often limited to the information contained in one specific metamodel, and cannot be defined by the developers themselves.

In this dissertation thesis, model-driven development techniques are used to define a view-based modelling approach based on the Orthographic Software Modeling concept by Atkinson et al. [7]. Dynamically created, so called *flexible views* are introduced to help the software developer focus on the parts of the system that are relevant for his or her current role, and offer an abstraction for the rest of the system. They can be defined by the lightweight domain-specific language (DSL) *ModelJoin*, and are part of a novel construction method for the single underlying model (SUM), which is a central prerequisite for any OSM-based approach.

The goal of the approach is to improve software quality by giving developers permanent access to consistent, up-to-date and complete information about the system under development, which is tailored to the information needs of different developer roles (e.g., domain experts, system architects, or software developers). Flexible views are customised to the needs of a single developer and can be defined by the developers themselves. They reduce the complexity by displaying only the type of information that is relevant at the time of modelling, and enable collaborative editing of model artefacts. Flexible views may also be used to hide information and thus to implement access control to parts of a software system.

1.2. Problem Statement

In this section, we will identify the problem areas and challenges in view-based software engineering and will motivate them with an example from component-based software engineering (CBSE).

1.2.1. Situation

In any large software development process, several formalisms, such as programming languages, domain-specific languages and metamodels, are used in the development process to describe the system under development from a specific view point or at an aedequate level of abstraction. Representing information about the software system in domain-specific models and languages has multiple purposes:

- The information is formalised in a *machine-readable* way, which makes it possible to define and check for constraints, and to re-use the information through model transformations.
- Appropriate *levels of abstraction* increase the understandibility of the models for developers.

- Language- or metamodel-specific *tools* offer a convenient way of modelling the software system.

Depending on the development process, some of the artefacts that are created with a specific modelling or programming language have a higher importance than others. In classical software development processes, software models such as component models or UML class diagrams are often seen as only an intermediate step for the creation of the implemention of the system in a general-purpose programming language. *Model-driven development* processes, on the contrary, put models at the centre of attention by making them the primary artefacts of software development [137], and giving them the same importance as executable program code, which is partially generated from model-based artefacts. Since there is, however, not one formalism that can offer the right abstraction level for all phases of a software development process, multiple metamodels and languages are usually applied.

1.2.2. Motivating Example

In Figure 1.1, the usage of multiple formalisms in software development is shown at the example of a component-based software engineering (CBSE) process. The *architecture* of the system is modelled using the Palladio Component Model (PCM) [13] as an architectural description language (ADL). PCM also supports the modelling of performance properties, which are the basis of simulations and analyses. The results of these methods are persisted in the format of the Palladio *sensor framework*. The *object-oriented design* of the system is modelled using UML class diagrams [125]. The class structure of the system refines the architecture: Several classes implement a component, including the composite structure and the interface definitions. The *runtime semantics* of the system are represented in object-oriented Java code, which refines the object-oriented design of the class diagrams.

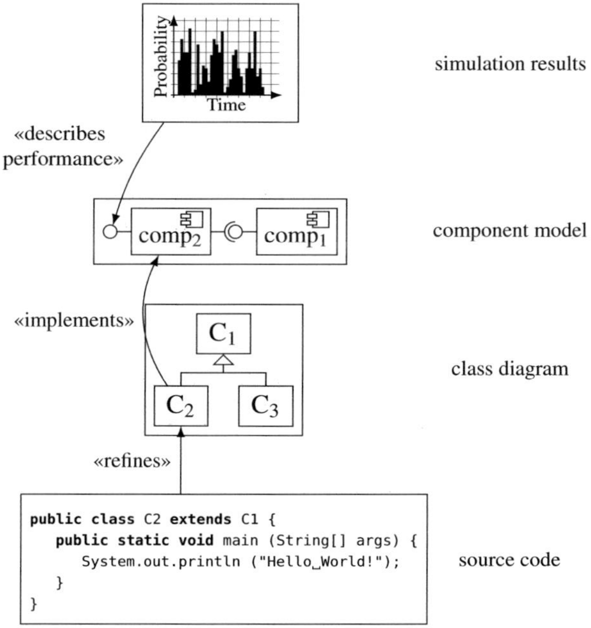

Figure 1.1.: Views in the Component-based Software Engineering Example Scenario

These artefacts represent the system under development from different view points, and are used to describe the same software system, but are developed technically independent of each other. Furthermore, the formalisms do not represent four completely disjoint view points of the system. The four standards that are part of the running example in Figure 1.1 share overlaps and redundancies, as well as implicit correspondences between the elements of the different views: The interfaces and method signatures of UML classes that implement PCM components have to be compatible to the interface definitions of this component. The same is true for the relation of Java classes to UML classes, and, as a transitive consequence, the Java implementation has to be compatible with the interface definitions of the components. Further relations between the architecture and the object-oriented structure of the system exist.

1.2.3. Problem Areas

We have identified the following primary problems, which arise from the usage of heterogeneous models in software development. We will illustrate each of these with the CBSE scenario.

- **Fragmentation:** Different aspects of one entity of the software system are spread over several instances of heterogeneous metamodels. Tracing the model elements that represent the same entity or parts thereof is difficult if elements are edited independently, since the mapping between elements is often not explicitely modelled, but rather depends on common identifiers, or other naming conventions, which are more ambiguous than identifiers. In the example of Figure 1.1, the simulation results refer to the software architecture in the component model, but are stored in an independent metamodel. In this case, the design decision to separate the models has been taken deliberately to keep the component metamodel free of performance-specific elements. Here, the overlap is minimal since simulation results of the sensor framework refer to assembly contexts in instances of the PCM through textual identifiers.

- **Redundancy:** The same piece of information is represented in multiple artefacts of heterogeneous formalisms. Although redundancy may be a desired property in some development scenarios, it is one of the reasons for inconsistencies in a system description. In the example, there is high redundancy between the class diagram and the object-oriented source code, since the object-oriented design, such as the class inheritance structure, element naming, and features, is expressed in both UML and Java. Further redundancies exist between the component model and code: the (normative) architecture of the system is defined in the component model. The implementation in Java, however, also defines an (implicit) software architecture. In both cases, the semantic overlap is high.

- **Inconsistency:** Inconsistencies between the artefacts can arise if they are modified independently and not synchronised manually. They occur since the artefacts share a semantic relation or overlap that is not formally defined, and for which consistency constraints are not available, so they cannot be checked automatically. In the example of Figure 1.1, inconsistencies lead to drift and erosion between the software architecture, the object-oriented design, and the implementation. Inconsistency can occur in two ways: First, if there is redundant information in the models, modifications have to be applied to all elements that represent the entity under modification. If only a subset of the models is modified, inconsistencies occur. For example, modifications to the Java code can violate the prescriptive architecture of the component model, if a class calls a method in another class, although this is not expressed by an interface definition in the component model. Second, if there are semantic relations between the elements that are not formalised and checked automatically, inconsistencies can occur if this relation is violated. For example, the simulation results in the example refer to a component by a common identifier. If the component is deleted, the simulation results become obsolete since there is no element with a matching identifier.

- **Complexity:** In large systems, the models of the software can grow so big that single developers cannot understand them in their entirety, and navigating the models becomes a time-consuming and frustrating task [52]. To satisfy the information need of developers, only parts of these models are of relevance, so there should be a means of selecting and displaying only these elements.

In addition to the main problem areas that we have just stated, we have also identified secondary problems, which apply to software engineering in general. These problems are not in the main focus of our research, but are affected by the view-based engineering approach.

- **Collaboration** Since most software projects are not developed by a single group of persons, they have to be partitioned so that different groups of developers can work on parts of the project. This applies especially to physically distributed projects, but also to projects that are developed at the same site but by several teams. The partitioning of software is however often quite inflexible and has to be adapted frequently if there are changes in the organizational structure of the development project or if new functional requirements are added. It would thus be desirable if developers (or any other role in the development process) could work on parts of the system that are relevant to his current interests without being limited by the borders of the modelling formalisms or programming language used. Of course, this should also be possible if several individuals are working on the system simultaneously. The latter is well supported in the implementation phases of the software development process, but not during architecture and OO-design of the system. Furthermore, the use of heterogeneous models in the different development phases induces problems of traceability and evolution; it is hard to identify what effect changes to code or OO-design will have on the software architecture.

- **Access control** could also be a reason for restricted views, e.g. in an outsourcing scenario where a certain group of developers should only be allowed to see the part of the system that is relevant to them, whereas other parts should be hidden in order to protect intellectual property, as is practised with databases, where views are also used for access control. Nevertheless, even developer groups of outsourcing partners should be included in all stages of development, which means that they should also be able to contribute to a system's architecture without gaining too much knowledge about the system that could be used in harmful way.

1.3. Approach

In this thesis, we present a view-based model-driven software development approach, which is based on the concept of Orthographic Software Modeling (OSM) [7], and which contributes to the VITRUVIUS approach [26, 95, 104]. The VITRUVIUS approach aims to realise the concept of the Single Underlying Model (SUM) of OSM by combining existing metamodels into a virtual, modular metamodel with information on the synchronisation between these parts. To our knowledge, VITRUVIUS is the first approach that aims to describe a systematic process for the creation of a SUM metamodel. The modular structure of the virtual SUM metamodel requires a special method for the definition of the view types, which serve as the exclusive interfaces by which the contents of a SUM can be accessed and modified.

1.4. Envisioned Benefits

Software Quality The goal of our approach is to improve software quality by giving developers access to consistent, up-to-date and complete information about the system under development, tailored to the information needs of different developer roles, e.g., domain experts, system architects, or software developers. Flexible views are customised to the needs of a single developer, and can be defined by the developers themselves. They reduce the complexity by displaying only the type of information that is relevant at the time of modelling.

Access Control A separation of views can be used to create a fine-grained access control mechanism for models without having to change or re-structure the model itself. For each role in the access control mechanism, a rule set should be defined that controls the set of elements that are displayed in the views that are adjacent to the respective role. Elements can also be subsumed into new elements at a higher level of abstraction or granularity.

Collaborative MDSD If flexible views are integrated into a collaboration workflow, the abstraction levels and access control methods can be used to enable distributed editing of parts of the model. The development process can contain a role that is analogous to that of the *methodologist* in the OSM approach, which is responsible for the definition of restricted, editable views.

The frequency of view updates can be adapted for different scenarios. In a completely real-time online scenario, changes to the underlying model are propagated to all views immediately, which is useful if the editors involved in the process are in contact via other means of communication, e.g. telephone. At the other extreme of possible update frequency, a classical check-in/check-out mechanism can be installed; mixtures of these two paradigms could also be implemented.

Metamodel Federation Flexible views support the displaying and editing of objects from heterogeneous metamodels. This would normally require the definition of a seperate "glue" metamodel that references elements from the original metamodels. With the rule set of a flexible view, displaying objects from heterogeneous models is possible in an easier way.

Usability of Modeling Tools If only certain parts or aspects of a model have to be edited, the complexity of a large model can be confusing to an editing person who only wants to see certains aspects of the model. With flexible views, the complexity of such a model could be abstracted in view types that are more intuitive to the editing developer.

Metamodel and view evolution Since views are treated as first-class entities in the proposed approach, they can evolve on their own and have to be maintained. While this introduces a higher maintenance effort at first, it has the advantage that the view type and the underlying metamodels can evolve independently. A change to the metamodel does not necessarily cause a change in the view type. Thus, developers and user can continue with the same formalisms and use the same tools, reducing maintenance effort since the tools do not have to be adapted. On the other hand, the effort of evolving the bi-directional transformations between views and the underlying model can also be high and should not be underestimated.

1.5. Contributions

We will list the contribution of this dissertation thesis here. The contributions of this thesis can be arranged in three groups:

Systematic Process for VITRUVIUS: The view-centric VITRUVIUS approach is currently developed by several researchers in the Software Design and Quality group at KIT. The goal of VITRUVIUS is to deliver a systematic construction process for a metamodel for Single Underlying Metamodels (SUM) of the Orthographic Software Modeling method. The contribution of this thesis to the VITRUVIUS approach is a formal specification of the core concepts in VITRUVIUS, such as the single underlying model and its metamodel, correspondences between sub-metamodels, and the relation between view types and the modular metamodel. Furthermore, a development process for VITRUVIUS has been developed, which describes the transition of software development with independent formalisms to the VITRUVIUS-based process.

Metamodel and Model Evolution For the description of changes to metamodels and models, this thesis contains an change metamodel that can be used for a unified representation of changes both at the metamodel level and the model level. Furthermore, a change impact analysis for changes to Ecore-based metamodels, based on the change metamodel and a state-based analysis of different metamodel versions, is presented.

Flexible View Types The definition of view types on a modular SUM metamodel poses special requirements on the description formalism. The flexible view types concept, which is presented in this thesis, offers a compact definition of the types of elements that can occur in a view, the selection of elements in an actual view, as well as information on how these elements can be modified, and how modifications are propagated back to the model. Besides the abstract definition of the concept, the ModelJoin language is presented, which offers a declarative description mechanism for flexible views. The formal definition of the semantics of this language is a contribution of this thesis.

1.6. Structure of the Thesis

This dissertation is strucured as follows: In chapter 2, we will present the technologies and concepts on which the approach is built, most importantly the *Orthographic Software Modeling* approach by Atkinson et al. Related work is described in chapter 3.

The first major contribution of this dissertation will be the definition of a construction process for the *single underlying model (SUM)* as part of the VITRUVIUS approach. We will describe our concept of a *modular SUM* in chapter 4.

The evolution of metamodels and models in VITRUVIUS will be discussed in chapter 5.

The second contribution is the concept of *flexible views*, which will be presented in chapter 6. For the realisation of this concept, the *ModelJoin* language has been developed and has been implemented prototypically. We will describe the design of the language and its realisation.

We will discuss scenarios for the validation of our approach in chapter 7. The thesis closes with a look at future work and the next steps in chapter 8, and the conclusion in chapter 9.

2. Foundations and State-of-the-art

In this chapter, we will present the conceptual and technical foundations on which this thesis is based. First, we will give an overview of view-based software development approaches and standards in section 2.1. In section 2.2, we will introduce the model-driven development paradigm and the OMG standards that are part of the Model-Driven Architecture (MDA), followed by a description of the Eclipse Modeling Framework and the Ecore metamodel in section 2.3. The *Orthographic Software Modeling* approach is presented in section 2.4. A short explanation of the notational conventions in this thesis (section 2.5) concludes this chapter.

2.1. View-based Software Development

2.1.1. Concept

The concept of *view-based software development* goes back even before the era of object-oriented languages. It can be traced back until 1985, when Wood-Harper [157] presented the multiview approach. The term *ViewPoint* was coined by Finkelstein et al. in the early 1990s to describe the structuring of software in certain methods, languages, formalisms and work plans:

> [A ViewPoint] is a loosely coupled, locally managed object which encapsulates partial knowledge about the system and domain, specified in a particular, suitable representation scheme, and partial knowledge of the process of design. [49, sect. 3]

Recently, the terms view and view point have been specified for software architecture engineering. The IEEE 1471/ISO 42010 standard [76, 77], which was finalised in 2011, contains a definition for the terms *architecture view* and *architecture viewpoint*. The term *architecture view* is defined as a "work product expressing the architecture of a system from the perspective of specific system concerns", and *architecture viewpoint* is defined as a "work product establishing the conventions for the construction, interpretation and use of architecture views to frame specific system concerns" [77]. These conventions may include "languages, notations, model kinds, design rules, and/or modelling methods, analysis techniques and other operations on views". In addition to these terms, the term *model kind* is introduced as "conventions for a type of modelling".

The usage of the term *metamodel* in the ISO 42010 standard deviates from the understanding of the term in model-driven development, for example as defined by the OMG [117]. Hilliard [74] has debated the usage of this term in the ISO standard. He has concluded that the ISO standard contains a *conceptual* model for architecture, which is expressed as a metamodel, but that existing architectural frameworks share a different notion, even although claming conformance to ISO 42010.

The ISO standard also differentiates between *synthetic* and *projective* view-based approaches:

> In the synthetic approach, an architect constructs views of the system-of-interest and integrates these views within an architecture description using model correspondences. In the projective approach, an architect derives each view through some routine, possibly mechanical, procedure of extraction from an underlying repository. [77, sect. A.4]

The IEEE 1471/ISO 42010 standard [76, 77] gives only a broad definition of the terms view and viewpoint. Most importantly, no distinction is made between the metamodel level and the instance level of views. The standard contains the term *model kind*, which can be understood as the metamodel of a view. We will use the more precise definition of Goldschmidt et al. [58,

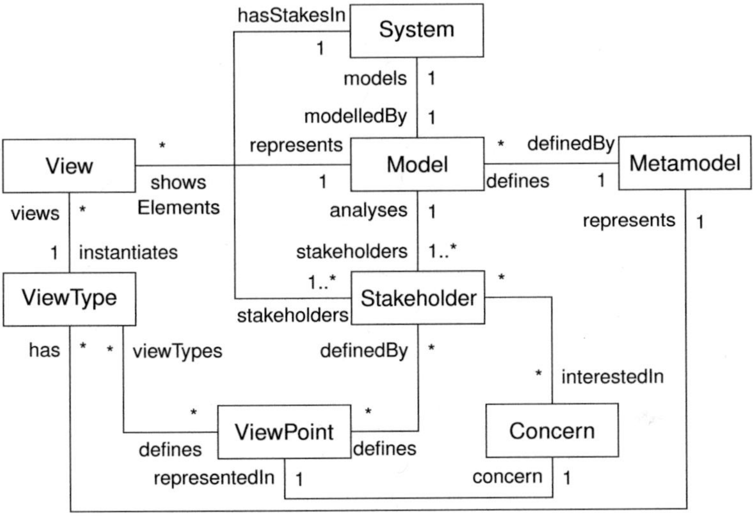

Figure 2.1.: Terminology for *view, view type* and *view point* (from [57])

57], which we have rephrased into Definition 1. The full terminology is displayed in Figure 2.1.

Definition 1. *A* view type *defines the set of metaclasses whose instances a view can display. It comprises a definition of a concrete syntax plus a mapping to the abstract metamodel syntax. The actual* view *is an instance of a view type showing an actual set of objects and their relations using a certain representation. A* view point *defines a concern.*

In UML, for example, diagram types such as sequence or class diagrams would be view types. A view is an actual diagram containing classes *A*, *B* and *C*. The static architecture or dynamic aspects of a system are characterised as view points of UML by Definition 1.

The main difference of this definition to the IEEE/ISO standard is the introduction of the term *view type*, which can be interpreted as a metamodel for actual views. Goldschmidt also defines different notions for completeness and partiality of view types and views, such as containment-completeness, selectional completeness, and a definition for overlaps of view types [58, sect. 4.4].

A developer will rarely use a complete view on a system because it is often too complex and tends to be confusing. This is why today's software modelling tools offer possibilities to restrict a view to certain elements; the possibilities for creating custom views are however limited to the selection mechanisms implemented in the tools, so that often only a manual selection of elements is possible. The idea of restricted views for developers goes back to the 1990s [49, 98, 131]. Today's model-driven techniques, such as model transformations and the support for textual syntaxes, offer new perspectives for model-driven view-based approaches.

2.1.2. Challenges of View-Based Approaches

The problem fields mentioned in subsection 1.2.3 are addressed in the field of multi-viewpoint modelling by presenting information to developer in specific views, which contain only the pieces of information that are of interest to the developer in a familiar formalism. These partial views reduce the complexity for the single developers, but raise other problems that are rooted in the inherent complexity of the definition and generation of view types.

The challenges of these view-based approaches do not apply to all kinds of approaches in the same way. Thus, we differentiate the challenges here by the type of approach (projectional, synthetic, see section 2.1). The challenges that we have identified for view-based approaches are:

- **Synchronisation:** With a growing number of views, synthetic approaches suffer from the complexity of synchronising information across the views, since the number of synchronisation relations grows quadratically with the number of views. Although not all views have to be synchronised with every other view, adding a view means that the effects of this view are to be determined for each of the other views, which does not scale well if a high number of views exists, and which always requires a modification of the complete set of views if a view is added.

- **Common Metamodel:** Projectional approaches avoid the problem of synchronisation complexity at the cost of having to define a formalism for a central model that covers all view points. Thus, the synchronisation relations only grow linearly with the number of views. The metamodel for this central model, however, has to be created for each development scenario and the combination of view types that are required in the scenario. If a fixed metamodel is defined a priori, the domains where the approach can be applied are limited by the expressional powers of this metamodel. On the other hand, if a metamodel has to be created from scratch for every scenario, the effort of instantiating a view-based process is very high, and re-usability is low since the metamodel can be used only for the specific scenario.
- **Compatibility:** Existing languages and metamodels must be supported in a view-based development process, either because of existing software tools and model transformations, or because compliance to a certain standard is required by external factors, such as legal regulations. Often, it is not possible to alter metamodels or language definitions, so they have to be supported without modifications, or an import/export function has to be included that offers compatibility to the standards.

Since these challenges apply to every software development process, we will differentiate the challenges by those which are caused by the *essential* or *accidental complexity* of the problem, as defined by Brooks [80].

Essential Complexity If a software development process involves several formalisms whose artefacts have to be synchronised, the relations between these artefaccts have to be made explicit, and the effects of changes to one of the artefacts on the other artefacts have to be formalised. View-based approaches cannot eliminate this kind of complexity. It is, however, possible, to shift the complexity away from developer and support them with a framework that offers means for synchronisation.

If a projectional approach is chosen, the definition of a common metamodel or language that covers all the information of interest is a problem that adds to the inherent complexity of the approaches. Finding the right abstraction level for the common metamodel is a difficult task: If the metamodel is to specific, the re-use in scenarios that are similar to the one for which it was defined is hindered; if it is too general, the expressivity of the models may be insufficient, and too much of the logic has to be put into the transformations to view types and other metamodels.

Accidental Complexity Accidental complexity in view-based approaches is caused by the multiple formalisms, which are the base of the view types. Although the usage of different formalisms helps to analyse the various properties of a software system, it also aggravates the problem of recognizing the semantic relations between the respective artefacts of the languages. Furthermore, not all information is persisted in well-defined, formal languages. Semantic relations between existing, formally defined artefacts may be or may not be known to the developers, and are often, if at all, only defined in natural language documents. This hinders the traceability of elements across heterogeneous formalisms, which is a necessary precondition for automatic support in synchronising the artefacts.

Furthermore, the definition of view types, views and the synchronisation policies requires the development of several artefacts (such as metamodels, transformations and tools) that have to be maintained manually, since there are no standardised languages for the description of view types and their synchronisation behaviour.

2.2. Model-Driven Development

2.2.1. Concept

Model-driven development (MDD), also called *Model-driven engineering (MDE)*, is a software development paradigma that raises the abstraction level in comparison to third-generation programming languages. The model-driven development process puts models in the centre of attention and gives them the status of primary development artefacts, in comparison to other development processes, where models serve only as intermediate artefacts for the development of program code, or for the documentation of software systems.

Model-driven development is essentially the combination of two concepts [137]: First, *domain-specific languages (DSL)* offer means for the expression of domain concepts to reduce the complexity in the modelling of systems. In contrast to general-purpose textual languages, which are usually defined using a grammar definition, domain-specific languages are defined using metamodels, which themselves are defined using a standardised, fixed meta-metamodel. Second, *transformations engines* are used to transform these models into instances of other domain-specific languages (model-to-model-transformation), or into textual representations (model-to-text-transformation) of other formalisms, which can again be programming languages, or textual data formats.

A core paradigma of model-driven development is the representation of all concepts and entities as model, often called "Everything is a model" [16]. The precise definition of the term "model" is often neglected in the specification of model-based or model-driven approaches. The common model theory of Stachowiak [144, sect. 2.1.1] is an appropriate foundation of the model notion in model-driven development. According to Stachowiak, a model has three main properties: First, models are *representations* of natural or artificial originals, which can themselves be models; second, models do not capture all attributes of the original that they represent, but are *reductions* that only contain the attributes that are relevant to the creator or user of the model; third, models are always tied to a certain purpose *(pragmatism)*.[1]

Bézivin [16] has also identified *representation* as one of the core concepts of model-driven engineering, which is given between a model and the system that it represents. The second core concept is the concept of *conformance*, which is the relation between a models and the metamodel. Bézivin argues that models should not be seen as *instances* of metamodels, since the semantics of conformance differ to the instantiation principle in object-oriented languages. Atkinson et al. [6] have developed this differentiation further by distinguishing the *ontological* classification (to which the instantiation relation belongs) from the *linguistic* classfication of elements (of which conformance is an example).

A key benefit of model-driven development is the possibility to define domain-specific languages and generate appropriate tooling rapidly and comparably easily. Developers can use several modelling languages in the different phases of a software development process, like models for requirements engineering, architecture and object-oriented design, specialised models depending on the domain for which the software is being developed, and code for the implementation and runtime behaviour of system, which can also be seen as a model.

During the model-driven development of an actual software system, several of these languages can be used, which may differ in the level of abstraction and the type of modelled information, but should essentially represent the same system. Developers have to take manual steps to achieve synchronisation of information across these models. This is why developers usually work in only one kind of model at a time.

[1] These concepts have been originally defined by Stachowiak in German as "Abbildungsmerkmal" (representation), "Verkürzungsmerkmal" (reduction), and "Pragmatisches Merkmal" (pragmatism). Translation by the author of this thesis.

2.2.2. Model-Driven Architecture

The model-driven architecture (MDA) standard has been defined by the Object Management Group (OMG) [112]. It describes the development of software systems using OMG's own standards such as UML [125], MOF [117], QVT [116], OCL [123], and others. In the MDA standards document, the terms *view* and *viewpoint* are used in the same way as in the ISO standard. The MDA standard thus specifies three view points (written as "viewpoint"): *computation independent viewpoint, platform independent viewpoint*, and *platform specific viewpoint* with the accompanying models *computation independent model (CIM), platform independent model (PIM)*, and *platform specific model (PSM)*. The more specific models are derived from the more abstract models by refinement, during which the step from PIM to PSM should ideally be performed by automatic transformations.

In this subsection, we will shortly describe the standards and models of MDA that are relevant in the further course of this thesis.

2.2.2.1. Unified Modelling Language (UML)

The Unified Modelling Language (UML) was developed in the 1990s as a graphical description language for the development of software systems [18]. As such, it precedes the conception of model-driven software development. Originally developed at Rational Software, it is now managed by the Object Management Group and has been established as the ISO/IEC standard 19505.

In the current version 2.4.1 [125], the UML specification contains 14 types of diagrams, called *language units*. In are recent survey [100], which investigated 121 UML models, UML class diagrams have been identified as the most frequently used diagram type by far (used in 100% of the investigated models), followed by use case diagrams (47%), and interaction diagrams (39%).

2.2.2.2. Meta-Object Facility (MOF)

The Meta-Object Facility (MOF) [117] is a language for the definition of domain-specific languages. The MOF standard was defined by the OMG as a most general metamodel, which is suited for the definition of arbitrary languages. It can be seen as a generalization of UML, and today serves as the metamodel in which the UML metamodel is described. Due to its high genericity, the MOF metamodel is self-descriptive, and can thus be understood as conforming to itself, in terms of ontological classification.

In the current version 2.4.1, the MOF standard specifies two flavours of the MOF language: Complete MOF (CMOF) and Essential MOF (MOF). While CMOF is supposed to be used for more sophisticated metamodelling purposes, EMOF offers a simpler and pragmatic standard, which is compatible to serialization formats and programming interfaces such as XMI [158] and JMI [81].

2.2.2.3. Modelling Layers and Instantiation Potencies

The MOF standard defines the fixed number of four meta-levels (M3-M0), where elements at the lower levels conform to elements of the next higher level. Figure 2.2 illustrates this with the WebGUI component from the running example, modelled in PCM. Since instatiation is only possible between neigbouring layers, the concepts of higher levels cannot be instantiated or modified if there is more than one meta-level between the elements. For example, the Ecore metamodel contains an EAnnotation element with which M2 elements, such as classes, attributes, or packages, can be annotated. Since the class EAnnotation is at the M3 level, it can be instantiated in an M2 metamodel, but not at deeper levels. If it is desired to use annotations at the M1 level, they have to be specified seperately in the respective metamodel.

In the implementations of MOF, such as JMI [81] and EMF [47], this is realised by the instantiation mechanism of Java, which has two levels of instantiation: Class level and object level. Depending on the context, an element of, e.g., the M2 level can be a obtained as a class or as an object; reflection operations are used to "lift" an element between the the two metamodelling levels. The mixture of the ontological and linguistical classification in these implementations further adds to the misunderstandings and complications that can arise during modelling.

In contrast to modelling with fixed layers, *multi-level modelling* [6] offers concepts for the definition of deep instantiation, which make the aforementioned observations explicit by equipping each element with a number of levels across which it can be instantiated, called *potency*. A potency of 2 of an element expresses, for example, that the element can be instantiated as an element, which can have instances of its own. In the example of Figure 2.2, the elements are based on Ecore, so the potencies are "hard-wired" by the definition of the Ecore meta-metamodel and the instantiation mechanisms. In Figure 2.2, we have added the potencies to illustrate these conventions.

In the Ecore metamodel, EClass and EStructuralFeature (and its subtypes) are the only concepts that have a potency of 2. All other concepts in Ecore, such as inheritance, composition, definitions of abstractness of classes, and so on, are elements that can only be instantiated once at the metamodel (M2) level. As explained above, it is not directly possible to use these concepts with M1 instances.

To analyse differences between instances, we have to determine which kinds of edit operations can be applied to instances of Ecore-based metamodels. Thus, we have to regard the elements of Ecore that can be instantiated twice, across two meta-levels. In the running example of Figure 1.1, there are four metamodels involved, which can all be expressed as instances of the MOF metamodel. For example, the class EClass in Ecore is instantiated as the class BasicComponent in the PCM metamodel. The class BasicComponent can be instantiated as the component WebGUI in a PCM instance.

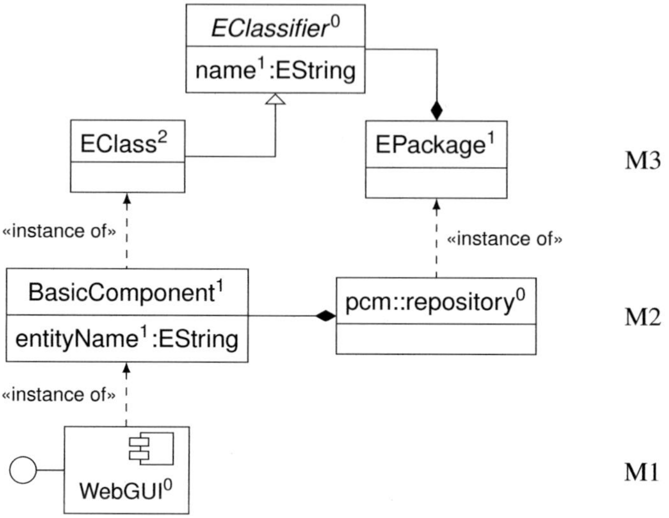

Figure 2.2.: Example: PCM Component with Excerpts from the PCM Metamodel and Ecore, Annotated With Multi-Level Modelling Potencies

The class BasicComponent contains attributes and references, which are instances of the Ecore class EAttribute and EReference. For example, BasicComponent contains the attribute entityName (inherited from NamedElement), which is instantiated as the String `WebGUI` in the PCM instance.

The instances of Eclass instances can be created and deleted, and their features can be set, changed, and unset. This is the most generic description of editability of instances of Ecore-based metamodels (see also Figure 2.2).

2.3. Eclipse Modeling Framework (EMF)

The Eclipse Modeling Framework (EMF) is a development framework for model-driven development that is implemented using the Java-based Eclipse platform. The EMF project[2] encompasses several sub-projects for managing, querying and transforming model-based data.

[2] `http://www.eclipse.org/modeling/emf/`, retrieved 13 May 2014

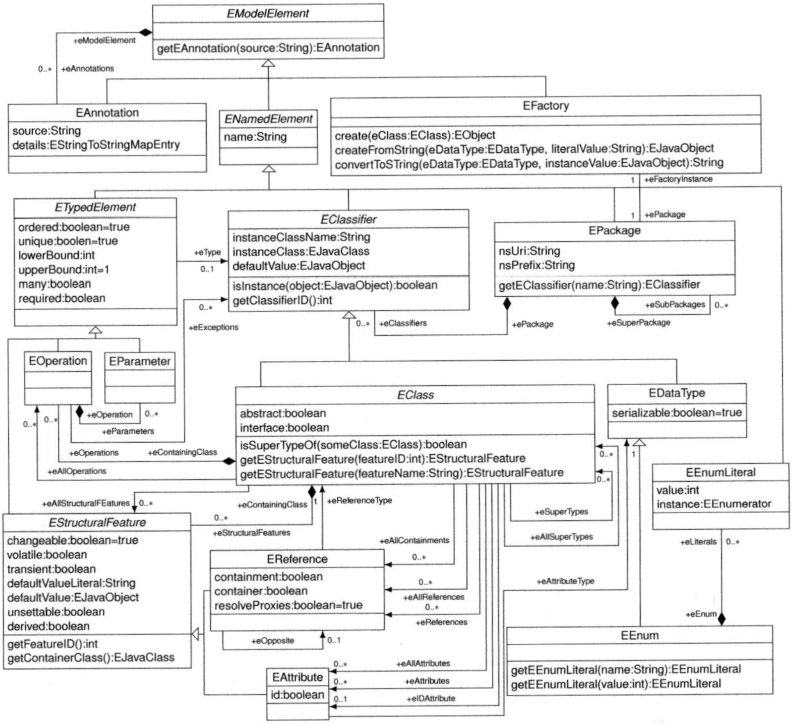

Figure 2.3.: Main Components of the Ecore Metamodel

In the following subsections, we will describe the *Ecore* meta-metamodel, which is part of the Eclipse Modeling Workbench. After that, we will adapt a set-based notation for MOF-based metamodels, so that it can be used with Ecore-based metamodels.

2.3.1. The Ecore Metamodel

The Ecore metamodel can be seen as the most popular implementation of the MOF standard. Originally created as an alternative to the flawed MOF 1.4 standard, some concepts of Ecore have been integrated in the newer

2.0 versions of Essential MOF, which is a pragmatic and more compact alternative to the Complete MOF standard. Perhaps most notably, Ecore does not contain a concept for *associations* between classes as first-order elements. Instead, Ecore only implements the concept of *references*, which are contained in classes and thus share the same life-cycle. Furthermore, Ecore metamodels have to be organised in a rigid containment hierarchy with a single root element.

Ecore is, in most points, aligned with EMOF. The documentation of Ecore describes it as a "dialect of UML".[3] The Eclipse Modeling Framework contains an Ecore-based UML metamodel, which can be used to create instances of UML, and which is the base of Ecore-based UML modelling tools, such as Papyrus.[4]

The core components of Ecore are displayed in Figure 2.3: As mentioned above, the EReference element is a structural feature that is always contained in an EClass element. While EReferences are typed with other EClass elements, EAttributes are typed with EDataTypes. This is a main difference to the MOF 1.4 standard, where class-typed attributes were possible.

2.3.2. Set Notation of Ecore Metamodels

The OCL standard [123, Appendix A] contains a set notation for MOF metamodels, which we will use in this thesis for the formalisation of metamodelling concepts. The OCL notation is based on MOF 2.0. Since the VITRUVIUS approach is based on the Ecore meta-metamodel and the EMF framework, we have modified this set notation so that it fits the properties of the Ecore metamodel. The elements of the notation are listed in Table 2.1.

Most of the concepts of MOF are also valid in Ecore. We can use, without adaption, the definition of types and classes. The definition of attributes has been adapted since EAttributes can only be typed with EDataTypes, but not

[3] `http://download.eclipse.org/modeling/emf/emf/javadoc/2.9.0/org/eclipse/emf/ecore/package-summary.html`, retrieved 13 May 2014

[4] `http://www.eclipse.org/papyrus`, retrieved 14 May 2014

with EClassifiers. While associations in MOF are first-class entities, which can also have more than two association ends, Ecore only has the concept of references (EReference), which have to be contained in an Eclass, and which have only two ends (the eContainingClass and the eReferenceType). The term *system state* in the OCL definition denotes the set of instances of the metamodels, and can be used to describe instances of Ecore metamodels.

Since the metamodel definition in the OCL standard is based on the notion of associations rather then references, we will redefine the term metamodel here, so that it fits the Ecore definition.

Definition 2 (Metamodel). *A* metamodel *is a structure*

$$M := (\textsc{Class}, \textsc{Att}, \textsc{Ref}, \textit{associates}, \textit{multiplicites}, \prec)$$

The sets $\textsc{Class}$, $\textsc{Att}$, and $\textsc{Ref}$ are described in Table 2.1. The set of references $\textsc{Ref}$ replaces the set of associations $\textsc{Assoc}$ of the OCL specification. The relation *associates* describes the signature of these references, while relation *multiplicites* describes the cardinality of features, i.e., attributes and references.

Note that the elements $c, c' \in \textsc{Class}$ represent class names; hence, $c = c'$ expresses that the (simple) names of two elements are identical, but not object identity. The identity of classes is expressed by the identity of their types: $t_c = t_{c'}$.

Type system The OCL standard contains generalization hierarchy $\prec$ with the reflexive extension $\preccurlyeq$. The sets $\textsc{Att}_c$ and $\textsc{Ref}_c$ contain the attributes and associations for a class c. The sets $\textsc{Att}^*_c$ and $\textsc{Ref}^*_c$ additionally contain the attributes and associations inherited from all superclasses of c.

The OCL standard contains the primitive types *UnlimitedNatural*, *Integer*, *Real*, *Boolean*, and *String*. The operator $=_t$ only allows the comparison of elements of the exact same type, so it is not possible to compare e.g. integers

$\mathscr{M}$	Metamodels (see Definition 2)
CLASS	Class names with a generalization hierarchy $\prec$
$\mathscr{N}$	Named elements, $\mathscr{N} = \text{CLASS} \cup \mathscr{T} \cup \text{ATT} \cup \text{REF}$
$\mathscr{T}$	Type names where $t_c \in \mathscr{T}$ is the type of a class $c \in \text{CLASS}$
$\mathscr{T}_B$	Hard-coded basic (=primitive) type names; $\mathscr{T}_B = \{\mathit{UnlimitedNatural}, \mathit{Integer}, \mathit{Real}, \mathit{Boolean}, \mathit{String}\} \subset \mathscr{T}$
ATT	Attribute signatures. The set of attribute signatures ATT_c of a class $c \in \text{CLASS}$ is defined as $a : t_c \to t; t \in \mathscr{T}_B$.
REF	Reference names
REF_c	References of a class $c \in \text{CLASS}$. A reference has a signature $\mathit{associates}(r) = \langle c, c' \rangle \in \text{CLASS} \times \text{CLASS}$
$\mathit{multiplicities}()$	Cardinality of attribute signatures and references. The function $\mathit{multiplicites}(a) = N$ assigns each attribute or reference a non-empty set $N \subseteq \mathbb{N}_0$ with $N \neq \{0\}$
$I(e) = \{\underline{e}_1, \underline{e}_2, \ldots\}$	Possible instances of an element $e \in \mathscr{N}$. The instances of classes, attributes, and references are called *objects*, *attribute values*, and *links*.
$I_*(c)$	For a class c, $I(c)$ is the set instances of c and all its subclasses. The set $I_*(c)$ contains direct instances only.
$\mathscr{I} = \bigcup_{e \in \mathscr{N}} I(e)$	all possible instances
$\sigma_{\text{CLASS}}, \sigma_{\text{ATT}}, \sigma_{\text{REF}}$	Snapshot functions that return all instances of a given class, attribute or reference, together forming the *system state*
$L(r)(\underline{c}_1) \subseteq I(c_2)$	Instances that are linked to $\underline{c}_1 \in I(c_1)$ via a reference r with the signature $\mathit{associates}(r) = \langle c_1, c_2 \rangle$

Table 2.1.: Sets and Functions in the Set Notation of Ecore

with real numbers. We weaken this requirement and allow coercion for the number types *UnlimitedNatural*, *Integer*, and *Real*.

Helper functions Several helper functions are defined in the OCL standard to ease the usage of the formal definition. We list the functions that will be used later in this thesis below:

- $parents() : \text{CLASS} \rightarrow \mathscr{P}(\text{CLASS})$ returns all superclasses of a given class;
- $class() : \mathscr{I}_{\text{CLASS}} \rightarrow \text{CLASS}$ returns the name of the most special class of which an object is an instance.

2.3.3. Textual Domain-Specific Languages

Recent textual concrete syntax frameworks such as Xtext[5] and EMFText [66] offer a convenient way of defining textual syntaxes for Ecore-based metamodels. These approaches suffer, however, from the synchronisation with other concrete syntaxes of the models, since formatting information may be lost if models are edited in other editors and re-opened in a textual editor; if models are edited in the textual editor, renaming and move operations must be detected so that unwanted deletions and creations of model elements are avoided. The FURCAS approach of Goldschmidt [56] is based on MOF 1.4 and offers algorithms for the detection and synchronisation of such cases. The approach furthermore supports the definition of partial and overlapping textual view types.

Framework-specific languages (FSML) [2] offer the usage of application programming interfaces (API) with specialised modelling languages. In contrast to model-driven engineering, the models are supporting artefacts, which assist developers in code-based development; they can be generated by reverse engineering and can be discarded rapidly if not needed anymore.

[5] `http://www.eclipse.org/Xtext/`, retrieved 26 May 2014

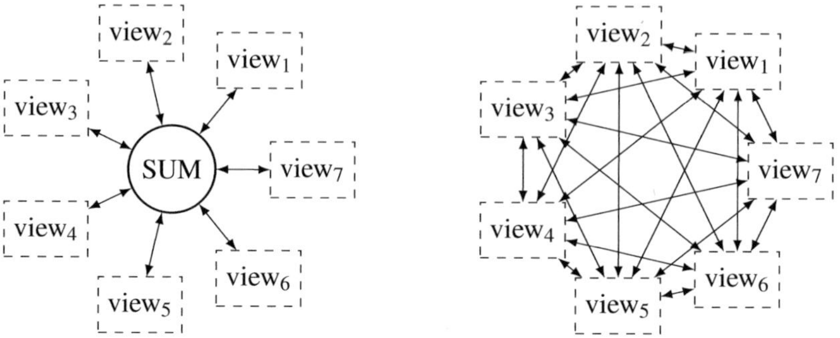

Figure 2.4.: Hub-and-Spoke vs. Peer-to-Peer

2.4. Orthographic Software Modeling

With the *Orthographic Software Modeling (OSM)* [7] approach, Atkinson et al. aim to establish views as first-class entities of the software engineering process. In the envisioned view-centric development process, all information about a system is represented in a single underlying model (SUM); thus, the SUM even transcends the function of being a model, but becomes the system itself. This makes the approach somewhat radical, as even source code is treated as only a special textual view. The SUM itself has to contain all execution semantics and could theoretically also be executed without the use of source code.

The OSM concept is based on three principles [7]:

1. Dynamic View Generation
2. Dimension-based View Navigation
3. View-oriented Methods

The authors of OSM suggest that user-specific custom views be generated dynamically based on transformations from and to the SUM. These views are organised in dimensions that are ideally independent from each other (orthogonal) – hence the name orthographic software modelling, which is an analogy to orthographic design in computer aided design (CAD). Technically, a view is a model of its own, which also has a metamodel. Model-to-model transformations create the views dynamically from the SUM. This also – theoretically – solves the issue of keeping views consistent, since every edit operation is immediately represented in the SUM and thus available to all other views. This concept requires however that bi-directional transformations exist for every view type (i.e. metamodel); they provide the synchronisation of views with the SUM, and edit operations are propagated back to the SUM likewise. Although bi-directional transformations are complex to develop, and bi-directionality cannot be easily ensured or even proven (see section 3.5), the complexity of a hub-and-spoke architecture like OSM is linear in terms of the number of transformations that have to be written and maintained, in contrast to the quadratic number of transformations in a peer-to-peer synchronisation scenario for views (see Figure 2.4).

OSM also encompasses a development process with a *developer* role, who uses the generated views, and a role called *methodologist*, who creates the different view types along the orthogonal dimensions. Atkinson et al. [5] have developed a prototypical implementation of the OSM approach, based on KobrA, which uses UML and OCL, and offers the dimensions abstraction (defined by notions of model-driven development), variability (defined by notions of product line engineering), compositionality (defined by notions of component-based development), encapsulation (e.g. public/private), and projection (structural/operational/behavioural). The approach lacks a method for the construction of the single underlying model (and the metamodel it is based on), which is supposed to carry all information of the software development lifecycle. Atkinson et al. have however proposed a multi-level modelling approach [6] that could theoretically solve many issues of MOF and UML, most importantly the deficiencies of the meta-level principle, which is fixed to four levels in MOF. The problem of bi-directional transformations has not been solved in this protopye either; the implementation of M2M transformations is based on the Atlas Transformation Language (ATL).

2.5. Notational Conventions

In this section, we will specifiy notational conventions for UML activity diagrams and Fundamental Modeling Concepts diagrams, which we will follow in this document.

2.5.1. UML Activity Diagrams

For the description of the control and data flow of processes, we will use UML activity diagrams [125]. For the concrete graphical syntax, we will use the SysML [124] variant of this diagram type. The elements of the syntax are displayed in Figure 2.5: An activity is labelled with the keyword **act** in the top left corner, followed by the activity's name. Inside the activity, the control flow is displayed in a similar way to the notation of finite state machines: Start states ● and final states ◉ are displayed as black circles. The activity contains actions, which are diplayed as rounded rectangles ▢. Input and output parameters of an activity are displayed as regular rectangles □. Inside an activity, the control flow is displayed as dashed arrows - - ►, while data and object flow are displayed as solid arrows ⟶. If data and control flow occur together, they are also displayed as a solid arrow. The input and output parameters of single actions are marked by pins □. To model the control flow inside an activity, fork and join nodes are used to describe parallelity in the execution of the action. They are displayed as black bars —. Branch and merge points in the control flow are displayed as diamond shapes ◇. Branches can have guards, as in the example of Figure 2.5.

Activity diagrams contain further concepts, such as swim lanes, events, and signals, which are not described here, since they are not used in this thesis.

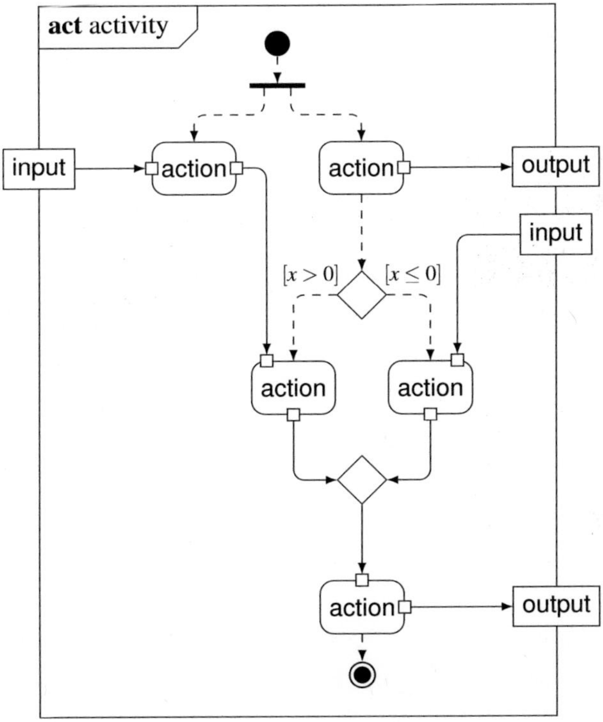

Figure 2.5.: SysML Activity Diagram Syntax

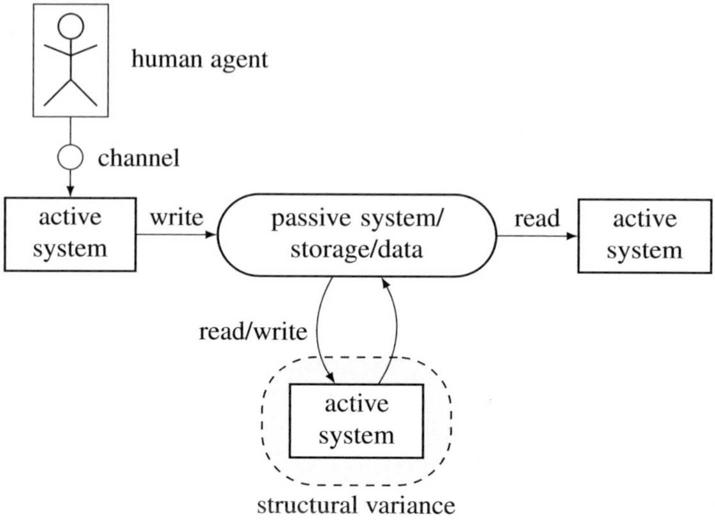

Figure 2.6.: Fundamental Modeling Concept: Elements in the Compositional Structure Diagram

2.5.2. Fundamental Modeling Concepts

The *Fundamental Modeling Concepts (FMC)* [89] are a simple description method for systems with a graphical syntax. The Compositional Structure Diagram of FMC is used to describe the structural view point of systems (see Figure 2.6). While acting nodes are depicted as rectangles ☐, passive nodes, which can represent data containers and artefacts, are depicted as rounded rectangles ⬭. Arrows indicate data flow: data flow to a passive node represents a write operation, and data flow from a passive node represents a read operation. The Compositional Structure Diagram also contains *structural variance* elements ⬭, which can be created, modified, or deleted at runtime of the system.

3. Related Work

The related work to the VITRUVIUS approach will be presented here in eight sections. First, we will present related view-based approaches in section 3.1. The field of *multi-paradigm modelling* (section 3.2) addresses similar problems of model synchronisation and specification of correspondences. Related work in model-driven engineering is presented in general in section 3.3, with a special focus on metamodel and model evolution in section 3.4. The topic of synchronisation is investigated in research about bidirectional transformations, which will be discussed in section 3.5. Aspect-oriented development approaches (section 3.6) follow a different approach to address the problems of concistency and complexity in software development. The definition of views and their updatability has been studied extensively in the field of relational databases, which will be covred in section 3.7. Finally, methods for modularization, view definition, and evolution in ontologies and the semantic web, and their relation to model-driven development are discussed in section 3.8.

3.1. View-based Approaches

The ViewPoints approach of Finkelstein (see subsection 2.1.2) has been implemented in the ViewPoints framework [122] for requirements engineering. The framework supports the specification of semantic overlaps with rule-based inter-view point corresondance definitions, and allows the management of desirable redundencies in heterogeneous view points. A development process for requirements engineering with view points is also described.

The first object-oriented methods like OMT [136] and Fusion [38] already featured several diagram types for structural, behavioural and operational view points. This was further extended in approaches like the 4+1 view points by Kruchten [98], leading to today's standards like RUP [97] and UML [125], which contain several (fixed) diagram types for the description of software architectures (see subsubsection 2.2.2.1 for details). The views described in these standards are *partial*, i.e. they do not represent all information contained in the underlying model.

Goedicke et al. [55] have applied distributed graph transformations to Finkelstein's ViewPoints modelling framework to synchronise the heterogeneous artefacts without unifying them to a single model. The approach formalises ViewPoints, so that a mathematical description of consistency is possible. Graph rewriting rules serve as a description language for in- and inter-viewpoint consistency.

The *ADORA* approach by Glinz et al. [54] takes a different approach to object-oriented modelling of systems, which, in contrast to UML, is not based on classes, but on *abstract objects* that are organised in a hierarchical decompositition structure. This structure is used for the visualization of a system at different levels of abstraction and formality. The aim of this reorganization of object-oriented models is to solve several problems of the UML language, such as weak semantics of the compositional structure, and bad integration of the different view points for structure, behaviour, and the execution environment of systems.

3.2. Multi-Paradigm Modelling

Multi-paradigm modelling approaches are concered with the modelling of software systems with multiple languages, metamodels, or schemata. *Mapping languages* [151] have already been defined in the 1990s to bridge the semantic gap between multiple models. Similar to transformation languages in model-driven engineering, these mapping languages have been developed in declarative, functional, and imperative style, as well as with knowledge-based rules.

3.2.1. Simulation Approaches

Multi-formalism approaches have been developed in concunction with methods for simulation coupling. The AToM^3 tool by Vangheluwe et al. [41] uses meta-modelling techniques and graph grammars to create visual modelling tools for simulations. The AToM^3 Kernel serves as a metamodel and model repository that is able to load, manipulate, and save models. The tool is based on the scripting language Python, so Python code can be embedded to describe constraints on the models, but constraints expressed in OCL as well as in graph grammar rules are also supported. These grammar rules also serve as the definition of the editability scope of the models: In the so-called *syntax-directed* approach, the allowed editing actions on a model are defined as graph grammar rules. The semantic relations between multiple formalisms is established by a Formalism Transformation Graph (FTG), which serves as a documentation of which formalisms can be transformed into other formalisms by a homomorphic mapping. The transformations themselves are described as graph grammar rules, which can be composed in the visual editor of AToM^3, and which can also be used to generate code from the models. Since the tool is targeted at the simulation of multi-formalism models, it does not provide means for the synchronisation of the models in different formalisms.

The OsMoSys framework [152, 119] is a multi-formalism tool with a focus on the analysis of systems with heterogeneous models. A modelling methodology has been defined for OsMoSys, which is based on metamodelling, and which is used to include existing modelling formalisms into an OsMoSys-based process. The approach differentiates between *explicit* multi-formalisms, which are visible to the user, and which can be used to model a system with different formalisms, and *implicit* multi-formalisms, which are only used internally to exploit existing analysis tools, solvers, and processes. Several OsMoSys-specific languages have been developed for the representation of models, metamodels, queries, and solution processes. The implementation of the framework contains a database backend that serves as a repository for the aforementioned artefacts. A disadvantage of this custom implementation of metamodelling concepts, queries, and processes is the incompatibility to established modelling standards and tools, which hinders the import and export of models, and which prevents the framework from profiting from advances in these standards and their implementations, such as EMF, QVT, OCL, and other languages.

3.2.2. Approaches for Model-based Data Exchange

The NAOMI platform [42] has been developed by the research department of Lockheed Martin. It contains an XML-based repository that stores models of multiple formalisms, and also offer version control. The formalisms themselves do not have do be adapted in order to work with NAOMI; for each formalism, however, a *connector* has to be specified that translates the native formats of the formalisms into the NAOMI XML representation. From there, correspondences and update actions can be specified in the multi-model manager (M3) of NAOMI. Rather than checking semantic consistency between the models, the information of interdependency is used to manage the modelling workflow with different formalisms. For this purpose, a workflow engine called Automated Multi-Mode Execution Engine (AMMEE) is connected to the NAOMI toolset. Despite the name, the engine is used for the execution of projects and their workflows, and does not execute the models themselves.

The exchange of information between heterogeneous systems has also been the focus of the Standard for the Exchange of Product Model Data (STEP), which has been standardised in ISO 10303 [130]. The standard is not targeted at software development, but rather at the software-supported mechanical and electrical development. It originated in the exchange of graphical and geometrical data in Computer-Aided Design (CAD), but is intended for the entire life-cycle of products in the field of eclectrical and mechanical engineering. The synchronisation of heterogeneous models is mostly described using common exchange file formats, and recommendations for the development process. The standard has been extended with ontologies [129] to represent the semantic relations between sub-elements, and to simplify models from different domains for the purpose of design review walkthroughs.

3.3. Model-driven Engineering

3.3.1. Architectural Frameworks

The approach of Cicchetti [33] uses model-driven technologies to create a *hybrid* view-based architectural framework that combines the projective and synthetic concept (as defined in ISO 42010 [77], see also section 2.1). It is based on the Eclipse Modeling Framework (EMF) and combines several model transformation and textual template languages to offer the creation and customization of user-specific views, similar to projective approaches, but without creating a single model where the information about the system under development is integrated. Instead, generated transformations synchronise the view types directly, similar to a synthetic approach. Although the approach is very customizable, the complexity of synchronisation still suffers from the quadratic increase of synthetic approaches.

The MEGAF infrastructure [75] is an implementation of the ISO42010 standard, and offers a repository for existing viewpoints. The models that are created with MEGAF are denoted as *megamodels*, since they consist of a combination of existing models, which are transformed into each other, or woven into new combinations of models. MEGAF can be used to define project- or system-specific architecture frameworks, which cover only the relevant viewpoints and their formalisms. Users of these architecture frame-

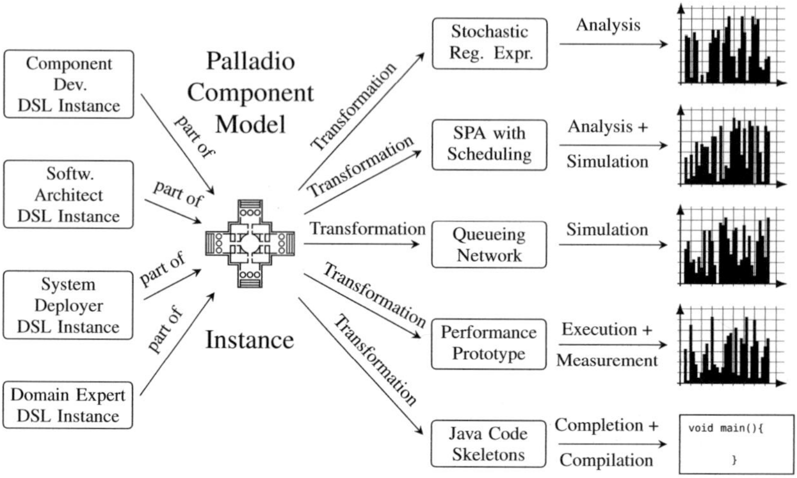

Figure 3.1.: Multiple Formalisms in the Palladio Approach

works can than instantiate architecture descriptions, for which consistency is automatically checked by the framework.

The Palladio approach [13] consists of a component-based software architecture development process, a metamodel for component-based modelling (Palladio Component Model) [134], and an architecture simulator (Palladio Simulator) that offers the coupling of Palladio models with different formalisms (see Figure 3.1). These formalisms include layered queueing networks [93], queueing Petri nets [113], Java code for simulation [115] and prototyping [109], and OMNeT++ models for simulation [69]. Furthermore, Palladio models can be converted into and from Use Case Maps [153] for intuitive modelling. The Palladio approach can thus also be seen as a multi-paradigm modelling approach that supports several formalisms for simulations, specification of semantics, and for compatibility to existing standards.

3.3.2. Round-trip Engineering

The VITRUVIUS approach presented in this thesis can also be seen as a special form of *round-trip engineering (RTE)* [73], which is concerned with the reflection of changes to a target model of a development process back to the source model. The proposed concept of a single underlying model requires however that the cycles of re-integrating changes to a certain view back into the SUM be short, essentialy after each editing step. Thus, many problems of RTE, like the merging of large sets of changes that were applied simultaneously, do not always apply to the approach presented here, but are dependent on the frequency of synchronisation.

Hettel [73] has used abductive logic reasoning to describe the synchronisation of heterogeneous models with partial, non-injective functions. The approach is used for round-trip-engineering (RTE) in heterogeneous models, which is similar to the synchronisation of editable views with a base model in view-based model-driven engineering. The synchronisation of changes is restricted to those cases of model changes that can be reflected back to a change in a source model. Thus, the ability for the synchronisation of changes is guaranteed by restricting the set of possible changes. The approach offers methods for distinguishing these kinds of changes and proves the synchronisation properties of possible changes with formal reasoning.

3.3.3. Collaboration

Classical code engineering follows an asynchronous paradigm: code parts are checked out from a repository, modified, and checked in again. If there have been any changes to the repository in the mean time, a line-based three-way textual merge can be performed before the changes are committed to the repository. This works well for the development of code. For modelling tasks, it is often desirable to work synchronously, so that changes are reflected to the underlying model immediately and seen by all users. Tools like EtherPad[1] or Google Docs[2] even offer synchronous real-time editing of (non-structured) textual documents.

Collaborative editing of documents online is a widespread practice as long as textual documents are edited. With the *SLIM* tool [149], Thum et al. have presented a browser-based collaborative editing tool that aims to be a "Google Docs for models". The tool is browser-based and offers synchronous editing of UML diagrams as well as XMI im- and export. Since the approach is designed for multi-user scenarios, synchronisation is also provided via locking mechanisms at the model element level. SLIM follows a complete online editing paradigm where changes are immediately reflected in the model repository.

The *ModelBus* approach [67, 3] aims to provide sharing mechanisms for models in a distributed and heterogenous model-driven process. A central repository serves as the store for models, which are then transformed into tool-specific formats using service-based invocation techniques. ModelBus also supports collaborative work on a software model using different tools, e.g. Enterprise Architect and Papyrus. ModelBus is a tool-centric approach an does not contain any mechanisms for the transformation of heterogeneous metamodels or DSLs; it is a purely technical solution that supports the interchange of EMF/MOF-based metamodels between modelling tools.

DuALLy [111] is a framework that aims to create interoperability between architecture description languages (ADL). It uses higher-order transformations to translate existing languages via a hard-coded core set of architectural models and weaving models. This is similar to the idea of the SUM in the OSM approach, but limited to the domain of architectural engineering. An implementation of DuALLy based on Eclipse and ATL exists.

[1] `http://etherpad.org`, retrieved 26 May 2014
[2] `http://docs.google.com`, retrieved 26 May 2014

3.4. Evolution of Models and Metamodels

In model-driven engineering, models and metamodels usually have different development cycles: While metamodels are often part of development standards, and thus remain unchanged during the develoment of a software system, models are instantiated, changed, and discarded frequently. Changes to metamodels require additional efforts to co-evolve existing instances, transformations, and tools. In this subsection, we will first describe the ways in which models and metamodels can be modified, and give an overview of existing approaches for the managing of changes to models and metamodels.

3.4.1. Editability of Ecore-based Metamodels and Models

Instances of Ecore-based metamodels can only be edited in a limited number of ways, since the kinds of elements of which such an instances consist are limited by the layout of the Ecore Meta-Metamodel and the way in which instantiation in EMF works. Since EMF and Ecore follow the classical four-layers instantiation model of MOF, there are two places where elements can be instantiated: The Ecore metamodel can be instantiated into metamodels, which themselves can have instances. (See subsubsection 2.2.2.2 for a detailed discussion of editability of MOF-based metamodels and models.)

Langer et al. [102] have presented an approach based on graph transformation, which offers an a posteriori analysis of changes to EMF-based metamodels and their instances, independent of the way in which the models were edited. The approach is able to extract complex change operations from atomic difference descriptions, which have been determined with EMF Compare. It has been validated in a metamodel evolution scenario using Ecore as the metamodel, thus being able to extract the change operators of Herrmannsdörfer [70]. The differences between models are not represented as models themselves, but rather as signatures, which serve as an input for an algorithm that computes the differences as operations in the EMF Modeling Operations language, based on pre- and postconditions expressed in OCL.

3.4.2. Changes at the Metamodel Level

The possible modifications to metamodels have been investigated in the field of *metamodel evolution* and *co-evolution* of metamodels and models. The basic principle of describing the difference between two metamodels in a metamodel-independent way has already been identified by Alanen and Porres [1] for UML class diagrams. They distinguish the two cases *element creation and deletion* as well as *feature modification*. The difference between two UML class diagrams is then described as a sequence of this atomic change operators. The approach offers a difference calculation algorithm, which converts a state-based description of two metamodel versions into the delta-based description in the form of sequences of these atomic change operations. These sequences are then used to merge different versions of UML models at the M2 level, rather than for co-evolving existing instances.

The approach of Wachsmuth [154] uses concepts from object-oriented refactoring and grammar adaptation for the purpose of metamodel evolution, and automatic model co-evolution. The approach uses model transformations to describe the refactoring steps. These steps can then serve as patterns in the construction of new metamodels, for the description of versioning of metamodels, for documenting changes to metamodels, and for the co-evolution of existing instances of these metamodels. The approach is based on MOF 2.0 and uses QVT-R for the declarative description of model transformations. The adaptation operations are categorised by the way in which they preserve the semantics of a metamodel. Inverses of adaptation operations are also identified.

The MOF-based change metamodel by the author of this thesis [27] uses the categorization of [12] to estimate the impact that changes to MOF-based metamodels have on existing instances. The change metamodel can be used to describe changes that have been determined either by state-based or by delta-based analysis of metamodel versions. It offers a worst-case analysis of the impact of changes on existing metamodels, which is agnostic of the actual set of instances, but computes the impact on any possible instances. The descriptions of the changes themselves as instances of a MOF-based metamodel allows the processing of change description using model-based technologies, such as model transformations or code generators.

The COPE approach of Herrmannsdörfer, which has been developed into the Eclipse project *Edapt* [72], offers a comprehensive catalogue of change operators for Ecore-based metamodels. To adress the problem that the completeness of such an operator catalogue cannot be proven formally, due to the lack of a formal basis of the Ecore metamodel, the authors have applied the change operators in several case studies to demonstrate the *practical completeness* (in constrast to theoretical completeness) of the change operations. The change operations are aligned with object-oriented refactoring operators and are classified into three categories, which express the effort for co-evolving existing instances. The operations contain low-level, atomic edit operations, as well as more complex, semantically richer refactoring operations, which can also be expressed as a sequence of atomic operations. The respective inverses of the operators are analysed to determine whether inverting the operations yields the same result, and also classified into safe and unsafe inverses. The table of change operations is included in the appendix of this thesis. (see Appendix B). Edapt has been implemented as an Eclipse plug-in that can execute the change operators and record the changes for the creation of co-adaptation scripts.

While the approach of Herrmannsdörfer is a delta-based approach and relies on manual definition of edit operations, the approach of Kehrer et al. [84] determines consistency-preserving edit scripts from state-based difference descriptions between two versions of a model. The authors use a rule-based approach to extract high-level edit operations, such as refactorings, from low-level descriptions of atomic edit operations. A similar approach has been taken by the author of this thesis in [30], where a difference-based analysis of metamodels is combined with a rule-based approach to determine a conformance relation between two Ecore-based metamodels.

3.4.3. Changes at the Model Level

The challenge of describing changes at the model level is to find a formalism that is generic enough to describe changes to instances of arbitrary metamodels. While metamodel evolution can always be described relative to a meta-metamodel, which is usually fixed, the evolution of models has to be described in a metamodel-specific, but still general way.

EMF Compare [22] is an extensible tool for the differencing of models in the Eclipse Modeling Framework. It uses a heuristic differencing engine to match elements and determine the delta between two models, even if the elements do not contain universal unique identifiers (UUIDs). The differencing engine can be extended by metamodel-specific filters to describe change types that are tailored to the metamodels of which the models under comparison are instances. EMF Compare offers a graphical user interface that displays the differences between two models in a tree structure, and a programming interface that can be used to query the results of a model comparison for specific elements. The differences are expressed as instances of a comparison model, which is described in the EMF Compare developer guide.[3] Besides matching and differencing, EMF Compare can also be used for a full three-way comparison of conflicting model revisions, and also for the resolution of these conflicts.

Cicchetti et al. [34] have developed a metamodel-based description for changes at the model level. The metamodel-specific *difference model* is generated by a metamodel-to-metamodel transformation and contains elements for the atomic change operations add, delete modify for each element in the metamodel of the elements that shall be modified. The model elements that describe the changes can be composed to change sequences, which can be concatenated in sequence, or in a parallel way. The detection of possible conflicts is, however, not covered.

[3] `http://www.eclipse.org/emf/compare/doc/21/developer/developer-guide.html`, retrieved 26 May 2014

The DeltaEcore approach [139] also uses a metamodel-based description of changes to models. Although mainly targeted at modelling variance in product lines, DeltaEcore provides means that are also suited for describing evolutionary steps between versions of metamodels and models. The description language for differences between models consist of a metamodel-independent base language, for which a specific *delta dialect*, which describes atomic changes, can automatically be created for actual metamodels. DeltaEcore also offers the possibility to extend the metamodel-specific dialects with domain-specific complex operations, so called *custom delta languages*. The languages themselves can be described using a textual concrete syntax, which is processed by the EMFText framework to yield model-based representations from the textual descriptions.

The approach of Taentzer and al. [148] provides a mapping of Ecore-based models to typed graph structures to describe state-based as well as delta-based modification to models. The aim of the approach is to support versioning of models, including the resolution of merge conflicts.

3.5. Bidirectional Transformations

Bidirectional transformations are used in model-driven view-based approaches for the synchronisation of the views with the underlying base models. To offer editable views, these transformation have to be bi-directional to reflect changes in the views as well as in the base models. Depending on the transformation language, bi-directionality can be a feature of the language, or can be guaranteed by proving certain properties of a transformation.

3.5.1. BX

Perdita Stevens distinguishes bidirectional transformations (abbreviated as *bx*) from bijective transformations [146], and identifies several requirements that bidirectional transformations should satisfy: In the context of QVT-R, the basic requirements are *correctness* (the transformation engine produces models that satisfy the relations), *hippocraticness* (models that satisfy a relation are not modified by the executions of the transformation engine), and additionally *undoability*. Diskin et al. [44] give a weaker definition for *undoability* and *invertibility*, which is more suitable for practical applications of bidirectional transformation, and which is based on lenses. They also argue that *delta-based* approaches are superior to *state-based* approaches: While state-based transformations have the complete models in their current status as input and output, delta-based approaches use the differences between models. These deltas may carry semantic information that cannot be computed by comparing model versions, such as refactorings like renaming and changes in containment. This is especially important in scenarios where UUIDs/primary keys are not always available, such as in EMF, where they are only optional for model elements.

Bidirectional transformations can be classified into *symmetric* and *assymetric* cases: In the symmetric case, both source and target models of a transformation can contain new information that is not yet present in the respective other model and has to be added there by the transformation. In the asymmetric case, one model does not contain new information, which is the case for (non-editable) views. In the general case however, views may be editable and thus, the framework must support changes on both sides of the transformation. For read-only views, it is sufficient to define only a unidirectional transformation, thus reducing the complexity.

Some transformation languages support bidirectionality better than others; for example, in the context of QVT [116], it is possible to define bidirectional transformations in QVT-R as well as in QVT-O; but while QVT-R supports bidirectionality by its design, it must be defined manually in imperative transformation languages, such as QVT-O, or in hybrid languages, such as the Epsilon Transformation Language (ETL) [90], by writing two transformations and ensuring that they fulfil bidirectionality manually. The Atlas Transformation Language [79] contains reverse operations for each of the language's primitive operations, to support bidirectionality.

Bi-directionality can also be achieved by allowing only injective functions for the definition of pairs of transformations between a source and a target model. The Inv language of Hu et al. [120] provides a reversible transformation language for the synchronisation of views and base models.

3.5.2. Lenses

The *lenses* approach by the Harmony group [50] offers a language for the definition of bi-directional mappings between tree-based structures. The authors define lenses as mappings between a "concrete" and and "abstract" domain, which does not describe the level of conceptual abstraction, but is used in the sense that the abstract domain contains less information. In the context of view-based modelling, the "concrete" entity is the model that contains the information of interest, while the "abstract" entity would be the view that contains information representing the model. The mappings consist of pairs of functions for the creation of views (called *get*) and the propagation of changes to the views (called *putback*). The get functions are designed in a way that the view can always be computed from the underlying data structure. For the put function, only the modified view and the original underlying data structure is needed as input; thus, the approach is *state-based.* Based on these operations, the authors define the laws GETPUT and PUTGET, which describe *hippocraticness* properties (see previous paragraph) for roundtrips from views to the source and vice versa: The GETPUT law describes that creating a view and writing back the information to the source, without modifying the view, should also leave the source unmodified; the analogous PUTGET law states that a view that is written to the source and created again should remain identical. If lenses fulfill both these laws, they are called *well-behaved.* If, in addition, the PUTPUT law is fulfilled, which states that the double propagation of the identical view update has the same effect as the single propagation, the lense is called *very well-behaved.* Based on these properties, the authors define composition operators on lenses and show that the set of well-behaved lenses is closed under these operators. Lenses have been applied to relational databases [17].

Diskin et al. have extended the lenses approach to delta-based synchronisation for metamodel-based structures in the symmetric [44] and the asymmetric case [43]. The delta-based approach aims to reduce problem of state-based bidirectional transformations such as incorrect sequential composition and poor modularity. Algebraic frameworks for delta-based lenses have been defined for the asymmetric case (based on category theory), and the symmetric case (so-called sd-lenses). The approach has been further developed by Diskin into the *tiles* formalism, which allows a visual combination of synchronisation blocks for the definition of mappings between models. The algebraic frameworks of Diskin offer a sound theoretical foundation, and prove important properties of the proposed operators, such as hippocraticness, well-behavedness, invertability, and undoability. To apply these theoretical proofs to existing metamodelling tools, a formal foundation for metamodelling languages such as MOF and Ecore would have to be provided first. Taentzer et al. [148] have provided a theoretical foundation for Ecore-based metamodels using a graph-based representation of models, which could serve as such a formal basis.

3.5.3. Triple Graph Grammars

Triple graph grammars (TGG) [138] are a formalism for the specification of interdependencies in graph-like data structures. The grammar rules of TGGs define the modification of three graphs (left, right, and correspondence). Each rule contains a pre- and a postcondition, which have to be satisfied before and after the rule application.

TGGs can be used for the declarative specification of bi-directional model-to-model transformations [53]. The concept has been implemented in various tools for Ecore-based metamodels, such as TGG interpreter [60], eMoflon [105], and EMorF[4].

Bergmann et al. [15] have used graph patterns and graph transformations to define a change-driven model transformation approach. This approach is similar to the synchronisation mechanisms in VITRUVIUS, which are also triggered by change operations to views or parts of the SUM. The approach of Bergmann processes change elements into other change elements, and thus offers a delta-based transformation approach for models.

The previously mentioned approach by Taentzer et al. [148] offers a formalisation of metamodels as graphs to define change operations and conflicts that can occur during editing and creation of new versions of a model.

3.6. Aspect-Oriented Software Development

The concept of *Aspect-Oriented Programming (AOP)* [87] is a method for the decomposition of software in code-based development processes. Approaches such as subject-oriented design [36] sought to improve the alignment between requirements, object-oriented design models and program code by re-structuring the software development process along system-wide, higher level concepts. The AOP approach has been extended to the field of model-driven development as *Aspect-Oriented Modelling*, and to generalised to *Aspect-Oriented Software Development (AOSD)* [35], which defines a complete development process that is based on aspect orientation. The rationale behind aspect orientation is "breaking the hegemony of the dominant decomposition" [10] in software development. In aspect-oriented approaches, software development is re-structured along system-wide, so called *cross-cutting* concerns, which have to be distinguished from non-cross-cutting concerns like component/object-structures. Changes to such a concern are not reflected in the underlying system immediately, but unified

[4] `http://www.emorf.org/`, retrieved 15 May 2014

afterwards in a *weaving* or *composition* process, which is a central concept of aspect orientation.

For the description of aspects, several languages have been developed. For code-based aspect-oriented programming, the AspectJ language extension for Java [86] is most notable, which is supported in the Spring framework for Eclipse [78]. Aspect-oriented modelling approaches usually come with a modelling language of their own, often an extension to UML, such as Theme/UML [31], or the approach of Klein et al. [88]. The survey of UML-based AOM approaches by Wimmer et al. [156] gives a good overall view of existing approaches. A more extensive survey by Chitchyan et al. from 2005 [32] also offers a comparison with non-aspect-oriented approaches.

The main difference between view-based modelling approaches and aspect-oriented approaches is the process of weaving and composing, which is special to aspect-oriented approaches. In AOM, the sub-models, which represent a specific aspect or concern, are edited independently and integrated into the system afterwards. Thus, in terms of view-based modelling, each aspect or concern is a partial, editable view of the system; the approach of weaving is comparable with the synthetic view-based approached, where the system description is derived from the information in the views in an integration step. The view-based approaches do, however, in general not distinguish between cross-cutting and non-cross-cutting view types.

The process of integrating the concerns into a model that describes all the aspects and concerns is called *unification* in AOM. The unification step can be performed at different points in the development process: If the concerns are unified statically (at modelling time), the resulting models can be used without changes to the tool chain, at the cost of losing traceability information. Dynamic unification requires an execution environment that supports the AOM constructs.

3.7. Databases

Many of the problems that are encountered in view-based modelling have counterparts in database research. The term *view* in relational databases can be understood as a stored database query in a relational algebra, for example, using the Standard Query Language (SQL).

Queries in relational algebra, and thus also views, define two dimensions of the result set: First, the schema of the result set, i.e. the attributes (columns in SQL), and second, a selection of tuples (rows in SQL), of which the attributes that have been specified in the schema are contained. The different types of operators have different effects on these dimensions: While projection affect the set of attributes, selection affects only the set of tuples. Join operators affect both these dimensions.

3.7.1. View Update Problem

If data in a partial view is manipulated, the *view update problem* [9, 37] arises, which is a central issue in relational databases research. Although it is well understood, and has been investigated since the 1980s, it is mainly unsolved [106]. The process of re-integrating changes on a partial view into the underlying database is called *translation*. Bancilhon and Spyratos [9] have defined translation as a co-evolution operator that converts updates on a view into updates on the underlying database. They also define the *complement* of a view, which is an other view on the database so that the whole database can be computed from the information in both these views. A view can have several complements; the updatability of a view is dependent on the choice of a complement. For a fixed complement, Bancilhon and Spyratos show that a view is updatable if and only if it is translatable in such a way that the complement remains invariant, which they call *translation under constant complement*. Buff [24] has shown that such a translation does not always exist for any kind of view update, and that it is undecidable if a unique translation exists. The problem can, however, be alleviated by carefully designing the views, so that every edit operation of a user in a certain view can also be reverted in that same view without losing information in the underlying database. The careful design of these views is, however, a manual process that requires of the view designer to estimate the translatability of the view definitions. Lechtenbörger et al. [107] have developed a heuristic algorithm for the computation of "resonably small" view complements, which can be minimal in special cases. Translation under constant complement fulfils the properties *correctness*, *hippocraticness*, *undoability*, *history ignorance*, and *invertability* [73, sect. 2.2.1].

Dayal et Bernstein [40] have formalised update translation for view updates, and thus defined the semantics of view updates. To this end, two graphs have been defined: The view-trace graph and the view-dependency graph. If updates in a view are translated to updates in a databes, these updates to the underlying database have to be *exact updates*, which means that a re-generation of the view from the updated databes yields the same result as the original view with the applied edit operation. Exact updates are possible if *clean sources* in the database exist for the edited tuples in the view. A change to a clean source does not have any effects on other views on the database except from the view where the initial update operation was applied.

Gottlob et al. [59] have defined a hierarchy of restriction in views on databases. The define the set of *consistent views*, which offer an unambiguous translation of update operations to database updates. These views contain the set of views that translate under constant complement as a subset. Thus, the concept of consistent views is a generalization of the definition of Bancilhon and Spyratos. Gottlob et al. concede that consistent views do not necessarily cover all *reasonable views*, since there are many examples of existing realistic views that do not fulfil this property.

In recent database research, the view-update problem has also been investigated using the lenses approach by Foster et al. [50] (see also section 3.5).

The approach operates on general tree-based structure rather than on relational databases. Based on translation under constant complement, as defined by Bancilhon et al., Foster et al. have investigated the properties *definedness* and *continuity* of bi-directional transformations over tree-based structures. The lens operators are assembled using lens combinators that are based on constructs from functional programming, such as composition, mapping, projection, conditionals, and recursion.

The view-update problem is closely related to the problem of bi-directional transformations in metamodelling and view-based approaches. The communality of both approaches lies in the fact that views on an underlying database can re-arrange and aggregate data, or present it differently, but do not add information that is not present in the underlying database. Views only contain information that is not in the underlying database after an edit operation. This is the same case in *projectional* view-based software development approaches (see section 2.1), where views are only transient projections on a base model of the system under development.

3.7.2. Schema Integration

If several databases are used in federation, identical data may be represented in heterogeneous schemata, which have to be integrated so that they can used in a unified way. Methods for the integration of such schemata [133, 140] require manual interaction of experts that have a semantic understanding of both domains, which is necessary to define the mapping between heterogeneous elements. This process cannot be fully automated since the semantics that are not formalised in the databases have to be added by human interaction. A global database schema is used to express data from various sources.

This insight can also be transferred to the field of model-driven development. Heuristic approaches, which attempt a mapping based on structural similarities or naming convention of heterogeneous metamodels are not able to capture certain semantic relations. These can only be determined by a human specialist who has the understanding of all the domains that are affected by a semantic overlap. The global database schema is similar to the concept of a single underlying model (SUM) in Orthographic Software Modeling (see section 2.4), for which a metamodel (which is analogous to a database schema) has to be defined first; with this metamodel, developers must be able to express all the concepts of those metamodels that are integrated into the development process.

3.8. Ontologies and Semantic Web

In model-driven development, metamodels describe exactly the elements and the relations that can be expressed in a domain-specific language. Thus, a metamodel can be seen as a special form of an ontology [62]. Aßmann et al., on the other hand, state that "ontologies are special models" [4, p.256]. They further destinguish between *descriptive* and *prescriptive* models and argue that prescriptive models should not be called ontologies. Despite the similarities in the concept of metamodelling and ontology modelling, model-driven development and semantic web technologies have been developed almost independently of each other. Ontologies are mostly used for knowledge representation in connection with technologies of the semantic web. They can be used as domain models, domain-specific languages, and description languages in software development processes [4].

The most important language standards for the definition of ontolgies are *RDF Schema* [19], and the *Web Ontology Language* (OWL) with its three species OWL Full, OWL DL, and OWL Lite [126]. Ontologies can contain a strong formal basis for the semantic description, which is usually expressed in description logics (DL) [8]. OWL implements several levels of description logic that differ in their decidability and and the time complexity for reasoning.

The sentences in description logic are categorised into two kinds of sentences: While the Terminological Box (TBox) describes the knowledge about a domain, the Assertional Box (ABox) describes facts about individual objects. In model-driven terms, the the metamodel is part of the TBox, while the models that are instances of a metamodel are part of the ABox.

Ontologies follow the *open-world assumption*, which means that everything that is not explicitly expressed by an ontology is *unknown*. This contrasts with the *closed-world assumption* of metamodelling, which states that everything that has not been specified is either implicitly disallowed or implicitly allowed [4].

3.8.1. Ontology Modularization

In general, ontologies suffer from similar problems as model-based approaches: With a rising number of elements in an ontology, no single user or developer has a full understanding of all the concepts in the ontology. Furthermore, ontology languages allow the mixing of data at the instance level and at the schema level, which is not possible in standard metamodelling approaches such as MOF [117] or EMF [47]. While working with a large ontology is cumbersome, the problem of complexity increases when several ontologies are used that represent overlapping parts of knowledge. Ontologies that cover fields of knowledge that are requested by many users often grow very large in terms of the number of concepts. For example, the Foundational Model of Anatomy [135] contains tens of thousands of concepts and classes and more than two million relations.

Techniques for *ontology modularization* aim to alleviate this problem. The goals of modularization have overlaps to the ones that have been identified in this thesis for view-based model-driven approaches [127]: Although some of the primary goals of ontology modularization, such as improving the performance of querying and reasoning of data, are not comparable with the goals of this thesis, the problem of scalability for evolution and maintenance, complexity management, understandability, personalization and reuse are very similar to the problems that we have identified for view-based approaches.

Ontology mapping approaches [20] are used for the composition of existing ontologies to form a larger, modular ontology. These approaches are concerned with automatic identification, as well as with the formalisation of ontology mappings. These mappings are usually defined declaratively, and can be categorised into three types [147]: equivalence, containment, and overlap. In [20], Brockmans et al. have created a metamodel that describes ontology mappings, and have defined a UML profile for the visual notation of them.

3.8.2. Queries and Views on Ontologies

Several query languages for ontologies have been developed, which are used for the retrieval of information from knowledge databases. Most of these languages are low-level languages comparable with the SQL language for relational databases, and can only be used to retrieve data elements, but not to define parts of a schema. The SPARQL language [61] is a query language for RDF that offers a SQL-like textual syntax. The RDF Query language (RQL) [82] is a semi-formal language, which can be used to query RDF schema and resource descriptions with minimal knowledge of the schema.

While the creation of views is a well-understood notion in the field of relational databases and in model-driven engineering, the concept of ontology views raises specific questions concerning the definition and technical creation of the views. This problem is similar to the definition of view types in the VITRUVIUS approach; unlike view in relational databases, the view types in VITRUVIUS and sub-ontologies that are defined for ontology views are not just projections of the underlying database or model.

Rajugan et al. [132] propose a layered view model, which offers formal semantics for ontology views. The RDFS/OWL visualization language

(RVL) [128] offers the mapping of RDFS/OWL concepts to graphical elements. Noy et al. [121] have presented a concept for the creation of views and ontologies that is similar to the concept of the ModelJoin language (see section 6.2): Starting from a core concept, they provide the definition of traversal specifications, which describe the relations and concepts of interest that should be included in the ontology view. Similar to ModelJoin, which defines a target metamodel and a set of target instances, traversal views collect the schema elements as well as the data. Traversal views define a subsect of the underlying ontology that is self-contained, and that is related to a specific concept.

3.8.3. Ontology Evolution

Like every formalism, ontologies also suffer from the problem of evolution. Ontology evolution occurs when new concepts have to be included into an ontology, for example, if changes in the domain that it describes occur, so that the ontology is developed into a new version. These modifications have a potential impact on consistency and coherence of the ontology. Zablith et al. [159] have surveyed ontology evolution approaches. They have identified the stages in the ontology evolution process, and defined an ontology evolution cycle that describes these changes and their interdependencies. The change cycle consists of five steps:

1. Detecting the Need for Evolution
2. Suggesting Changes
3. Validating Changes
4. Assessing Impact
5. Managing Changes

This process is also viable for the evolution of metamodels and their instances in general, and for the VITRUVIUS approach in particular. Although the formalisms for describing validity and consistency between the artefacts differ from those in metamodel definitions, the process model itself is, however, applicable to the evolution scenarios in VITRUVIUS as well.

With the evolution of ontologies, the problem of inexpressibility arises: Ontologies can be evolved in such a way that the result of the evolution is not an element of the description language in which the ontology was formulated. This problem is adressed by restricting the expressibility of the languages to a set elements that are closed under evolution [85]. The evolution of ontologies that are expressed in different languages is managed by separating the linguistic layer from the knowledge layer [45], similar to the concept of separating the linguistic classification of models from the ontological classification in multi-level modelling [6].

4. An Approach for View-Based Engineering using VITRUVIUS

In this chapter, we will present a view-based software development approach based on VITRUVIUS and Orthographic Software Modelling (OSM). The contributions of this chapter include a construction method for a modular single underlying model and the management of views, which are used to retrieve and modify information in the SUM.

After the description of the overall approach in section 4.1, we will present the method for constructing the single underlying model in section 4.2. In section 4.3, the terminology for view types and views in VITRUVIUS is defined. The development process for the view-based approach is presented in section 4.4, followed by evolution scenarios in section 4.5. The application of the whole approach to the example scenario is described in detail in section 4.6.

4.1. The VITRUVIUS Approach

The VITRUVIUS[1] approach, which we will present in this dissertation, is a view-based software engineering approach. It is currently (2014) being developed at the Chair for Software Design and Quality [26, 95, 104]. VITRUVIUS is based on concepts of Orthographic Software Modelling ([7]. In this section, we will introduce the design rationale of VITRUVIUS as well as assumptions and limitations of the approach. In the remaining sections of this chapter, we will describe the core concepts (sections 4.2,

[1] **Vi**ew-Cen**tr**ic Engineering **U**sing a **Vi**rtual **U**nderlying **S**ingle Model, after the roman architect *Marcus Vitruvius Pollio* (ca. 80-70 B.C. – 15 B.C.)

4.3), the development process (section 4.4), and give an extended example (section 4.6).

4.1.1. Design Rationale

VITRUVIUS is a *projectional* approach ([77], see section 2.1), which implements the following core ideas of Orthographic Software Modelling:

- All information about the system under development is represented in a single underlying model (SUM).
- This model can be accessed exclusively by specific views.

Using a single underlying model is a theoretically elegant solution to the aforementioned problems of fragmentation, redundancy, and inconsistency. Specific views serve the purpose of taming the complexity for developers. Existing research on OSM is, however, lacking a description of how such a single underlying model should be created, so that it can be used in arbitrary software development scenarios. If a SUM is created using model-driven technologies, a metamodel for SUMs would have to be defined first, but such an all-purpose metamodel has not been defined yet for the OSM approach.

There is a prototypical implementation [5] for component-based software development, for which a SUM metamodel was constructed manually as an extension to UML 2.0 [125]. This *monolithic* SUM metamodel contains all the necessary concepts for the CBSE scenario, such as structural, functional, and behavioural views on the UML components. As a general procedure for the creation of a SUM metamodel, however, we deem this approach to be impractical due to the problems listed in section 1.2: A monolithic SUM metamodel causes high effort in construction and is difficult to reuse, since the SUM metamodel has to be defined anew for each scenario. Furthermore, existing software development processes make use of several pre-defined metamodels, called *legacy* metamodels in the following, to which compatibility has to be preserved. Thus, import and export functionality has to be added to the monolithic SUM metamodel.

4.1.2. Proposed Benefits of the Modular SUM Metamodel

The VITRUVIUS approach addresses these shortcomings and proposes the usage of a *modular* SUM metamodel rather than a monolithic SUM metamodel. The modular SUM metamodel consists of existing metamodels, mapping between these metamodels and rules for semi-automatic synchronisation of elements. The concept is described in detail in section 4.2. The proposed benefits of using a modular SUM metamodel over a monolithic SUM metamodel are listed in the following:

- **Maintainability and Re-use:** Many projective view-based approaches, such as DuALLy [111], or KobrA [5], rely on a fixed metamodel, which represents all the concepts that are necessary for the modelling task. If functionality is added to this metamodel, the developer who modifies the metamodel has to possess knowlegde of the complete, and possibly large, metamodel. In a modular SUM metamodel, the sub-metamodels and explicit correspondences between them can be maintained separately by experts of the respective domain. Furthermore, parts of the modular SUM metamodel can be re-used to build a different scenario-specific SUM metamodel.
- **Compatibility to Existing Metamodels:** Software projects usually have to adhere to certain languages and standards, such as UML, Java, and further domain-specific models. If a project is realised with the VITRUVIUS approach, changes to the metamodels are unnecessary for the inclusion into the modular SUM metamodel. Thus, existing instances of the metamodels, tools, and transformation can be re-used. For this purpose, the metamodel can be exposed as a view type that offers import and export functionality.

- **Evolution of Metamodels:** If a new version of a metamodel has to be supported in the development process, only the sub-metamodel and the adjacent correspondences and view type have to be modified to include this new version into the modular SUM metamodel. The impact of such a change can be estimated better than for a monolithic SUM, since the relation of the metamodel elements to the rest of the SUM metamodel is modelled explicitly.

The usage of a modular SUM metamodel requires a novel way of creating view types, which are used to display and manipulate the information in the SUM. In section 4.3, we will define the properties of view types in VITRUVIUS and introduce the notion of *view type scope*. The development process of VITRUVIUS (section 4.4) is based on the development process of OSM and contains the developer role of the *methodologist*, who is responsible for the definition of the modular SUM metamodel and the view types. The developers who use the SUM metamodel for the development of software systems can instantiate SUMs as well as views to describe the system. The SUM metamodel can however also be extended by custom view types, which are defined by the developer.

4.1.3. Assumptions

In this subsection, we will state the assumptions that we make for the cases where the VITRUVIUS approach is applicable.

The VITRUVIUS approach is intended for software development processes that make use of several formalisms, such as metamodels, languages, or developer tools, during the specification, planning and implementation of software. Although it is based on model-driven technologies such as model transformations, it is not only targeted at model-driven development processes. It is however a precondition for the approach that the formalisms that are used in the process can be expressed as a metamodel. Since there are model-based representations for many formalisms, including programming languages such as Java [23, 66], we do not see this as a severe limitation. Furthermore, it is often possible to define a metamodel for existing standards with reasonable effort, for example, by creating the metamodel from a given grammar.

In development processes where several formalisms are used to describe a software system from different perspectives, we assume that there are implicit relations between the artefacts of these formalisms that are not specified formally. It is possible that the information in the different artefacts complements each other or is overlapping.

We claim that the VITRUVIUS approach is especially helpful if there are more view types than metamodels. This is the case either if there are already different view types for the single metamodels or if there is the demand for view types that integrate information from several metamodels.

While the view types in the OSM approach are organised along orthogonal dimensions, this is not a requirement for the design of view types in the VITRUVIUS approach. This requirement has been loosened to support legacy view types, which may follow a different pattern of organization than orthogonal dimensions. It is, however, of course possible to define the view types with VITRUVIUS in such a way that they are orthogonal to each other, and to implement a fully OSM-compatible development process with it.

4.2. A Modular Way of Defining Single Underlying Models

In this section, we will describe the construction of the modular SUM metamodel. Since existing OSM publications [5, 7] do not contain a formal definition of the term *single underlying model*, we will first define it here to clarify our understanding of a SUM and its metamodel.

4.2.1. Definition

Definition 3 (Single Underlying Model (SUM)). *A* single underlying model (SUM) *is a complete definition of a software system. It contains all available* *information about the system. The information in the SUM is displayed or manipulated exclusively by specific views, which adhere to these description formalisms.*

The formalism that is used to describe the SUM is called a SUM metamodel.

As suggested in the OSM approach [7], the SUM metamodel is specific to the software development process, the domain where the software system is used, and the modelling standards that have to be supported. The information in a SUM metamodel is expressed using well-defined description formalisms, such as domain specific languages, metamodels, or general-purpose programming languages. In the CBSE example, the SUM metamodel has to contain concepts for the representation of software architecture (components), object oriented design, Java code, and performance simulation. The SUM metamodel is instantiated for every software system that is developed, so the same SUM metamodel can be re-used for multiple software projects.

To our knowledge, no generic SUM metamodel for software development has been defined yet. There are several approaches (see subsection 3.3.3) that use a single underlying model (although not labelled as such) as a hub for the synchronisation of diverse development artefacts. For example, DuALLy [111] uses an A_0 model to which all the other models have to be synchronised. These approaches rely on a monolithic metamodels that are either very general, so that they support the most common concepts in a specific area (such as architecture modelling in DuALLy), or have to be created manually for each specific scenario, so that they support a specific development process, domain models, or modelling languages (such as the UML2 extension for KobrA [5]). For arbitrary development scenarios, there is however no method for the construction of a single underlying metamodel based on the formalisms that have to be supported in the development process. This is why we propose a method for the construction of a *modular SUM metamodel*.

Definition 4 (Modular SUM metamodel). *A* modular SUM metamodel $M_{sum} \subseteq \mathcal{M}_{sum}$ *is a structure of metamodels that are connected by* correspondence mappings. *These mappings express the semantic relationships and overlaps between the metamodels.*

$$M_{sum} := \{\mathcal{M}, corr\}$$

with the correspondence relation

$$corr = \langle e_1, e_2 \rangle \in \mathcal{M} \times \mathcal{M}$$

The metamodels that are part of the modular SUM metamodel can be divided into *legacy metamodels* and *additional metamodels*. Legacy metamodels have been defined outside the VITRUVIUS-based development process, and are also used independently of the SUM metamodel. Metamodels that are created for existing formalisms are also counted as legacy metamodels, although they are specifically created for the VITRUVIUS-based process. Since the formalisms, such as a textual language or a file format, are developed by external parties, the specification and evolution of these formalisms is not under control of the developers of the VITRUVIUS-based process, so these metamodels are also considered as legacy. Additional metamodels are defined especially for the VITRUVIUS-based process to represent further information, which shall be included into the modular SUM metamodel, such as mapping information between elements of the legacy metamodels, and additional information that is not represented in any of the legacy metamodels. An instance of a modular SUM metamodel, i.e., a SUM representing an actual software system, is a set of heterogeneous models, which are instances of the metamodels that are part of the modular SUM metamodel.

Since these heterogeneous models represent the same software system, a meaningful connection between the metamodels exists, which is made explicit in the *mappings* in the modular SUM. In an implementation of a VITRUVIUS-based framework, these mappings have to be complemented with rules for checking and restoring consistency between instances of the metamodels. Since there is no restriction on which metamodels can be used in the modular SUM metamodel, the semantic overlap between the metamodels can be of various size. The modelling of these mapping and the checking of consistency constraints is the subject of ongoing research [95], but not in the focus of this dissertation. We will outline the possible methods of specifying these mappings in 4.2.3.

Finally, the *view types* are also part of the SUM metamodel definition. View types decouple the inner structure of the SUM from the way that it is presented to the developers. Despite the modular structure, the SUM shall be perceived as a single entity that it represents, which is the software system under development. The view types serve as the interface for the interaction between developers and the system. The definition of view types make it possible to change the layout of the SUM metamodel without altering the way in which it can be accessed. View types will be described in detail in section 4.3.

4.2.2. Structure of the Modular SUM Metamodel

In this section, we will describe the parts of a modular SUM metamodel through the example of the CBSE scenario depicted in Figure 4.1 (We will exclude the performance view point for now).

In general, any facet of software development can be integrated into the approach in this way as long as a metamodel exists. Since the SUM is *method-specific*, as suggested by [7], the selection of metamodels for the SUM metamodel can vary from project to project: Depending on the domain for which software is being developed, metamodels for security, performance, real-time properties etc. can be included; depending on the development paradigm, component models, class models, aspect models etc. can be included. The CBSE example here is just one case that we have selected as a running example.

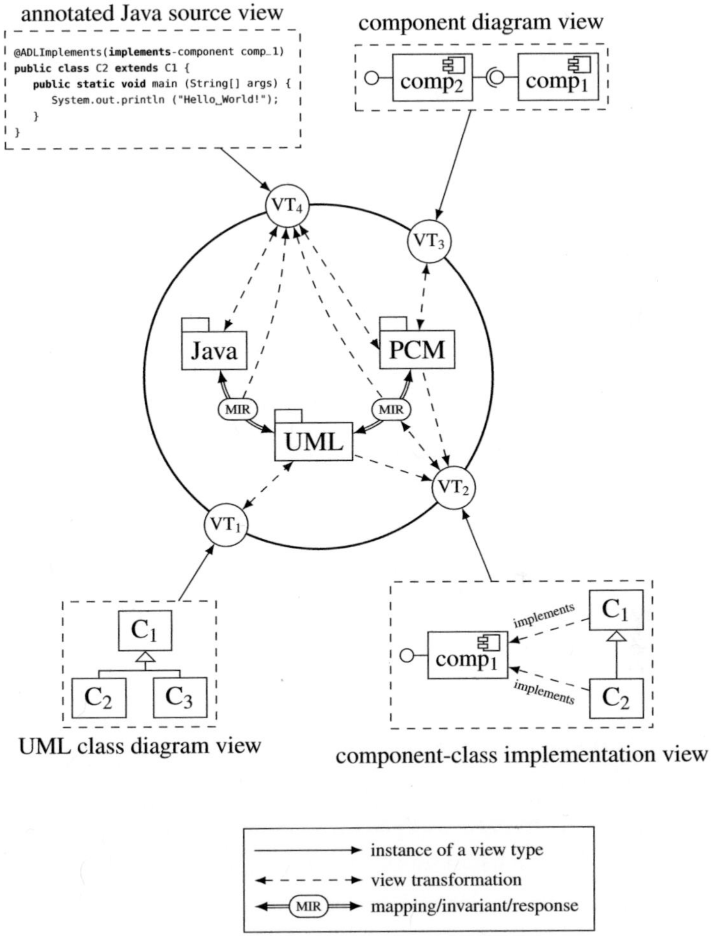

Figure 4.1.: Structure of the Modular SUM Metamodel in the CBSE Example Use Case

4.2.2.1. Metamodels

In the CBSE scenario, three formalisms are used: The Palladio Component Model (PCM) for the definition of software architecture, UML for the object-oriented design, and Java for the runtime semantics and implementation. PCM and UML are already based on a metamodel definition, so the PCM and UML metamodel are included into the modular SUM metamodel as *legacy metamodels*. Java is not originally based on a metamodel definition, but defined as a textual programming language with a specific grammar. There are, however, possibilities to express Java code in a metamodel-based format, such as the KDM Java metamodel of MoDisCo (Model Discovery) [23], or JaMoPP (Java Model Printer and Parser) [66]. Based on the availability of import and export tools that offer the conversion of textual and model-based Java programs, one of these approaches has to be chosen. In our example, we have decided to use the JaMoPP approach, since, at the time of writing, it offers stable tool support. Thus, the JaMoPP metamodel is also part of the modular SUM metamodel. These three legacy metamodels serve as sub-metamodels, but have not been modified in any way before being embedded into the modular SUM metamodel.

4.2.2.2. Correspondences

The elements in the respective sub-metamodel in the modular SUM metamodel share semantic relations, which are reflected by *correspondence mappings*. These mappings can be understood as an implementation of the correspondence concept in the ISO 42010 standard [77], which proposes the usage of correspondence elements to detect and express inconsistencies in architecture descriptions. The standard also contains a concept for *correspondence rules*, which are used as a declarative description of consistency and semantic relations.

To express the correspondence mappings between the sub-metamodels in VITRUVIUS, several methods exist (see subsection 4.2.3 for a detailed comparison). In the CBSE example, *MIR* elements [95] (mapping/invariant/resonse, depicted as ◄(MIR)►) have been chosen. MIR elements contain the actual *mapping* of classes and features in the different metamodels, *invariants*, which express consistency constraints between the metamodels, and *response* actions for consistency conservation, which guarantee that the SUM is always in a consistent state if changes are made to one of the submodels. In the example, MIR elements are defined for the combinations PCM/UML and UML/Java. It is not necessarily the case that there are mappings for every combination of metamodels in the modular SUM metamodel, either because the semantics of the connection could not be determined, is left undefined on purpose, or because none exists. The constraints and the mechanisms to establish consistency ensure that the conglomerate of models can interact in a uniform way with the outside, i.e. the views that are defined on top of the SUM.

4.2.2.3. View Types and Views

View types (depicted as (VT)) are defined based on the information in the metamodels of the SUM metamodel, and the additional mapping information. For each legacy metamodel, at least one view type is defined, which represents the complete metamodel or parts thereof. In the example, these legacy view types are UML class diagram (VT_1), component diagram (VT_3), and Java source (VT_4). While the PCM and UML view types only represent information from one metamodel respectively, the Java Source view type also contains information from the software architecture, i.e., the PCM metamodel. This information is displayed in Java annotations, which are a language element of Java, so the Java view type itself is a legacy view type that is fully compatible with the Java language definition. In addition to this enriched Java code view, a pure Java view without these architectural annotations can also be defined. The information about the mapping of Java classes to architectural element is, however, acquired by an analysis of the ←(MIR)→ elements between the metamodels of Java, UML, and PCM. Since the UML is only needed as the linking metamodel between object-oriented Java code and PCM instances, view type VT_4 does not display any explicit information from the UML metamodel, but only from PCM, such as component names. While the Java and PCM information can be edited in this view type (indicated by the bidirectional arrow ← →), the mapping itself cannot be altered, since this would affect elements in the UML metamodel, which is not modified by this view type.

In addition to these legacy view types, VT_2 is a specific view type for this SUM metamodel. It displays classes from UML, components from Java, and information on which classes implement which components. For this view type, a specific metamodel has to be defined, which contains the necessary concepts for the elements and relations. The information in the view type is acquired from the UML and PCM metamodel, as well as from the ←(MIR)→ element between these metamodels, which store the information of the implements-relation. Only this relation can be modified in VT_2; the classes and components themselves are not editable in this view type.

The actual views (depicted as [ ]) instantiate the view types. Of course, view types can be instantiated several times to express different parts of the SUM. Since the generation of views from the SUM instance is deterministic, multiple instantiation of the same subset of a SUM yields, however, the identic set of view elements. The definition of view types and views is described in detail in section 4.3.

4.2.2.4. Modelling Levels

The SUM metamodel and the view types consist of meta-elements, which are instantiated in actual SUMs and views. Using the terminology of MOF [118], SUM metamodels and view types reside on the *M2* layer, whereas SUMs and views reside on the *M1* layer. In Figure 4.2, the SUM metamodel and the instantiating views from Figure 4.1 has been extruded into the third

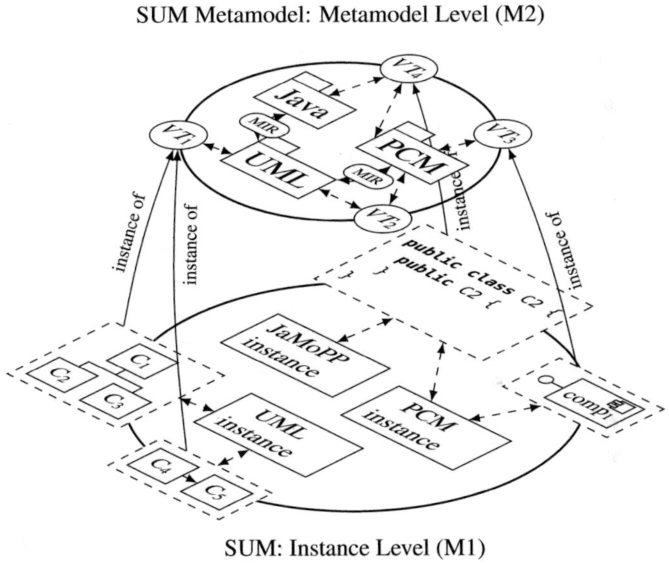

Figure 4.2.: The MOF Modelling Layers in VITRUVIUS

dimension to demonstrate the affiliation of the elements to the metamodelling layers.

4.2.3. Modelling of Intrinsic and Extrinsic Information

The information that is expressed in the SUM can be distinguished into two types: *Intrinsic* and *extrinsic* information. *Intrinsic* information is the information that is expressed by instances of the legacy sub-metamodels of the SUM metamodel. In the CBSE example, this kind of information consists of the following parts: the component-based architecture is expressed by instances of the PCM metamodel, while the class structure is expressed as a UML model, and the implementation is expressed as Java code (more specificly, a model-based representation thereof). Although these artefacts represent the same system from different viewpoints, there may be inconsistencies between them, since, in contrast to a pure OSM approach, the SUM in the VITRUVIUS approach is not redundancy-free. It is possible that the information in the sub-metamodels overlaps, complements, or is contradictory [122]. Furthermore, there may be semantic links between the elements of the sub-models that are not expressed formally, but are only expressed in natural language documents, or not persisted at all.

The semantic correspondences between the sub-models are called *extrinsic* information. This information is not explicitely modelled in the legacy metamodels. We can distinguish two cases of extrinsic information:

- information that can be *derived* from the information that is modelled in the legacy metamodels, e.g., by a set of rules;
- information that has to be *specified manually*.

As an example of information that can be derived by rules, we can use the correspondence between the component model and the simulation results metamodel in the CBSE example: The simulation results can be traced to the components to which they belong by a naming convention of the sensors, which contain the universal identifier of the AssemblyContext of the PCM component. An integrated view that displays this relationship can be computed automatically from this information. Of course, the rules and transformations themselves have to be defined manually, or can be determined by an automatic matching of similar elements, which is however not in the scope of this thesis.

As an example for the second case, the implements-relation between classes and component is one kind of additional information that cannot be derived automatically, but has to be specified manually. The *component-class implementation view* shows the correspondence links and offers means for the manipulation of them.

In either case, extrinsic information is made explicit in the VITRUVIUS approach, and thus persisted in the SUM metamodel. In contrast to the legacy metamodels, which are integrated without change, extrinsic information can be modelled in various ways, depending on the nature of the information and the way in which it is determined. Thus, for a certain combination of legacy metamodels, there can be various SUM metamodels, which differ in the way that the extrinsic information is modelled. This is, however, not relevant for the access to the information in the SUM, since view types fulfil the purpose of conceptual interfaces in the VITRUVIUS approach, so that the access to a SUM is decoupled from its inner representation. Thus, it is possible to use the same view types with different internal representations of the additional information.

In our previous work [64], we have investigated ways of extending metamodels with additional information. In the following subsections, we will apply these methods in the context of VITRUVIUS to persist extrinsic information in SUM metamodels, and estimate the advantages and disadvantages of each solution.

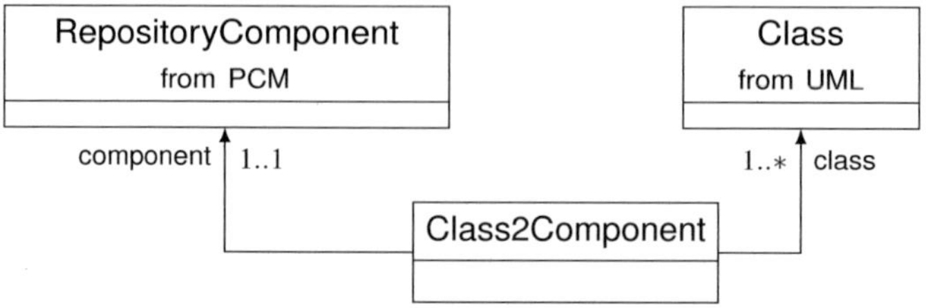

Figure 4.3.: Example for Mapping in an Additional Metamodel

4.2.3.1. Additional Metamodel

The simplest way of expressing the additional information is a special metamodel, which serves only the purpose of expressing the mapping between elements of other metamodels. This metamodel can be described as a "bridge" or "glue" metamodel. Furthermore, the set of valid mappings can be restricted in the metamodel using constraints in a declarative language, such as OCL in Ecore-based metamodels.

In the CBSE example, the component-class implementation relation of the example would be stored in a separate metamodel that contains an element for the mapping of components to classes, as displayed in Figure 4.3.

Advantages: The mappings can be expressed for any kind of metamodels. The mapping metamodel can be amended with arbitrary additional information, which as modelled as additional classes and references in the mapping metamodel.

Disadvantages: An additional view type is always necessary to display the information, since the information is stored in neither of the participating metamodels.

4.2.3.2. Metamodel Extension Mechanisms

The VITRUVIUS approach follows the principle that the involved metamodels are included non-intrusively, meaning that no changes to the metamodels are necessary for the inclusion in the modular SUM. Some metamodels already offer means for extension and customization, which preserve the compatibility of existing instances. Thus, they can be used in VITRUVIUS for the persistence of correspondence information.

In the CBSE example, the component-class mapping information could be stored either in the PCM metamodel, or in the UML metamodel, or in both. This is possible since these metamodels contain extension mechanisms, so that arbitrary information, such as the structural information in this example, can be added to the instances without having to change the metamodel. In UML, this is the *profiles* extension mechanism, with which instances can be extended by additional, user-defined information. In PCM, a profile extension mechanism is under development [96] based on the EMF Profiles project [101]. In Figure 4.4, an example application of the profiles approach is displayed: The stereotype UMLClassImplementation is defined using the EMF profiles approach for PCM. It expresses that a PCM component is implemented by a set of classes in UML, through a cross-metamodel reference to the Class element in the UML metamodel. To model a concrete mapping between a PCM component and a UML class, the stereotype is applied to a PCM element and linked to the UML classes that implement the component.

The profile approach offers a type-safe mechanism for adding custom information without breaking compatibility to tools and instances. From a metamodelling point of view, the stereotypes and profiles in this example are used a standardised method for creating a decorator model [91].

In general, all instances of Ecore-based metamodels can be extended using textual annotations. This method is however not very convenient, since there is no type safety, and information has to be serialised to a

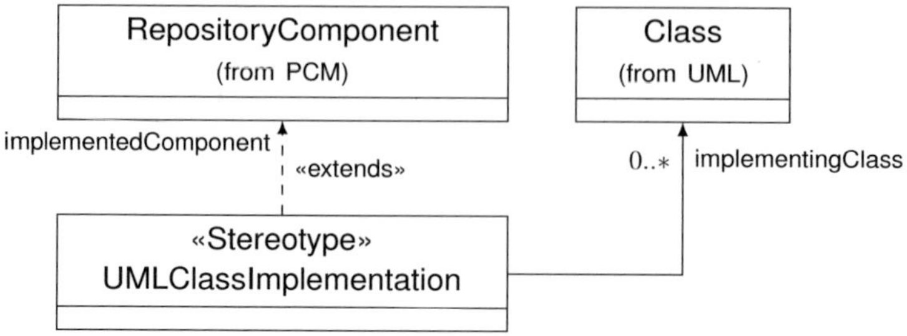

Figure 4.4.: Example for Mapping with Profiles and Stereotypes

textual representation. Furthermore, this annotation is only available at the meta-level by default and has to be explicitely included in the respective metamodels, if it is to be used at the instance level, e.g., by including a reference to the EAnnotation class.

Advantages: The information can be displayed in legacy view types that support the metamodel extension mechanism. The stereotypes can contain arbitrary additional information and references to other metamodels.

Disadvantages: This method is only applicable to metamodels that contain an extension mechanism.

4.2.3.3. Declarative Definition

If the correspondence between the elements of the different sub-metamodels can be determined automatically, it is possible to describe the mapping using a declarative language, such as the Mapping/Invariant/Response language by Kramer et al. [95]. The links between actual elements can then be derived from this declarative definition. An example for such a definition, using a textual domain-specific language, is displayed in Listing 1. In this example, the *interface* concept of PCM is mapped to UML class diagrams. Lines 5–13 describe the correspondences between the interface concepts of both

```
import "http://sdq.ipd.uka.de/PCM/Repository/5.0" as repo
import "http://www.eclipse.org/uml2/2.1.0/UML" as umlcd

// correspondence rules
map repo:OperationInterface to umlcd:Interface
  with signatures::OperationSignature
      to ownedOperation::Operation
    with returnType::DataType
      to ownedParameter::Parameter.type::Type
      when ownedParameter.direction = return
    and with parameters::Parameter
      to ownedParameter::Parameter
      when ownParam.direction <> return

// consistency invariant
context repo:Repository
inv uniqueInterfaceNames(i::repo:Interface,j::repo:Interface):
 self.interfaces->forAll(i,j | i.entityName <> j.entityName)

// response action
var interfaceNameCount : Map<String,Integer>
on creation of interface:repo:Interface
restore inv interfaceNamesUnique(i::repo:Interface, j::repo:Interface)
by {
  var occurrences = interfaceNameCount.get(i.entityName)
  occurrences = (occurrences == null) ? 2 : occurrences++
  interfaceNameCount.put(i.entityName, occurrences)
  interface.entityName += occurrences
}
if (occurrences == null) {
      occurrences = 2
    } else {
      occurrences++
}
```

Listing 1: Example for Declarative Mapping of Components and Classes (from [95]) languages: PCM interfaces are mapped to UML interfaces; signatures are mapped to operations; return types and parameters are mapped to parameters. In addition, an invariant is defined in lines 16–18, which realises a naming convention between PCM and UML. The response action in lines 21–34 is not necessary for the mapping itself, but describes a behaviour that reacts to changes in one of the models, in this case the creation of an interface in PCM.

Since the declarative definition is an all-quantified expression that applies to all instances in a SUM, this method does, of course, not apply to information that has to be specified manually. For such correspondences, the MIR elements would have to hold explicit mappings between actual instances (e.g., component $comp_1$ corresponds to class c_1), which is exactly the first approach described above, using a glue metamodel.

Advantages: The declarative description offers a compact method for the definition of general correspondences that are applied to all elements in a SUM. The automatic application avoids the manual definition of correspondances for every element in the SUM

Disadvantages: The declarative definition is not suitable for special cases at the instance level that cannot be described with general rules. It would be possible to encode these exceptions in the declarative definition using naming conventions or identifiers of elements, although this would mix the definition levels (M2 and M1). Thus, exceptions from the declarative mapping rules have to be handled by a framework that implements the VITRUVIUS approach and that provides an execution engine for the declarative mappings.

4.3. View Types and Views in VITRUVIUS

In this section, we will define the notions *view type* and *view* in the context of VITRUVIUS. For the formal definition of the terms, we will use the set notation for metamodels and instances presented in section 2.2.

4.3.1. Definition

In VITRUVIUS, views are the means by which a developer interacts with the SUM to retrieve or manipulate information of the software system. The VITRUVIUS concept of a view is based on Atkinson's understanding of the view concept in the Orthographic Software Modeling approach:

> "a view is a normal model which just happens to have been generated dynamically for the purpose of allowing a user to see the system from a specific viewpoint" [7, section 3.1]

Thus, the elements in a view *represent* elements in the SUM. The notion of *view type* has been introduced by Goldschmidt et al. [57]. It describes the kinds of elements that a view can contain; thus the view type is the *metamodel* of the view. In VITRUVIUS, the term *view point* is used to group view types by the concerns that they serve (cf. Figure 2.1 and the ISO 42010 standard [77]). View points are not modelled explicitly by a model element in the SUM metamodel.

The relation of the terms view, view type, and view point, as well as model and metamodelmodel is depicted in Figure 4.5: Views and view types are special models and metamodels, which *represent* elements from other models and metamodels. The models and metamodels of Figure 4.5, which are represented by the views and view types, are part of the SUM and the SUM metamodel respectively.

In the categories of the ISO 42010 standard [77], VITRUVIUS is a *project ive approach*, since the views are generated artefacts that are derived from the single underlying model (SUM). In a consistent model, views do not

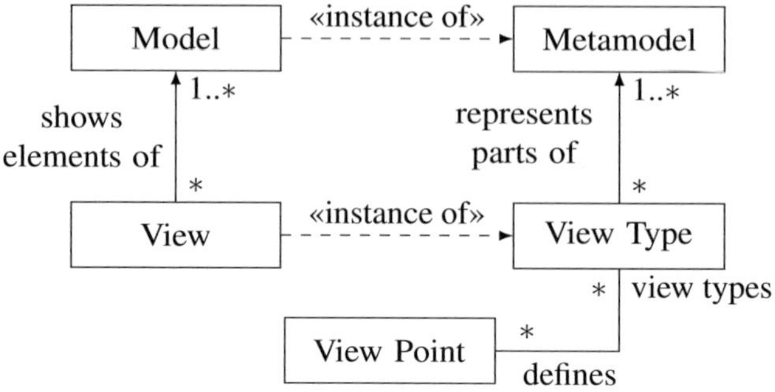

Figure 4.5.: View and View Type Terminology

contain any information that cannot be computed from the information in the SUM. VITRUVIUS contains, however, also concepts of synthetic approaches, since the "single repository", which is demanded for a projective approach, is indeed a modular SUM, where correspondences between sub-models are explicitly defined, which is a characteristic of synthetic approaches. Thus, the approach is not synthetic in the sense that correspondences are defined directly between the views, but between the model elements in the SUM.

Although views and view types are "normal" models and metamodels, they have special properties that the models and metamodels in the SUM and SUM metamodel do not posess, and that are specified in the following definitions.

We will use the symbols listed in Table 4.1 to denote the differents sets of elements. A complete overview of the elements at the metamodel level and at the instance level is given in Figure 4.6.

4.3.1.1. View Type

Definition 5 (View Types in VITRUVIUS)**.** *The set of view types is a subset of the set of metamodels* $\text{VIEWTYPE} \subseteq \mathscr{M}$. *In a view type* $VT \subseteq \text{VIEWTYPE}$, *an element* $e_{vt} \in VT$ *represents information of elements in a metamodel*

symbol	meaning
$\mathscr{M}_{sum}$	SUM metamodels
SUM	SUM instances
VIEWTYPE	View types
VIEW	Views
rep	is represented by, metamodel↔view type
$\underline{rep}$	is represented by, model↔view

Table 4.1.: Notation for SUM Metamodels and SUMs

$e_{sum} \in M, M \subseteq M_{sum}$, which is part of a modular SUM metamodel $M_{sum} \subseteq \mathscr{M}_{sum}$. This is expressed by the is-represented-by *relation*

$$rep = \langle e_{sum}, e_{vt} \rangle \in \mathscr{M}_{sum} \times \text{VIEWTYPE}$$

To respect the generalization hierarchy in the SUM metamodel and in the view type, we define an extension of the relation rep that covers also the representation information in the superclasses of the elements:

$$rep^* = \{\langle e_{sum}, e_{vt} \rangle \in \mathscr{M}_{sum} \times \text{VIEWTYPE} \mid$$
$$\exists \langle e'_{sum}, e'_{vt} \rangle \in parents(e_{sum}) \times parents(e_{vt}) : rep(e'_{sum}, e'_{vt})\}$$

The relation of elements in a view type to elements in a SUM metamodel can be seen in Figure 4.6: The view type VT_1 contains an element e_5, which represents information from a modular SUM metamodel (M_{sum_1}), specifically from two different sub-metamodels M_1 and M_2. This semantic connection is expressed through the relation *rep*. Note that the direction of the relation *rep* is from the metamodel to the view type. We have chosen this direction since it follows the direction of the transformation of information in the SUM metamodel to the view type. We will use this relation to describe properties of the view types in the following.

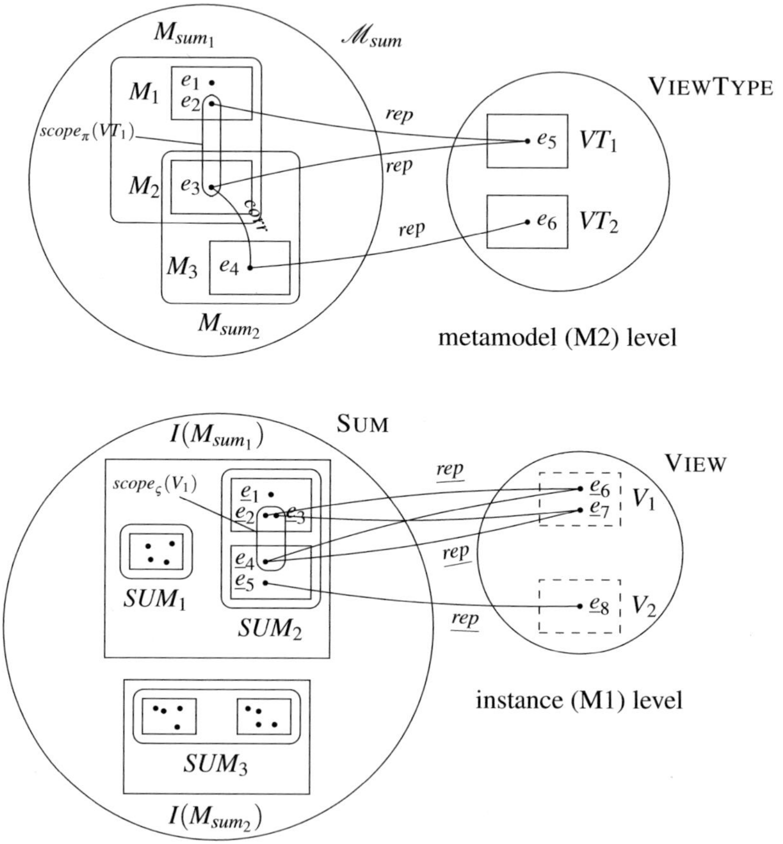

Figure 4.6.: Sets of Elements in VITRUVIUS: SUM metamodels $\mathscr{M}_{sum}$, SUM instances SUM, view types, and views

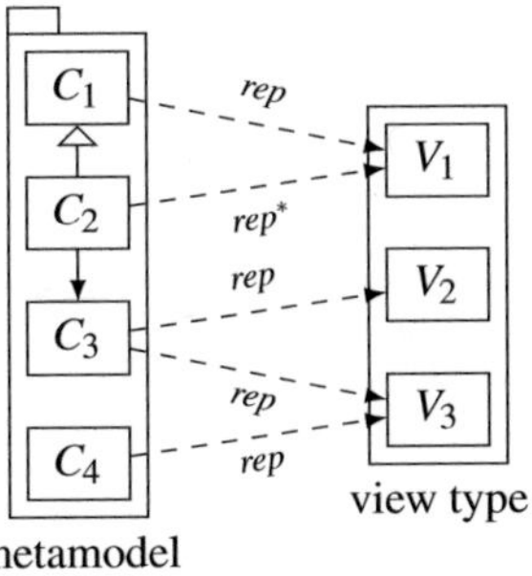

Figure 4.7.: The *is-represented-by* Relation *rep* and its generalization closure rep^* between Classes $C_1,\ldots,C_4$ in a Metamodel in the SUM Metamodel and View Type Elements $V_1,\ldots,V_3$ a View Type

A view in VITRUVIUS is transient, wich means that all the information that is contained in a view must also be contained in the SUM, so that the view can be generated from it. As a consequence of this, for the elements of a SUM metamodel and its view types, the relation *rep* has the following properties:

- It is *surjective*, since all elements in a view type represent at least one element in the SUM metamodel or of another view type.
- It is in general not *functional*, since an element of the SUM metamodel may be represented by several elements in the view type.
- If the view type is a subset of the underlying SUM metamodel, e.g., it is identical with one of the metamodels $M \subseteq M_{sum}$ of the modular SUM, the relation is *injective*.

As introduced in the preceding section, VITRUVIUS is based on a modular SUM that is not free of redundancies and overlaps, and contains additional information to make the semantic relations between the sub-models explicit. Since the views serve as a uniform way of accessing the information in the SUM, they must be able to abstract from these redundancies and to re-organise information in such a way that the developer is presented only the desired parts of the SUM. This is why the view types in VITRUVIUS are *strongly decoupled* from the SUM metamodel regarding the structure of the view type metamodel: It is not necessary (although still possible) that the elements in the view type are a subset of the elements in the metamodels of the SUM, so that $\text{VIEWTYPE} \subseteq \{M_1 \cup \ldots \cup M_n\}$. A view type can reproduce, re-arrange, or aggregate information from these metamodels.

4.3.1.2. View

Definition 6 (Views in VITRUVIUS). *Let $VT \in \text{VIEWTYPE}$ be a view type. The instances $I(VT)$ of this view type are called* views. *An element $\underline{e}_v$ in a view $v \subseteq I(VT)$ represent an element $\underline{e}_{sum}$ of a SUM. This is expressed by the* is-represented-by *relation at the instance level:*

$$\underline{rep} = \langle \underline{e}_{sum}, \underline{e}_v \rangle \in \text{SUM}, \text{VIEW}$$

The relation $\underline{rep}$ respects the is-represented-by relation at the meta-level. That is, an element $\underline{e}_v$ in a view v can only represent an element $\underline{e}_{sum}$ in the SUM if the respective elements of which they are instances are also in the is-represented-by relation:

$$\forall \underline{e}_{sum} \in I_*(e_{sum}), \underline{e}_v \in I_*(e_{vt}) : \underline{rep}(\underline{e}_{sum}, \underline{e}_{vt}) \Rightarrow rep^*(e_{sum}, e_{vt})$$

The relation $\underline{rep}$ is a relation at the instance level (M1). It has the same properties as the relation *rep* at the metamodel level: It is surjective and in general not functional.

In the consistent state, views contain only *transient* information, which is also persisted in instances of the sub-metamodels of the SUM that it represents. Thus, a view can always be generated from the elements in the SUM with a *view defintion function*:

Definition 7 (View Definition Function). *A view is defined by a* view definition function, *which calculates a view of a specific view type VT from an actual single underlying model $\underline{M}_{sum} \subseteq I(M_{sum})$:*

$$\text{DEF}_{VT} : \text{SUM} \rightarrow I(VT)$$

During editing, temporary inconsistencies may occur, which have to be propagated back to the SUM (see subsection 4.3.4 for details), so that the view can always be generated from the information in the SUM.

This difference in the role of models and views results in a fundamental difference between the consistency relations (represented by double arrows ↔ in Figure 4.1) in the SUM, and the bidirectional transformations between the SUM and the views (represented as single arrows ← → and - - →): The consistency relations provide the semantic links between the modular sub-metamodels of the SUM in the form of explicit models or constraints. They also contain update policies and strategies to restore consistency if an update violates a constraint. The bidirectional transformations between views and SUM serve the purpose of keeping the views up-to-date with the SUM and to update the SUM likewise.

In the following subsections, we will introduce the term *view type scope* to express the relation of view types to the SUM metamodel. Then, we will define view categories based on the scope definition. Finally, we will describe how editability and synchronisation of view types are managed in VITRUVIUS.

4.3.1.3. Relation of View Types and Views

As displayed in Figure 4.6, and specified in Definition 6, elements at the instance level can only be part of the relation $\underline{rep}$ if their corresponding metaelements are in the relation *rep*. This structural similarity can be expressed as a homomorphism of the instantiation relation $I_*()$ between the elements.

Corollary 1. *Let* $\mathbf{I} = (\mathscr{I}_{\text{CLASS}}, \underline{rep})$ *and* $\mathbf{C} = (\text{CLASS}, rep^*)$ *be relational structures. Then the function* $class : \mathscr{I}_{\text{CLASS}} \to \text{CLASS}$ *is a homomorphism of* $\mathbf{I}$ *in* $\mathbf{C}$.

Proof. The helper function $class()$ (see subsection 2.3.2) determines the class $c \in \text{CLASS}$ of an instance element $\underline{c} \in \mathscr{I}$. Thus, the function is an inverse of the instance-relation I_*:

$$class(\underline{c}) = c \Rightarrow \underline{c} \in I_*(c)$$

Using Definition 6, we can conclude that for any instances $\underline{c}, \underline{e}_v \in \mathscr{I}_{\text{CLASS}}$, the following relation holds:

$$\underline{rep}(\underline{c}, \underline{e}_v) \Rightarrow rep^*\left(class(\underline{c}), class(\underline{e}_v)\right)$$

Thus, the function *class* is a homomorphism for the fundamental operations $\underline{rep}$ and rep^*. □

4.3.2. Scope of View Types

4.3.2.1. Projectional Scope

As a consequence of the strong decoupling of view types from the metamodels that they represent, a single view type in VITRUVIUS can represent more than one metamodel. In the example of Figure 1.1, the *component-class implementation view* contains components and classes, which are elements from two distinct metamodels: PCM and UML. As a consequence of this, Definition 1 is insufficient for the purposes of VITRUVIUS, since in this definiton, view types only contain a definition of a concrete syntax and a mapping to elements of a single metamodel, which the view type represents. (cf. Figure 2.1 on page 15). Due to the modular nature of the SUM, we will extend this definition so that views on heterogeneous models are possible.

Definition 8 (Projectional Scope). *The* projectional scope *of a view type is defined by the relation of the elements in the view type to elements of the metamodels that the view type represents:*

$$scope_{\pi}(VT) := \{e \in \mathcal{M}_{sum} \mid \exists e' \in VT : rep(e,e')\}$$

If there exists a metamodel $M \in \mathcal{M}$ so that $scope_{\pi}(VT) \subseteq M$, then we say that VT has a single-metamodel projectional scope, *which means that it contains elements that represent elements from one metamodel; otherwise, we say that VT has a* multi-metamodel projectional scope, *since it contains elements that represent elements from multiple metamodels.*

The projectional scope of a view type is a subset of a SUM metamodel, since a view type cannot represent information from several SUM metamodels.

$$\exists M_{sum} \subseteq \mathcal{M}_{sum} : scope_{\pi}(VT) \subseteq M_{sum}$$

In the example of Figure 4.6, the view type VT_1 has a multi-metamodel projectional scope (M_1 and M_2), while view type VT_2 has a single-metamodel projectional scope (M_3).

Since a view type is a metamodel, it can also serve as a source metamodel for other view types. View types that represent elements from other view types are called *composed view types*.

Definition 9 (Composed View Type). *A view type $VT \subseteq$ VIEWTYPE with*

$$scope_{\pi}(VT) \cap \text{VIEWTYPE} \neq \emptyset$$

is called a composed *view type.*

A view type can represent elements of one or multiple metamodels. If a view type represents all the elements of the metamodels that are in its projectional scope, the view type is called *total view type*.

Definition 10 (Total View Type). *A view type $VT \subseteq$ VIEWTYPE with*

$$\forall e \in scope_\pi(VT), \forall M \in M_{sum} : e \in M \Rightarrow M \subseteq scope_\pi(VT)$$

is called a total *view type.*

The totality of view types is aligned with the notion of totality in the *lenses* approach [50]: A total view type is able to represent all elements that are in a particular sub-metamodel of a SUM metamodel. This property alone would only qualify for *left-totality* in the terms of the totality in lenses. For *right-totality*, the co-domain of the *rep* relation has to be a superset of the view type metamodel. In VITRUVIUS, the view type metamodel is part of the view type definition, and does not contain elements that do not represent any elements of the SUM metamodel. Thus, view types in VITRUVIUS are always right-total, and left-totality is sufficient for the totality of a view type.

4.3.2.2. Selectional Scope

Definition 11 (Selectional Scope). *The* selectional scope *of a view type is determined by a logical function $\varphi : \mathscr{I} \mapsto \{true, false\}$, which imposes restrictions on the instances of the view type:*

$$scope_\varsigma(VT) := \{i \in \bigcup_{e \in scope_\pi(vt)} I(e) \mid \varphi(i)\}$$

The selectional scope of a view type can be expressed by constraints in the view type metamodel; although defined at the metamodel level, it affects the instances of the view type, which are the views. Of course, the actual set of elements in a view is determined by a manual selection, which can only be a subset of the elements in the view type's selectional scope.

In the CBSE example, VT_2 shows the implements-relation between classes and components. The selectional scope of this view type restricts the elements to only those that are part of an implements-relation; if a class or component is not connected to a component or class repectively, it is not part of the view. Since the selectional scope of the view type affects all possible instantiating views, it has to be defined in a constraint language such as OCL.

An actual view also has a selectional scope, which is usually determined manually by selecting the set of elements that should be displayed in the view. The view shown in Figure 4.1 displays a subset of the possible instances (the elements $comp_1$, C_1, and C_2).

4.3.3. Projectional and Combining View Types

In VITRUVIUS, view types are divided into two categories, which depend on the property of the relation from elements in the SUM elements in the views that are instances of the view types. For the black-box usage of the SUM, the category of a view type is irrelevant. It is however relevant for the definition of the modular SUM metamodel, since the complexity of the SUM-to-view transformation and the definition of update semantics differ in their complexity for the view type categories. In Table 4.2, the categories for the CBSE examle in Figure 4.1 can be seen.

4.3.3.1. Projectional View Types

A view type is called *projectional* if every element in the view type represents only a single element of the SUM metamodel. This means that the *rep* relation of metamodel elements to view type elements is *injective*. Projectional view types do not necessarily have a single-metamodel projectional scope; it is possible that a projectional view type contains elements from several metamodels in the SUM metamodel.

Existing view types are integrated in the VITRUVIUS approach as *legacy view types*. These view types are projectional and have a single-metamodel projectional scope. In the example shown in Figure 4.1, the PCM *component diagram* view types and the UML *class diagram* view types are legacy view types. Projectional view types require less effort in defining, since

view type	categories
component diagram	projectional (legacy)
class diagram	projectional (legacy)
component-class implementation	combining
annotated Java source	combining

Table 4.2.: View Type Categories in the CBSE example of Figure 4.1

the underlying metamodel can be used as the view type metamodel, so no specific metamodel has to be created, and the represents-relation is just a projection of a subset of the underlying metamodel.

4.3.3.2. Combining View Types

View types that contain elements that represent multiple elements of the underlying metamodels are called *combining view types*. The *rep* relation for these view types is not injective.

In the CBSE example, the component-class implementation diagram and the annotated Java Source view type are examples of combining view types: The component-class implementation diagram combines information of the UML class diagram and the MIR element into a class element in the view type that contains a reference to the component that it implements. Combining view types are always necessary to display intrinsic and extrinsic information together in an integrated view type, like in this example.

4.3.4. Editability of Views Types and Synchronisation with the SUM metamodel

The views in VITRUVIUS are created by transformations from the SUM (depicted as ← → in Figure 4.1). The transient nature of views (cf. Definition 6) guarantees that the SUM always contains sufficient information to generate the views. Since the views are the only vehicle by which information in the SUM can be modified, rules for the editability of view types have to be specified.

Definition 12 (Editability of views). *For views in* VITRUVIUS, *the set of elements that can be modified is called the* editability scope. *This scope is defined for a view type at the metamodel level, but can be refined for actual views.*

Furthermore, a view type definition contains rules for the propagation of changes back to the metamodels that the view type represents.

4.3.4.1. Constraint Violations through Edit Operations

If a view type has a multi-metamodel projectional scope, the views that instantiate this view type can represent several heterogeneous models, which are affected by edit operations on the views. It is possible that there are further consistency constraints in MIR elements that exist between the metamodels, and also between the affected metamodels and further metamodels in the modular SUM metamodel. In the running example (see Figure 4.1 on page 69), the component-class implementation view type affects instances of UML and PCM, between which a MIR element exists. Furthermore, a MIR element exists between UML and Java.

An edit operation on the class-component view can, theoretically, affect the following constraints:

1. constraints of the PCM or UML metamodel;
2. constraints in the MIR element between PCM and UML;
3. constraints in the MIR element between UML and Java.

The constraints in the first and second case affect elements that are represented in the view type, and are thus inside the projectional scope of the view type, whereas the constraints in the third case are outside the projectional scope of the view type.

It would be desirable that the rules of the view type were so restrictive that edit operations in views cannot introduce inconsistencies by violating any of these constraints inside the scope of the view type. This would require that the definition of the view type rules is coupled to the consistency constraints between the metamodels whose elements the view type represents. Since the consistency rules can be defined in arbitrary languages, this coupling can neither be determined nor checked automatically due to the undecidability of language inclusion [14]. Thus, the rules of the view types have to be specified manually in such a way that inconsistencies in the scope of the view type are avoided.

In VITRUVIUS, we allow that view types are constructed in such a way that edit operations can cause constraint violations in those parts of the SUM that are outside the view type scope. If view types had to be restricted manually to edit operations that can never cause constraint violations, the editabilitiy restrictions for each view type would always have to respect the complete set of constraints in the SUM metamodel, which would add the complexity of the whole SUM metamodel to each view type. If all possible cases of inconsistencies had to be regarded in the rule definition for view types, it would mean that the person who defines the view types would have to know all the sub-metamodels in the SUM metamodels and all consistency rules between them. Furthermore, each of the view type definitions would have to be adapted at any changes to the SUM metamodel.

This would violate the concept of modularity and would also aggravate the problem of evolution of the sub-metamodels, since any change to the modular SUM metamodel, such as a modification to a metamodel or a MIR element, would cause a complete refactoring of all view types, since every one of them could possibly be affected. Since it is not possible to check automatically if a view type definition may introduce inconsistencies, we follow a different approach:

Instead, the view types in VITRUVIUS only have to respect the constraints of the metamodels and those MIR elements that are inside their projectional

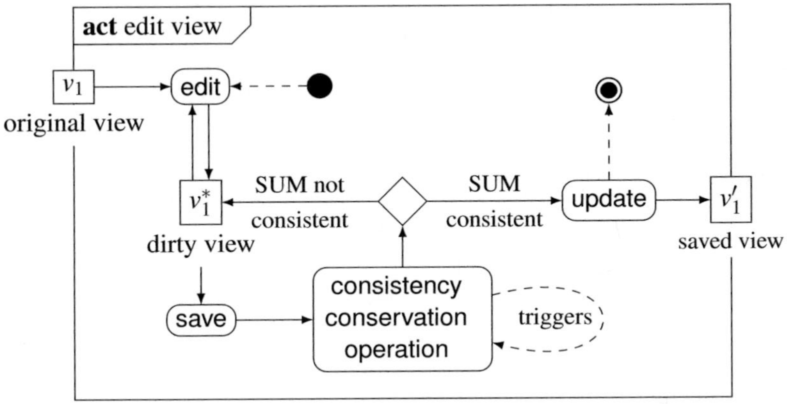

Figure 4.8.: Editing Workflow in Views

scope. This way, if a metamodel or MIR element in the SUM metamodel is added, deleted, or modified, only the view types that are directly accessing these elements have to co-evolve. Furthermore, this property reduces the strain on the *methodologist*, since it is not required that an "omniscient" methodologist is present who is an expert for every part of the SUM metamodel. Thus, the methodologist role can also be distributed between multiple persons with expert knowledge of the respective metamodels and the dependencies between them. Of course, it is recommended that the editability and propagation rules respect as many consistency constraints as possible, since it is not possible to exclude inconsistencies completely by static checks of the view types.

4.3.4.2. Semi-Automatic Checking and Resolution of Consistency

The VITRUVIUS approach includes a semi-automatic process for the checking and resolving of consistency constraint violations, which involves users in re-establishing the concistency in the SUM.

The process of editing a view can be seen in Figure 4.8: While a view is being edited, it can contain information that is not yet part of the SUM. If elements in the view v_1 are edited, the view enters a *dirty state* (indicated as v_1^*) where the elements in the view are not synchronised with the underlying model. Since the edited information in a view is not persisted in the SUM, it is lost if the view is closed and re-opened, thus re-generated. To persist the changes, the edit operations have to be written back to the SUM by a *save* operation so that they are still available on re-opening. The modifications in a view can, however, violate consistency constraints in the SUM, either because constraints inside a sub-metamodel are violated, or because the inter-metamodel constraints in the MIR elements are violated, or both. To restore the consistency, the MIR elements define response actions, which conserve the consistency of the SUM. These actions can themselves cause further responses, which attempt to conserve consistency within the SUM. It is possible that the conflicts that were raised through the edit operation in the view, or by the subsequent response actions, cannot be resolved automatically, but have to be fixed manually. These further editing operations can be performed either by the user role who committed the initial edit operation, or, if access restrictions are in place that limit the edit operations on other parts of the SUM, by other user roles.

If the consistency check was successful, i.e., the SUM is in a consistent state, the view returns to the non-dirty state (indicated as v_1') and can be edited anew. If the operation was not successful and a sequence of consistency conservation operations that leads to a consistent state could not be determined, the conservation operations have to be rolled back, and the view remains in the dirty state. The user of the view is informed that the edit operation was unsuccessful and can perform further editing steps in the view to avoid the inconsistency.

4.3.4.3. Discussion

The editing process in VITRUVIUS requires that the views are synchronised with the SUM at every save operation. Thus, the consistency check is an *online* operation. If a view is edited offline, it is not possible to check whether the changes in the view violate consistency constraints in the SUM. We have deliberately chosen to design the views in VITRUVIUS this way, since the advantage of modularization would be lost if every view type contained all the constraints that are necessary to prevent consistency violations. If this were the case, the complexity of each view type would be equal to the complexity of the total SUM metamodel. Furthermore, the constraints would have to be synchronised manually with the correspondence mappings and rules in the SUM. We expect that an automatic extraction of these constraints is not possible or only possible in special cases. Thus the consistency of a view in VITRUVIUS is not checked statically, meaning without applying changes to the SUM and analyzing the result.

4.4. Development Process

The VITRUVIUS development process is an extension of the development process of the Orthographic Software Modelling approach [7]. The process distinguishes between the role of the *methodologist* and the role of the *developer*. It is of course possible that specialised instantiations of VITRUVIUS contain further roles, depending on the domain that the development happens in. For example, in a component-based software engineering process such as Palladio [13], the developer role is refined to system architect, component developer, system deployer, and domain expert. These roles are subsumed as a single developer role, i.e., user of the modular SUM, in the VITRUVIUS process as displayed in Figure 4.9.

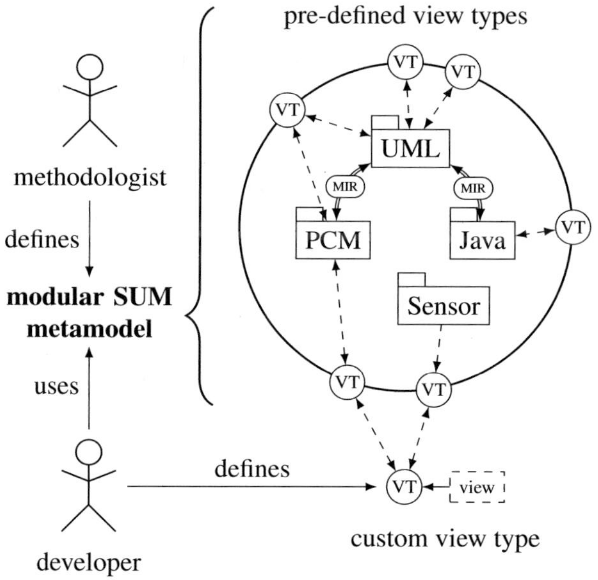

Figure 4.9.: Roles in the VITRUVIUS Development Process

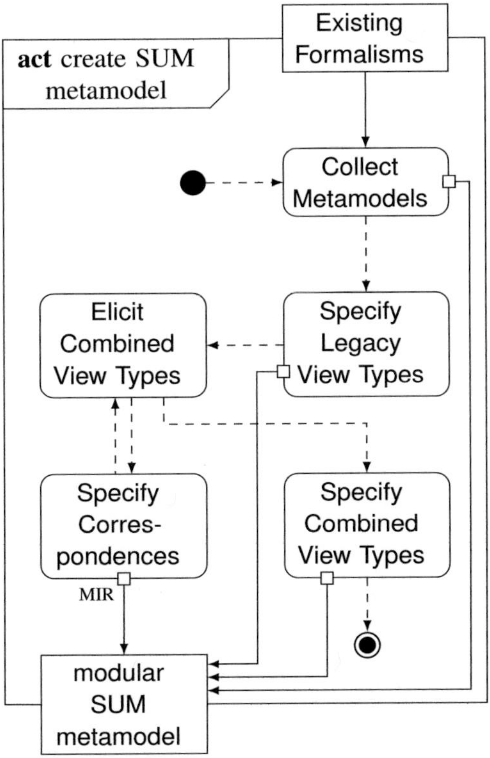

Figure 4.10.: Process for the Creation of the Modular SUM Metamodel

4.4.1. Process Model

In this subsection, we will describe the process for the definition and usage of the modular SUM metamodel and the view types. We will describe the responsibilities and the process for each of the roles.

4.4.1.1. Methodologist

The methodologist role is responsible for the creation of the modular SUM metamodel for a specific development scenario. This task includes the elicitation of the set of legacy metamodels that has to be supported in the scenario and the definition of the mappings between these metamodels (cf. Definition 4). In the example in Figure 4.1, these legacy metamodels are PCM, UML, and Java (a model-based representation of Java has to be chosen by the methodologist).

For each of the legacy metamodels, at least one legacy view type exists, which has projectional-complete view type scope (after the definition of [56, sec. 4.4]). The view type contains the complete legacy metamodel, which is exposed as a view type by the SUM metamodel, and possibly augmented with additional information. Legacy applications can use the view type as an import/export function. In the example, the Java source view type is able to display all elements of Java; architecture information is added in Java annotations of the respective classes, which are elements of the Java language.

Since a view type expects edit operations as a sequence of atomic editing steps, it is not possible to export a model through a view, modify it and re-import the modified model directly, since this state-based modification of instances is not support by VITRUVIUS. To use external tools to modify models, they either have to provide means to record the atomic editing steps, which are compatible to the view type definition of VITRUVIUS, or use algorithms for change detection to extract the atomic editing steps from a difference calculation of two model versions.

Further existing legacy view types are integrated by the methodologist. In the CBSE example, the different contexts of PCM (assembly, deployment, usage), and the diagram types of UML (class diagram, package diagram, ...) are integrated as legacy view types.

The methodologist role aggregates information about existing metamodel and elicits the semantic connections and overlaps that may exist between them. The elicitation process is view-driven: The methodologist identifies which kinds of information need exists, and, based on this information, defines additional view types that aggregate information from several metamodels. Since semantic correspondences between the metamodels may often not be represented formally in any of the metamodels, it is the task of the methodologist to decide between the different methods for adding this information to the modular SUM (see subsection 4.2.3).

As shown in Figure 4.9, the methodologist is responsible for the elicitation and specificatino of all the parts of the modular SUM metamodel.

4.4.1.2. Developer

The developer uses the pre-defined view types, which have been specified by the methodologist, to create, access, and manipulate the SUM for the system under consideration. Depending on the specific development process of the domain, the developer role can be sub-divided into several roles. In the running example, the CBSE process defines the roles system architect, component developer, system deployer, and domain expert. All these roles use a subset of the view types of the SUM metamodel.

The developer role is primarily concerned with the elements at the model level, such as the elements in the SUM and the views (see Figure 4.11). The SUM metamodel cannot be changed by the developer. It is however possible that developers define *custom* view types. This feature of VITRUVIUS supports the use case that developers have information needs that have not been foreseen by the methodologist (see next subsection).

4.4.2. View Type Categories by Developer Role

As described in the preceding subsection, the view types in VITRUVIUS can also be distinguished by the developer role that specifies the view type. We will call these categories *pre-defined* and *custom*.

4.4.2.1. Pre-defined View Types

The view types that are defined by the methodologist are called *pre-defined view types*. These view types include the existing formalisms, which have

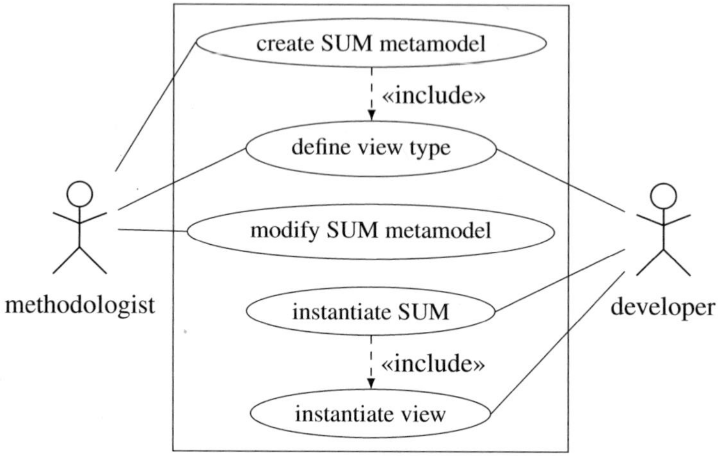

Figure 4.11.: Use Cases for Developer Roles in VITRUVIUS

been included into the VITRUVIUS-based development process by the methodologist. These are called *legacy* view types.

The pre-defined view types are seen as a part of the modular SUM metamodel, since a SUM metamodel specification only makes sense with a minimal number of view types, so that information from a SUM instance can be displayed and modified. Pre-defined view types have the same development cycle as the sub-metamodels of SUM metamodel. This means that they are usually not modified during a development project that makes use of the modular SUM metamodel.

4.4.2.2. Custom View Types

The SUM metamodel is a black-box entity for the developer role of the VITRUVIUS development process. The only means of accessing and modifying information in a SUM are instances of the pre-defined view types. It is however possible that the developer would like to combine information from the SUM in a way that has not been specified by the methodologist. Using the legacy view types, the developer can access information of the single sub-metamodels, or use other pre-defined view types, and re-arrange this information into new projectional or combined views, which are instances of a newly created view type.

VITRUVIUS provides means for the definition of such user-specific, *custom view types*. These view types can of course not violate the black-box principle of the SUM metamodel, so they are restricted to the available view types and their editability definitions. In the example of Figure 4.9, the developer creates a custom view type that combines information from the component model (PCM) and performance result data (Sensor model). Since the sensor view type is read-only (indicated by the direction of the arrow), the resulting custom view type can only modify instances of the PCM, but not the sensor data.

4.4.3. Collaboration

The benefits of a single underlying model and view-based modelling make a new type of collaborative process for software development possible. In this subsection, we will outline two possible collaboration workflows for the VITRUVIUS approach in an asynchronous and a synchronous scenario.

In classical asynchronous check-out/check-in collaboration workflows, developers retrieve working copies from a central repository, modify the working copy, and resolve concurrent changes when checking in the modified artefacts. This is also feasable in the VITRUVIUS approach. Existing metamodelling frameworks such as EMF [47] support versioning systems and offer means of displaying the differences between varying versions of model-based data [22]. Depending on the size and complexity of the SUM, developers can choose to check out the complete SUM as a working copy, or to work only on the relevant parts of the SUM that they plan to modify. The modular structure of the SUM makes it possible to modify the parts independently, and to analyse the impact of changes to parts of the SUM on the consistency with the rest of the SUM. In addition to the internal consistency of the view that is used to manipulate thc part of the SUM, which is continuously checked, the consistency check with the rest of the SUM is only performed before saving of checking in the modifications. The repository infrastructure has to support this similar to the way that build infrastructures support code-based development today.

In contrast to the asynchronous check-out/check-in collaboration workflow, synchronous online modelling can also be supported. The editability scope of view types and views defines the actions that the developers can perform. A framework that implements synchronous editing for VITRUVIUS must offer ways of locking parts of the SUM. This locking can also be done by checking out certain parts of the SUM and then editing these parts synchronously [160]. After the editing process, a new revision is created by a commit in the versioning system. This way, classical versioning systems can be used together with the synchronous approach. The SUM itself should be constructed while having in mind that parts of it may be checked out and edited separately. The editing tools should be aware of other parts in the SUM that may become inconsistent by the current modifications and should warn the user (but should not prohibit the editing step). During the restoration of consistence, edit operations of the user can be reverted or modified, which may not have been the intent of the user; in this case, the development framework should offer a possibility of interaction for the developer to resolve the incosistency [92]. In combination with access control, it is possible to show the user that editing steps may have an effect on other parts of the SUM, which would have to be changed to preserve consistency, but for which the user's role has no editing permissions (see subsection 4.4.4).

In the running CBSE example, the developer roles *system architect* and *component developer* may work independently and modify the architecture of the system using the componentn diagram view, or modify the object-oriented design using a class diagram view. In the asynchronous case, the workflow is identical with working at the single component or class model. Temporary inconsistencies are allowed in the views, can be persisted in the local working copy, and are not resolved until the user checks in the current set of changes. In the synchronous case, the developers are notified immediately if changes to the SUM are performed by other developers, and have the possibility to update the view in order to see the concurrent changes. This kind of real-time online modelling [149] requires that the developers are connected to a central repository, so that the notifications of changes can be propagated to the views. The synchronous case has, however, the advantage that, e.g., the component developer always has up-to-date about the system architecture, and can estimate the impact of editing operations immediately.

4.4.4. Access Control

The collaborative process that has been proposed in the previous subsection can also be used to introduce access control for development artefacts into the view-based developement process. As mentioned in preceding section, editable custom views may warn the user if they create an inconsistent state by editing a part of the SUM (the part that is affected by their custom view). Since not all developers are familiar with all parts of the system, or should not be allowed to change important parts like e.g. the software architecture, the view-based approach can also be used to enforce access control on the development artefacts.

If a developer tries to make a change to the system that would require a change of parts of the SUM for which he or she has no editing permission, the development framework would at first not allow the editing operation, but create an issue that could be delegated to a senior developer that is entitled to decide about this change. This could be realised technically by using issue-tracking or task management software. Depending on the collaboration scenario (synchronous, asynchronous or mixed), the developer may not be able to perform the editing operation or may not submit his/her changes to the repository until the senior developer has allowed the edit operation and/or made the appropriate changes to the rest of the SUM to ensure consistency.

If a user edits a model, the modelling tool can assist the user in limiting the part of the model that is visible in the editor, which is common practice in graphical editors. This mechanism could be extended in a way that the user can determine certain parts of an arbitrary model that he wants to edit – for example by marking an area in a graphical editor. The parts of the model that are removed from the view could then be abstracted in a specific element that represents the not visible parts, like a kind of "firewall" behind which the rest of the model is hidden, as seen in Figure 4.12. In the scenario depicted there, to users are editing parts of a component model, but are only allowed to see the part they are editing. Partial views are used here to enable the following workflow:

① User 1 tries to bind the required interface of Component 2 to a provided interface of a component that he is not allowed to see.

② The framework then decides, based on a set of pre-defined rules, if the the user is allowed to set this connection at all, and, if successful, delegates to the user who is responsible for the respective part of the component model, in our case User 2.

③ User 2 then decides to bind the incoming request to the provided interface of Component 4. He could also decide to bind it to a different component, depending on the nature of the request. The workflow messaging system should also provide for a possibility of sending messages to support the decision.

Additional constraints limit the kinds of elements that the modeler can create or edit. If a user tries to create an element that would not be permitted

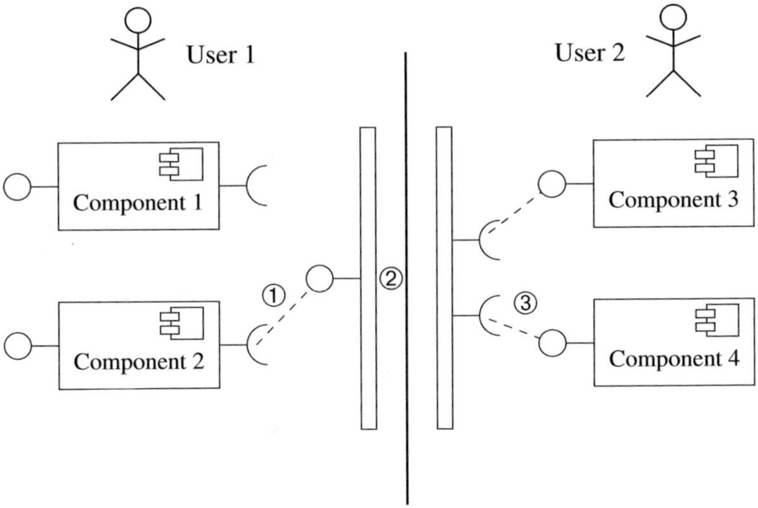

Figure 4.12.: Distributed Component-Based Modelling with Component Façades

in his current view, the modelling environment can forbid the action and abort the modelling step, or, if possible, offer auto-correction proposals.

The benefit of this representation would be that associations to elements that are not in the current view could still be displayed, unlike in current editors where the removal of elements also causes the removal of the associations to it from the view. This abstraction could also be useful for collaborative modelling scenarios: If the user wants to model an association that reaches outside the scope of his current view, which would normally be forbidden, a collaborative environment could send a message to modellers that have the appropriate view or permission to handle this kind of request.

4.5. Evolution of the SUM Metamodel

A SUM metamodel that has been created by the methodologist can be instantiated multiple times to model different systems that use all or a subset of the metamodels and languages that are part of the SUM metamodel. In the running CBSE example, multiple systems can be modelled using the SUM metamodel that contains PCM, UML, and Java. Like every metamodel, the SUM metamodel is also subject to modifications that affect the internal structure of the SUM as well as the interface definition, i.e., the view types. In the following, we will describe change scenarios for the SUM and the view types. We will categorize these scenarios using the terminology of Lientz and Swanson [110] (adaptive, perfective, corrective and preventive changes).

4.5.1. Adding Additional View Points

Category of Change: Adaptive, Perfective

If additional view points have to be respected in the SUM metamodel, e.g., if requirements on the system are modified, the SUM metamodel has to be extended by new concepts, which can be represented in additional sub-metamodels, additional correspondences between existing sub-metamodels, and new view types. The elicitation of these metamodels and correspondences follows the same principle as the development of a new SUM metamodel: First, the methodologist collects the new view types that have to be supported, and derives the additional metamodels and correspondences from these view types.

The strong decoupling of the SUM metamodel and the view types allows the methodologist to add elements to the SUM metamodel without breaking the compatibility to existing tools that use the view type definitions of the SUM metamodel as an interface description. Thus, compatibility problems at the metamodel-level can be avoided by continuing to support the existing view types.

Existing SUMs that are instances of the SUM metamodel have to be co-evolved to the new version of the SUM metamodel. Depending on the severity of the changes to the SUM, this requires manual effort by the methodologist (see subsection 4.5.3). In the case of additional changes, the effort is usually small, since this kind of changes usually does not break compatiblity to existing instances.

4.5.2. Converting Custom View Types to Pre-defined View Types

Category of Change: Perfective

Custom composed view types that have proven to be useful, since they are repeatedly used by developers, can be integrated into the SUM metamodel and become pre-defined view types. The methodologist can persist these view types as composite view types, which are synchronised with existing view types, or re-organise the synchronisation in such a way that the information is related directly to the sub-metamodels in the SUM metamodel.

A further cause for integration of a custom view type is the enhancement of the view with editability, which may not be possible due to editability restrictions of the view types that are the source of the custom view type. After the conversion to a pre-defined view-type, the view type can be enhanced by allowing additional edit operations, which could not be defined before by the developer because of the black-box principle of the SUM.

4.5.3. Refactoring of the SUM Metamodel

Category of Change: Preventive

If a VITRUVIUS-based development process is installed in a software development project, the modular SUM metamodel is created from the existing metamodels that are used in the development, and additional information that should be represented in the SUM. For the additional information, a model-based representation is chosen and integrated into the SUM metamodel. A SUM metamodel that has been created this way will contain controlled redundancies, which are specified in the MIR elements and managed by the synchronisation mechanisms of the implementations of VITRUVIUS.

The decoupling of view types, which are used as an interface definition, and the structure of the SUM metamodel makes it possible to change the internal structure of the SUM metamodel without modifying the interface. Thus, it is possible to refactor the SUM metamodel, for example to reduce the redundancies by combining sub-metamodels into new, redundancy-free metamodels. Candidates for the refactoring can be determined by an analysis of the number of view types that access information from a certain subset of the SUM metamodel. If there is a high number of combined view types for a certain combination of sub-metamodels, it could be beneficiary to combine these sub-metamodel into one metamodel. This reduces the number of synchronisation operations that are necessary after an editing step to one of the combining views. Furthermore, it is possible to consolidate the consistency information into constraints of the new sub-metamodel, and align the constraints of the view types with these constraints. Thus, offline editability of the views without the need to synchronise with the SUM is made possible while preserving the consistency of at least the sub-model that is modified by the view.

In the example of Figure 4.9, this could be the case for the PCM metamodel and the Sensor model, since the performance results in this scenario relate only to the component-based architecture, but not to other parts of the system description. The connection to the components to which the performance simulation results relate is achieved via common identifiers, which are stored in String attributes.

4.6. Example

In this section, we provide an extended example for the running CBSE scenario. The application of the VITRUVIUS approach to the scenario is shown in Figure 4.13.

The example describes a scenario where software is developed using PCM as a component-based representation for the software architecture, UML

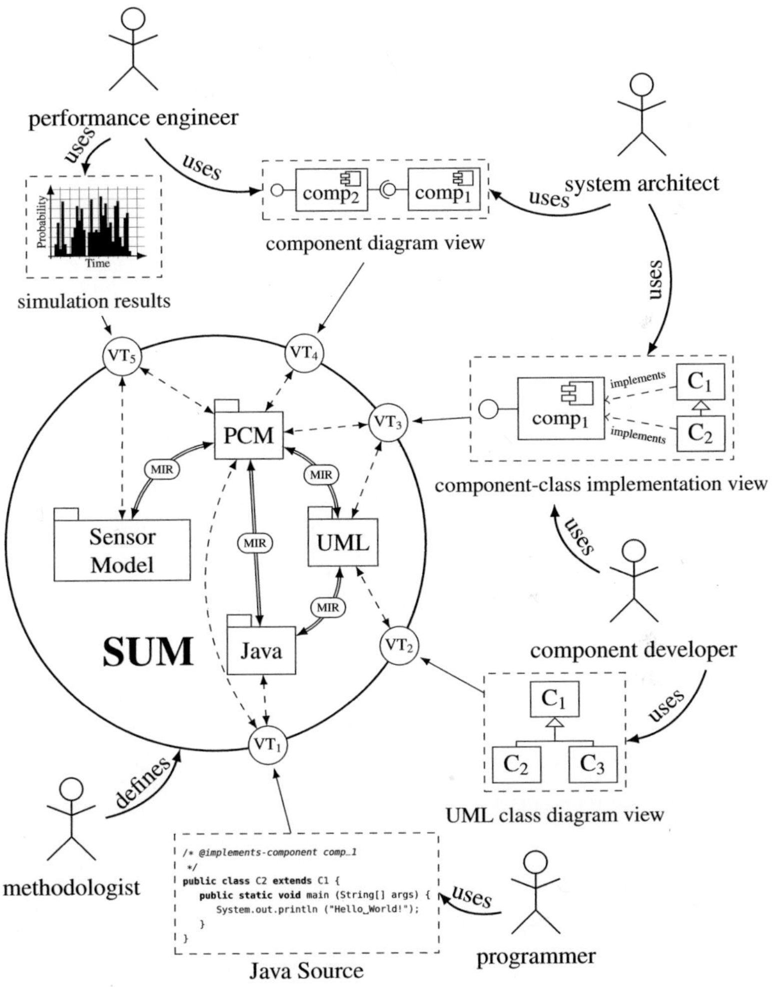

Figure 4.13.: Example: View-centric Component-based Development Process

as a class-based representation for the object-oriented design, and Java as the implementation language. Furthermore, results of performance analyses from PCM are persisted in a model-based format for sensor data (Sensor Model). The development process itself is not model-driven, meaning that the artefacts are developed independently of each other and are not transformed into other representations.

The developer roles in this scenario are divided into the four types *system architect*, *component developer*, *programmer*, and *performance engineer*.

The developer roles use (legacy) view types, such as component diagrams (VT_4) or class diagrams (VT_2) to access the information in the metamodels, but would also like to have integrated views, such as the *component-class implementation view* (VT_3) displayed in the example. The SUM metamodel (indicated as the large circle in the middle) consists of four sub-metamodels (PCM, UML, Java, Sensor Model) and also stores extrinsic information, e.g., the class-component mapping, which is not part of any of the single models. Developers can continue to use their legacy view types, such as class diagrams and Java source code, but can also use combined views that gather information from heterogeneous metamodels.

The SUM metamodel is created and maintained by the *methodologist* role. The methodologist elicits the existing metamodels, view types, and the correspondences between them. He defines the ←(MIR)→ elements that formalise the correspondences, store extrinsic information and provide rules for checking and restoring consistency between the sub-metamodels.

In a forward engineering scenario, the *system architect* first creates a component model using the component diagram view. He or she uses a real-time synchronous editor to develop the model and to discuss the layout with other developers. Since performance is also an issue, he or she collaborates with a *performance engineer*. The performance engineer uses a simulation framework, such as SimuCom or EventSim, which store the results as an instance of the SensorModel metamodel. The results can then be displayed in a custom view that combines simulation results and information from the component model. Afterwards, the *component developer* defines the class structure of the system, and a programmer implements the system using Java.

System architects and component developers both use a *component-class implementation view* to display the implements-relationship between classes and components. For both roles, it is irrelevant where the information about this relationship is stored – it could be persisted as an annotation on either side, or in the Java code, or in a third metamodel that is part of the SUM – the architect or developer can edit the implements-relationship transparently in the custom view. Other information that is displayed in the view cannot be edited, e.g. class or component names. If the architect or developer removes a class or component from a view, it is not deleted in the SUM; a deletion operation can only be performed in the specific component or class diagrams.

The programmer has a pure code-view in Java and works with asynchronous check-out/check-in versioning. There are however consistency constraints that limit the modifications to the code: the code structure must always be aligned with the UML class structure ($cons_2$); e.g. if the user adds new classes in Java, the UML class model must be updated accordingly. Furthermore, the calls to methods of other classes (which may implement a different component than the calling class) are only allowed if there is an appropriate interface in the component model ($cons_3$) and if the respective components are bound to each other. In Figure 4.13, the code also contains information about which component is implemented by a Java class in the commentary; this information is woven into the textual view, but can be stored anywhere in the SUM, similar to the implements relations in the component-class view.

A view type can be understood as a metamodel, with the single views as instances of this metamodel respectively (indicated by the solid arrow ⟶). To create a view, a model transformation has to be executed from the SUM to the view type. In the example of Figure 4.13, this is indicated as

←- - -►. In case of the legacy view type VT_1 (class diagram), the view type corresponds to only one sub-metamodel of the modular SUM metamodel; hence, the view type is fully editable, and the transformation is the identity relation. (Additional operations between the sub-models of the SUM may be necessary so that all consistency constraints are satisfied after an editing step.) The legacy view types enable the usage of existing modelling tools and can also be used for im- and export. View type VT_2 represents a more complex example: A developer would like to have a "class-component implementation view" that shows instances of two heterogeneous metamodels (PCM and UML) and an *implements*-relation between them. The purpose of this view type is to edit the mapping information between classes and components, but not to edit the class or component model. Thus, the developer creates a custom view with the following parameters:

- PCM components and UML classes can only be displayed, but not be deleted or edited, e.g., renamed
- details of classes and components are omitted, e.g. attributes are not shown for classes, only provided interfaces are shown for components
- the *implements*-relation is editable

The synchronisation between the view and the SUM depends on the design decision of where to store the extrinsic information of the *implements*-relation; since it is neither present in the PCM nor in the UML metamodel, it could be stored as an annotation on either side, or in an additional artefact, e.g., a mapping model, which would have to be added to the SUM then. Let us assume that a methodologist has decided to store the information as an annotation in the UML sub-model of the SUM. Since components cannot be edited by a view of this view type, the transformation from PCM to VT_2 will be unidirectional; although classes themselves are not modified by the view either, but the mapping information is added as an annotation, the transformation from UML to VT_2 is bi-directional. Neither of the metamodels has to be modified, since the existing UML annotation mechanism is used. The user of the view need not know how the implements-relation is technically represented in the SUM; it is even possible to change the representation strategy without modifying the view type.

In general, readability and editability restrictions in views can also be used to implement access control to the system: A software engineer who is responsible for the object-oriented design of a system may not be authorised to change the software architecture, since this is the responsibility of a software architect. In the example, the component-class implementation view type VT_2 guarantees that the software engineer does not change the architecture by making the components read-only, but gives the ability to update the class-component mapping. This prohibits changes in the descriptive system architecture by unauthorised developers; nevertheless, the implicit architecture of the object-oriented structure of the Java code can be influenced by modifications of the component developer or programmer. These inconsistencies are detected by the declarative correspondences rules in the ↔(MIR)↔ elements, and, if possible, resolved automatically.

The scenario presented in this example shows the benefits of a modular SUM compared to a monolithic SUM: developers can use the languages to which they are used (PCM, UML, Java), but are made aware that changes to their parts can affect the whole system and lead to inconsistencies. These inconsistencies are resolved with the help of the collaborative process. This does not require a white-box view of the SUM: a Java programmer may not know all parts of e.g. the component model, but only the parts that are relevant for the part of the code on which he or she is working; access control prohibits that the other parts are visible. Although the programmer is not able to change the component model, even the parts that are visible, he or she can request a change if it is necessary to fulfil the consistency constraints, which will then be carried out by the system architect. Thus, the explicit system architecture is always consistent with the implementation, and the rest of the SUM.

5. Metamodel and Model Evolution

In this chapter, we will present a method for the description and handling of the evolution of metamodels and models. After the motivation of the problem in section 5.1, we will present a metamodel that can be instantiated to describe changes to metamodels that are instances of Ecore, as well as changes to instances of these metamodels (section 5.2). Based on this metamodel, a change impact classification with a state-based analysis method has been developed for Ecore-based metamodels, which is presented in section 5.3.

5.1. Motivation

Model-driven development processes suffer from the problem of metamodel evolution and model co-evolution [48]. If metamodels are modified, existing instances may become invalid, which means that they no longer conform to the metamodels. Furthermore, existing model transformations or tools, which are based on a certain version of metamodel, can also become incompatible after changes to the metamodel.

Co-evolution approaches address this problem by describing changes to metamodels in a well-defined format [34, 27], and by creating adaptation scripts or transformations for existing instances [72]. For Ecore metamodels, the most sophisticated approach is the Edapt tool by Herrmannsdörfer et al. [70]. Edapt is a *delta-based* approach (see section 3.4), where refactoring steps to metamodels are explicitly defined by the user and recorded to generate adaptation scripts for existing models, and to estimate the impact of changes to metamodels on existing instances.

The delta-based refactoring mechanisms work well for manual changes to metamodels, since the user can express the intent of a modification by choosing the appropriate refactoring operation from a pre-defined set. Furthermore, changes to metamodels do not occur frequently in model-based development processes, since they require the adaption of the aforementioned artefacts. In VITRUVIUS, however, metamodels and transformations are generated automatically from declarative textual descriptions, such as the ModelJoin view type definitions (see section 6.2). On the one hand, the automatic generation of metamodels and matching transformations alleviates the problem of evolution, since these artefacts co-evolve automatically. On the other hand, the development cycles for metamodels are significantly shorter than in classical model-driven engineering, since new metamodels are generated on-the-fly, instead of being modelled manually.

Thus, the automatic generation of view type metamodels in VITRUVIUS poses three challenges in the context of metamodel evolution:

- **State-Based Evolution:** Since metamodels are generated automatically, the change impact analysis and co-evolution mechanisms cannot rely on a manual delta-based description, but have to work in a *state-based* way, comparing different versions of a metamodel.

- **Evolution at the Instance Level:** Metamodel evolution approaches describe changes at the metamodel level and generate adaptation scripts at the model level. The change description language is thus specific for Ecore as the fixed metamodel at the M3 level, and metamodels as instances at the M2 level.

  In the VITRUVIUS approach, it is however also necessary to describe modifications to instances of metamodels, e.g., for editability of views, or for the synchronisation mechanisms between the sub-models of a SUM. Thus, changes have to be detected and described at the M1 level for instances of arbitrary metamodels. A metamodel evolution mechanism is not usable here since it contains only change descriptions for the concepts of Ecore. A formalism for change descriptions at the M1 level must be generic enough to express changes to instances of arbitrary metamodels.

- **Compatibility of View Types:** Declarative descriptions of view types in VITRUVIUS can be used to automatically generate transformations that translate information from the SUM metamodel to a specific view type. Such a transformation requires, however, a specific target metamodel with a compatible structure. Although it is possible to derive the view type metamodel from the declarative definition, an existing view type metamodel may be used as the target of the view type transformation. In this case, the compatibility of the declarative definition of the view type with the existing metamodel has to be checked to determine whether the transformation can be used with the existing view type.

In the following sections, we will present a method for determining metamodel conformity based on the change impact classifications of Herrmannsdörfer and our own previous work [27]. We will then present a method for state-based determination of this classification.

5.2. A Change Metamodel for Metamodel and Model Changes

5.2.1. Requirements

A change operation to a metamodel, which is an instance of the Ecore meta-metamodel, or to a model, which is an instance of an Ecore-based metamodel, can only occur in a finite number of ways. As discussed in the foundations section (see section 2.2), this is due to the fact that the meta-metamodel, the *Ecore metamodel* is fixed, which means that it is normally not modified or extended for the usage in tools and transformations. The Ecore metamodel contains, of course, only a finite number of concepts, so the kinds of changes can also be classified into a finite number of categories.

Such a classification of the kinds of changes that are possible in Ecore-based metamodels, and their instances, can be organised along several dimensions:

- **Modelling Level**: Changes can affect metamodels (M2) or instances of metamodels (M1).
- **Granularity**: A change can describe a minimal difference or editing operation, or a more complex operation, which carries higher semantic information.
- **Impact**: Changes affect the internal consistency of models, or the conformance of instances and other models to the model under change.

Change descriptions for the co-evolution of metamodels and models, such as in [72] and [27], often only offer possibilities for the description of changes to metamodels. As such, they are specific to the meta-metamodel that is used in the approach, usually MOF, UML, or Ecore, and describe the effects of specific refactoring operations, or other, more complex changes. The approach of Cicchetti [34] can be used to describe changes to arbitrary models. Change descriptions are generated automatically for all the elements in the respective metamodel, so a type-safe description of changes is possible, but due to the automatic generation, the semantics of complex changes are not considered, and the change descriptions contain only atomic changes (add/delete/change). The diff metamodel of EMF Compare [22] uses a mixture of atomic changes and Ecore-specific changes such as containment or resources. The DeltaEcore tool [139] follows a similar approach and offers a textual DSL for the definition of change descriptions between arbitary instances of MOF-based metamodels.

In contrast to the description of changes in a textual language, changes to metamodels and models are often described as models themselves, so they can be used as input for further model transformations. The approaches of Cicchetti [34] and our previous work [27] also follow this approach. Herrmannsdörfer et al. [72] use a set of change operators, which can be invoked in the *Edapt* plug-in in Eclipse the perform metamodel changes. These operators can also be seen as a classification of change types and could be described in a model-based format, although Herrmannsdörfer et al. have not explicitly included this option.

5.2.2. Structure of the Metamodel

We also follow the approach of describing changes in a model-based format and have created an extensible *change metamodel* (see Figure 5.1), which can be used for Ecore itself, and for any Ecore-based metamodel. Since the topmost level of the metamodel hierarchy in MOF is self-descriptive, the Ecore metamodel can be seen as an instance of itself. Our change metamodel offers the solution that covers the aforementioned dimension: It can be used for several *modelling levels* (M2 and M1), since changes to Ecore-based metamodels can be described with the same formalism as changes to instances of such metamodels; changes to metamodels are a special case of changes to models, where the metamodel is Ecore itself. The change metamodel also covers several levels of *granularity*, since it contains concepts for the description of fine-granular atomic changes and or several coherent changes, which together form a sequence of changes. Finally, the metamodel can be specialised into metamodel-specific parts, which can be used to describe the specific *impact* of changes in the respective domain of the metamodels.

The change metamodel consists of a core part, which is called *metamodel-independent change metamodel* (see Figure 5.1). This core is specialised by metamodel-specific change metamodels (see Figure 5.2), whose classes inherit from the abstract classes in the core part. The metamodel-independent part is reduced to the most abstract kinds of changes that can occur in Ecore-based instances of metamodels. As discussed in section 2.2, the only classes in the Ecore metamodel that have a potency of 2, meaning that instances of these classes can themselves have instances, are the classes EClass and

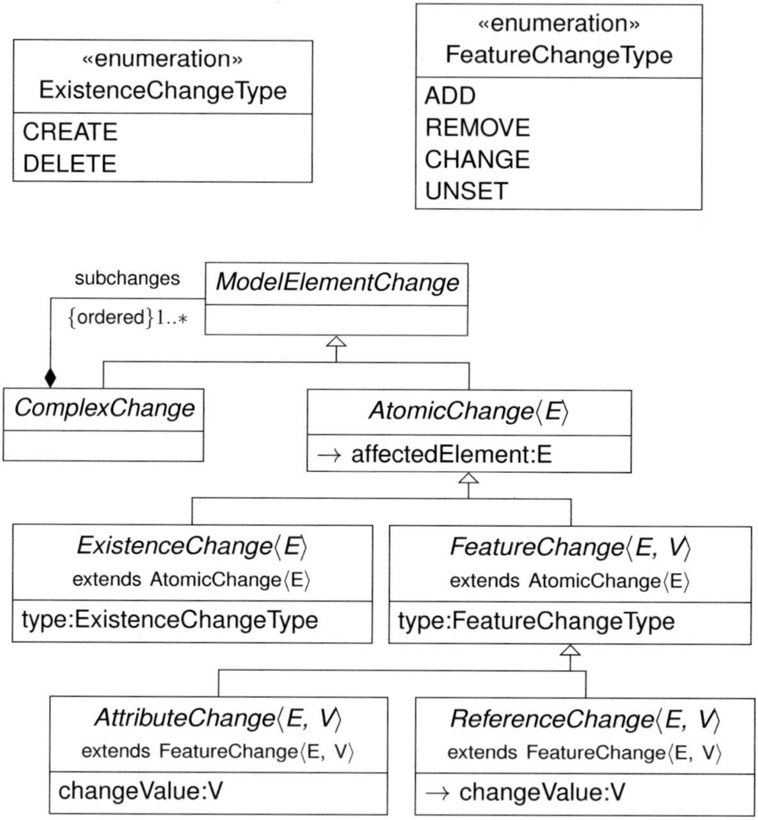

Figure 5.1.: Metamodel-Independent Change Metamodel

EStructuralFeature with its subclasses EReference and EAttribute. Thus, the two main classes in the metamodel-independent change metamodel are ExistenceChange and FeatureChange, which concern these two types of elements.

The main difference between instances of classes and instances of features at the M1 level is object identity: While objects (instances of classes) possess object identity, and can be seen as first-class elements, features such as references and attributes can only exist in the context of their containing objects. This can be exemplified by the generated Java code of Ecore metamodels: While Ecore objects are represented by Java objects, references and attributes are only fields in the objects, which do not have object identity. This fact is represented in the change metamodel by the class ExistenceChange, which represents the creation and destruction of objects. The type of change (CREATE/DELETE) is modelled as the enumeration-typed attribute type. While objects can be created and deleted, the same is not true for instances of features: Attribute values and links (instances of references) can neither be created nor deleted, but only changed, and, if the property unsettable is set to true for the feature in the metamodel, can be put into the unset state. (The unset state is a special state in Ecore, which is different from setting the feature to `null`.) For single-valued features, the change type CHANGE indicates a modfication. For multi-valued features, the change types ADD and REMOVE indicate that elements are added to or removed from the set of instances and values.

The change types ExistenceChange and FeatureChange constitute the kind of *atomic changes*. Although the difference between two models can be always expressed with these elementary operations [1], such a description may be undesirable, since atomic changes carry only little semantic information. For example, a change in an Ecore-based metamodel during which an attribute is moved up to a superclass (called *pull up feature* after Fowler et al. [51]) should be perceived as a single contingent change operation. Using only atomic changes, it would, however, have to be expressed as two elements of the type FeatureChange: The containment link between the attribute and the containing class is deleted for the original class and created for the superclass. Since containment is stored on the containing side of the association, and since links do not have object identity, this change cannot be expressed as a single atomic change, but has to be expressed as two changes: the removal of the containment link in the subclass, and the addition of a containment link in the new containing superclass. It should also be noted that an atomic change can damage the consistency of the model, so that several atomic changes may be necessary to restore consistency in a model; in the example here, deleting the containment link without setting a new link would lead to a feature that is not contained in a class, which leads to an invalid metamodel (that violates the constraint of Ecore that every feature has to be contained in a class). The *pull up feature* change is an example for a *complex change*, which consists of several atomic changes, but has specific semantic information attached to it. In this case, we say that the complex change *subsumes* a sequence of atomic changes. Depending on the purpose of the change analysis, complex changes can be used to cover the relevant cases for co-evolution, impact analysis, synchronisation, or other purposes. The process of deriving complex changes from a series of atomic changes is also called *semantic lifting* by Kehrer et al. [83].

In the change metamodel presented in this section, complex changes are represented by the abstract element ComplexChange, which is specialised by inheritance in the metamodel-specific change metamodels. A Complex-Change consists of at least one other change element, which can again be a complex change, or an atomic change.

5.2.3. Specification of Metamodel-Specific Submodels

If changes to a metamodel shall be described with the change metamodel presented in this section, a metamodel-specific change metamodel (see Figure 5.2) has to be created first. For the atomic change types, the specific change metamodel is straightforward: For each EClass, a class that specialises the class ExistenceChange has to be created, and for each EStructuralFeature, a specialization of FeatureChange has to be created. The reference affectedElement points to the element that is subject to modification. For ExistanceChanges, the affected element is the instance that is created or deleted; for FeatureChanges, the affected element is the instance that contains the attribute value or the link, whose new value is stored in the field changeValue.

Ecore contains the concept of *generics*, with which we have parameterised the classes ExistenceChange and ParameterChange, so that the type of affectedElement can be specified by the subclasses in the metamodel-specific change metamodels. Thus, the subclasses of ExistanceChange and FeatureChange are typed, with the limitation that any EObject can be inserted for the parameters E and V. The type safety for E and V cannot be achieved by generic supertypes of theses parameters, since there is no common superclass of all metamodel classes and features except EObject. Since the straightforward definition of metamodel-specific atomic changes is not possible with the means of Ecore, we have chosen a generator approach similar to the one of Cicchetti [34]: For each class and feature in a metamodel, the appropriate atomic change elements are generated automatically, along with OCL constraints that guarantee the right type for the affectedElement and newValue features of the change models. The algorithm for the creation of the metamodel-specific change metamodels is displayed in pseudo-code in Algorithm 1. In contrast to the approach of Cicchetti, the classes in the generated metamodels can be distinguished by their supertypes ExistenceChange and FeatureChange, instead of naming conventions. Furthermore, the information whether a change is additive/destructive or changing/unsetting is not represented by distinct elements at the meta-level, but at the instance level of the change model, as an attribute value in the enumeration-typed attribute type.

Algorithm 1 Generation of an Atomic Change Metamodel D for a Metamodel M

Require: $M = (\text{CLASS}_M, \text{ATT}_M, \text{REF}_M)$
  for all $c \in \text{CLASS}_M$ **do** ▷ c is a class name
    if $\neg isAbstract(c)$ **then** ▷ only non-abstract classes can be instantiated
      $d_c \in \text{CLASS}_D \leftarrow c+$"Change" ▷ naming convention
      $d_c \prec$ ExistenceChange ▷ d_c inherits from metamodel-independent classes
      $genericType_T(d_c) \leftarrow t_c$
    end if
    for all $a : t_c \rightarrow t \in \text{ATT}_M$ **do**
      if $\neg isDerived(a)$ **then** ▷ derived features cannot be changed directly
        if $t = Boolean$ **then**
          $d_a \in \text{ATT}_D \leftarrow$"Is"$+a+$"Change"
        else
          $d_a \in \text{ATT}_D \leftarrow a+$"Change"
        end if
        $d_a \prec$ AttributeChange
        $genericType_T(d_a) \leftarrow t_c$
        $genericType_V(d_a) \leftarrow t$
      end if
    end for
    for all $r \in \text{REF}_M, associates(r) = \langle c, c' \rangle$ **do**
      if $\neg isDerived(r)$ **then**
        $d_r \in \text{REF}_D \leftarrow r+$"Change"
        $d_r \prec$ ReferenceChange
        $genericType_T(r_a) \leftarrow t_c$
        $genericType_V(r_a) \leftarrow c'$
      end if
    end for
  end for
Ensure: $D = (\text{CLASS}_D, \text{ATT}_D, \text{REF}_D)$

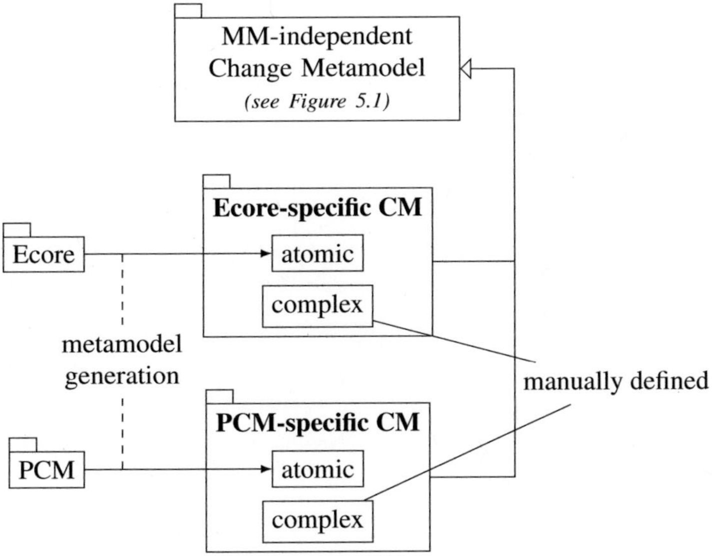

Figure 5.2.: Example for Metamodel-Specific Change Metamodels (CM) that inherit from the Core Metamodel: Ecore-CM and PCM-CM

The metamodel-independent change metamodel contains the element ComplexChange, which is used to express the semantic connections between a sequence of atomic changes. In contrast to the atomic changes, which can be derived from any metamodel using the algorithm displayed in Algorithm 1, the semantic connection between atomic changes is specific for the domain to which the metamodel belongs, and specific for the purpose of the change description. For example, a change metamodel for Ecore (which is used to express differences between Ecore-based metamodels) serves the purpose of describing metamodel evolution. This is used for co-evolution of existing instances, and for impact analysis of how instances are affected by changes at the metamodel level, which will be described in detail in section 5.3. Change metamodels for other metamodels, such as PCM or UML, as in the running example of this thesis (see Figure 1.1 on page 4) can be used to estimate the effects on existing simulations, transformations, or synchronisation in the context of a modular single underlying model in VITRUVIUS. Since the elements are domain- and purpose specific, the complex change elements at the metamodel level are specific to the semantics of the metamodel, and have to be specified manually. At the instance level, the complex change descriptions can either be determined by recording changes in a modelling tool that supports them, or by analysis of the atomic changes. In section 5.3, we will present a method for deriving complex changes from atomic changes to Ecore-based metamodels.

5.2.4. Change Sequences as Delta-Based Representation of Model Changes

The instances of the change metamodel describe the difference between two models, usually two versions of the same model, as a sequence of atomic and complex change operations. The change metamodel is agnostic of the way that this change sequence is determined; it can either be determined by tracing change operations in an editor, or by the comparison of two existing versions of a model. Indepently of the way that a change description is determined, a change model is always a complete delta-based description of the difference of two models. This property is described in Figure 5.3: If a change model describes the difference between a model $\underline{M}$ and a model $\underline{M}'$, then the model $\underline{M}'$ can be calculated (indicated as (merge) in the figure) from the information in M and the change model. The change descriptions are invertible, since every change can be undone by a corresponding inverse change: CREATE operations can be undone by DELETE operations, ADD operations by REMOVE operations, and so on. It is, however, not possible in general to derive the inverse of a change model (or a single change element) automatically. For example, the inverse of a delete operation cannot be determined if the source model is not known, since the properties of the deleted element are not contained in the change model itself; thus, the change model cannot be used to determine $\underline{M}$ from $\underline{M}'$. A change model is only automatically invertible in the special case that none of its operations leads to a loss of information. For the Ecore-specific change metamodel, this is true for the operations that have *safe inverses* according to the catalogue of Herrmannsdörfer [72].

The single change elements that are instances of subclasses of ModelElementChange have to be arranged in a sequence to form a complete change description. This is why the reference subchanges in the change metamodel is ordered.

Definition 13 (Change Sequence). *Let $D = \{d \in \textsc{Class} \mid d \prec ModelElementChange$ be the set of classes in the change metamodels that inherit from the metamodel-independent change metamodel. A* change sequence *$\underline{D}$ is a sequence of instances of this classes:*

$$\underline{D} = (\underline{d}_1, \underline{d}_2, \dots, \underline{d}_n)$$

where $\underline{d}_i \in I(D)$ and $i, n \in \mathbb{N}, i \leq n$. For every change sequence $\underline{D}$, there exists an evaluation function *$eval_{\underline{D}} : \mathscr{I} \to \mathscr{I}$, which applies the change*

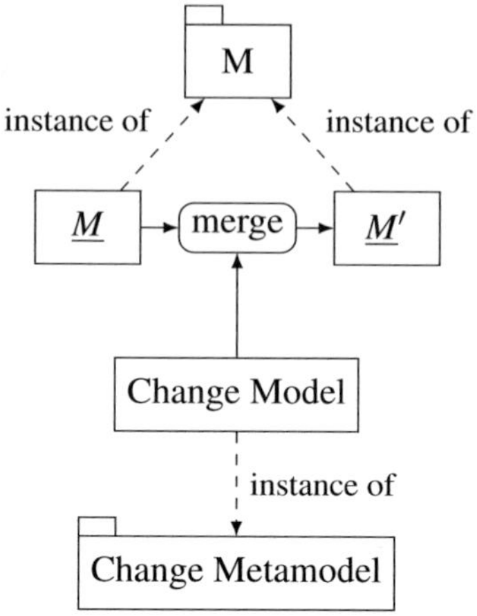

Figure 5.3.: Applying a Change Model to a Model $\underline{M}$ to obtain the new version $\underline{M'}$

sequence to instances of metamodels, so that a change sequence $\underline{D}$ that describes the difference between models $\underline{M}, \underline{M'} \in \mathscr{I}$ can be applied to $\underline{M}$ to calculate the model $\underline{M'}$:

$$eval_{\underline{D}}(\underline{M}) = \underline{M'}$$

The description of the difference between two models as a sequence of changes is ambiguous: Multiple change sequences can describe the same change between two models. As a pathologic example, a change sequence that contains two ExistenceChange elements that create and delete the same element, describes the same change as an empty change sequence.

Definition 14 (Equivalence and Minimality of Change Sequences)**.** *Two change sequences $\underline{D}, \underline{D'}$ are called* equivalent *if the evaluation of these sequences yields the same result for all possible instances:*

$$\underline{D} \sim \underline{D'} \Leftrightarrow \forall \underline{M} \in \mathscr{I} : eval_{\underline{D}}(\underline{M}) = eval_{\underline{D'}}(\underline{M})$$

A change sequence $\underline{D}$ *is called* minimal *iff*

$$\forall \underline{D}' : \underline{D} \sim \underline{D}' \Rightarrow |\underline{D}| \leq |\underline{D}'|$$

Depending on the layout of the metamodel-specific change metamodel, there may be several minimal change sequences for an actual change, since a sub-sequence of atomic changes can be replaced by a complex change that subsumes the atomic changes. There may, however, be different possible combinations for the subsumption of atomic to complex changes. For example, if there are three atomic change types $\{a, a', a''\}$ and two complex changes c, c' with $c.subchanges = \{a, a'\}$ and $c'.subchanges = \{a', a''\}$, then there can be two equivalent, minimal changes $\{\underline{c}, \underline{a}''\} \sim \{\underline{a}, \underline{c}'\}$.

5.2.5. Delta-based vs. State-Based Change Description

5.2.5.1. Comparison of Methods

To determine a change sequence between any two models, which can be two versions of one metamodel, two fundamental methods exist: First, the changes can be determined by tracking the changes during the editing of the model *(delta-based comparison)*, and second, the resulting models can be compared directly *(state-based comparison)*. The description of changes with the change metamodel presented in section 5.2 is based on a sequence of change operations. Both methods can be used in conjunction with the change metamodel, since the change metamodel is agnostic of the way that the change descriptions are determined. Each of the methods has advantages and disadvantages, which are displayed in Table 5.1: Delta-based approaches that capture the editing operations of a user have the advantage that the user can be prompted to specify his or her intent during the change operation, as it is the case in the Edapt approach by Herrmannsdörfer [72]. If the editing tool captures only atomic operations, or if the developer does not make use of the advanced operations, then this advantage does not apply. Thus,

Delta-based	State-based
⊕ user intent can be captured with complex change operations	⊕ can be used with generated metamodels
⊕ change sequence does not have to be calculated	⊕ minimal (for atomic changes)
⊖ only applicable if metamodels are edited manually	⊖ change sequence has to be determined by diff tool
⊖ generally not minimal	
⊖ tool support in editor is necessary	

Table 5.1.: Comparison of Methods to Determine a Change Sequence Between Two Metamodels

the quality of the change description depends on whether the developer plans the editing steps well. In general, a recorded change sequence is not minimal, since a developer can perform editing steps that are reverted later on. Furthermore, the delta-based approach is not applicable if models are generated automatically, or if the editing tool does not support the recording of changes. State-based analysis tools such as *EMF Compare*[1] [22] are independent of model editing tools. The result of such a comparison yields a minimal change description, which, however, only contains low-level differences between metamodels, which can each

The algorithms of EMF Compare contain heuristics to detect basic refactoring steps, such as moving an element into another container. For more complex changes, a post-processing of the change sequence is necessary.

[1] `http://www.eclipse.org/emf/compare/doc/21/developer/developer-guide.html`, retrieved 26 May 2014

5.2.5.2. Mapping of EMF Compare Changes to the Change Metamodel

To determine the changes that are necessary to gain one model from another, we use EMF Compare to calculate the difference between two models. EMF Compare also stores information in a model-based format, so that difference descriptions are instances of the *comparison metamodel* of EMF Compare. A comparison model stores information about the difference between two models, and also matches and conflicts, which are used for the merging of three-way comparisons of models. For our considerations, a two-way comparison is sufficient, so only the class Diff of the comparison metamodel and its subclasses have to be regarded. These classes can be mapped exactly to the atomic changes of the change metamodel (see Table 5.2).

EMF Compare does not distinguish between the creation or deletion of an element and the addition or removal of a reference, as the change metamodel does. It is possible to model every creation or deletion of elements as a change in a reference due to the strict containment hierarchy of EMF; for changes in the root element of a resource, EMF Compare contains the class ResourceAttachmentChange. Furthermore, the change kinds in EMF Compare do not represent distinct change operations, but are used to express multiple actions: In contrast to our change metamodel, changes in containment are expressed by the special kind of change (MOVE). This change kind is mapped to two seperate atomic changes of the type EContainingClassChange or EPackageChange, depending on whether a feature or a class/package is moved in our change metamodel. The MOVE kind is, however, also used to express the re-ordering of a multi-valued feature. Apart from the special meaning of MOVE when containment is changed, the change kind CHANGE also has an ambiguous meaning depending on the kind of feature that is changed: In mono-valued features, CHANGE represents a modification of the value, while for containment references, the same is expressed by MOVE.

EMF Compare	**Change Metamodel**
ResourceAttachmentChange	
ADD	ExistenceChange(CREATE)
DELETE	ExistenceChange(DELETE)
MOVE	—
AttributeChange	
ADD	AttributeChange(ADD)
CHANGE	AttributeChange(CHANGE)
DELETE	AttributeChange(REMOVE/UNSET)
MOVE	AttributeChange(CHANGE) *(re-ordering)*
ReferenceChange	
ADD	ReferenceChange(ADD), ExistenceChange
CHANGE	ReferenceChange(CHANGE)
DELETE	ReferenceChange(REMOVE), ExistenceChange
MOVE	ReferenceChange(CHANGE) *(re-ordering)*
	ReferenceChange(DELETE, ADD) *(containment)*

Table 5.2.: Mapping of EMF Compare Diff Elements to the Change Metamodel

In EMF Compare, the creation and deletion of elements is expressed as a ReferenceChange. This unintuitive wording arises by the fact that all Ecore instances have to follow a strict containment hierarchy, and every element except the root package has to be contained in another element. The EMF Compare metamodel treats these cases specially with the class ResourceAttachmentChange, which describes the fragementation of models, which means that a subpackage of a model is moved to a resource of its own. Furthermore, the containment relation is treated especially by the additional MOVE kind. In our change metamodel, we have refrained from treating containment specially to preserve the generality of the model. In the Ecore-specific change metamodel, these changes are represented by the aforementioned change classes for the explicit containment references.

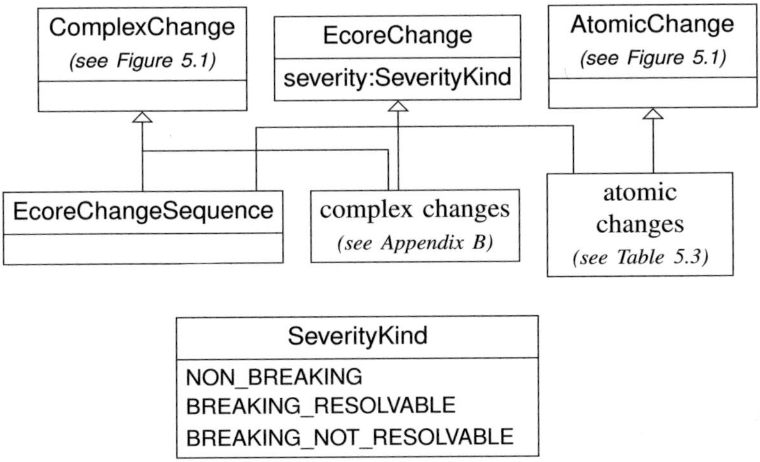

Figure 5.4.: Structure of the Ecore-Specific Change Metamodel

5.2.6. Example

In this subsection, we will give two examples of change metamodels: The change metamodel for Ecore, which is used for the description of metamodel evolution, and the change metamodel for the Palladio Component Model (PCM).

Ecore The modification of a metamodel is a special case of model evolution, where *Ecore* is the metamodel of the models that are modified. Apart from that, the description of changes is identical to the description of changes of other models. The Ecore metamodel is relatively small, with 12 classes, 30 attributes, and 18 references. The atomic change classes for these elements are displayed in Table 5.3. While this table has been created manually, the atomic change classes for a metamodel can also be created automatically using the method presented in section 5.3.

The complex change classes for a specific metamodel can, however, not be determined automatically, since they are specific for the semantics of the

ExistenceChange	AttributeChange	ReferenceChange
*(EModelElement)**		EAnnotationsChange
*(ENamedElement)**	NameChange	
*(ETypedElement)**	IsOrderedChange	ETypeChange
	IsUniqueChange	
	UpperBoundChange	
	LowerBoundChange	
	IsManyChange	
	IsRequiredChange	
*(EStructuralFeature)**	IsChangeableChange	EContainingClassChange
	IsVolatileChange	
	IsTransientChange	
	DefaultValueLiteralChange	
	DefaultValueChange	
	IsUnsettableChange	
	IsDerivedChange	
EClassChange	IsAbstractChange	ESuperTypesChange
	IsInterfaceChange	EStructuralFeaturesChange
		EOperationsChange
EOperationChange		EParametersChange
		ETypeParametersChange
		EExceptionsChange
EParameterChange		
EReferenceChange	IsContainmentChange	EOppositeChange
	IsContainerChange	EReferenceTypeChange
	IsResolveProxiesChange	EKeysChange
EAttributeChange	IsIDChange	EAttributeTypeChange
EPackageChange	NsURIChange	EClassifiersChange
	NsPrefixChange	ESubPackagesChange
EFactoryChange		EPackageChange
EDataTypeChange	IsSerializableChange	
EEnumChange		ELiteralsChange
EEnumLiteralChange	ValueChange	
	InstanceChange	
	LiteralChange	
EAnnotationChange	SourceChange	DetailsChange
EStringtoString-	KeyChange	
MapEntryChange	ValueChange	

* Abstract classes, for which no change classes are generated, are listed here in *italics* to group the attribute and feature changes.

Table 5.3.: Atomic Change Classes in the Ecore-specific Change Metamodel (without Generics) metamodel and the purpose of the change description. Herrmannsdörfer et al. have defined a catalogue of change operations to Ecore-based metamodels [72], which consists of 61 change operators. The full table of change operators is displayed in Appendix B. Each of these operators is represented by a class in the Ecore-specific change metamodel. These classes inherit from ComplexChange and contain OCL constraints that limit the types and ordering of the contained atomic changes. For example, the subchanges of a *pull up feature* operation have to contain a set of arbitrary EStructuralFeatureChange elements of type DELETE, and one of the type CREATE, for which the containing classes of the deleted features are (possibly indirect) subclasses of the containing class of the added feature. The affected elements (features) must have the same name, type, and multiplicity.

A concrete example can be seen in Figure 5.5: A part of the IMDB metamodel (see Figure C.2) is modified by introducing the new abstract class Person as a superclass of existing classes User and Actor. Then, the common attribute name is moved from these two classes to the new superclass. The table below the class diagrams in Figure 5.5 shows a change sequence that consists entirely of atomic changes, and that describes the change between the two versions of the metamodel depicted in the figure. The elements 1.–10. can be contained in one root change sequence element, which is of the type EcoreChangeSequence (see Figure 5.4). The example change sequence shows the special case of the *pull up feature* operation: In the Ecore-specific change metamodel, PullUpFeatureChange is a change type that inherits from ComplexChange. Thus, it can contain several other change elements in its reference subchanges. In this example, the change elements 6.–10. can be subsumed as one element of the type PullUpFeatureChange. By subsuming the elements into a complex change, the effect of the change sequence on the metamodel is not altered in any way. The additional information that these changes are grouped to a *pull up feature* change is, however, relevant for the impact of the change sequence on existing instances of the metamodel.

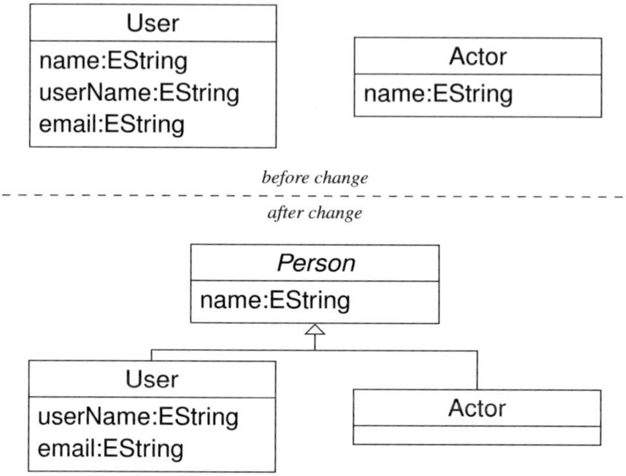

#	Change	type	affected el.	value
1.	EClassChange	CREATE		
2.	NameChange	CHANGE	(new class)	Person
3.	IsAbstractChange	CHANGE	Person	true
4.	ESuperTypesChange	ADD	User	Person
5.	ESuperTypesChange	ADD	Actor	Person
6.	EAttributeChange	DELETE	User.name	
7.	EAttributeChange	DELETE	Actor.name	
8.	EAttributeChange	CREATE		
9.	ENameChange	CHANGE	(new attr.)	name
10.	EContainingClassChange	ADD	name	Person

Figure 5.5.: Example for a Metamodel Change: Pull Up Feature

PCM In this paragraph, we will give an example of a change description at the instance level. We use the Palladio Component Model [134], which is part of the running example in this dissertation, and the standard example MediaStore [94] to illustrate the description of a change to an instance of PCM. Since the PCM is a larger model ($\sim$100 classes), we have not reproduced the complete atomic change metamodel for PCM here; the adjacent elements of the change descriptions can, however, be derived using the naming conventions introduced in Algorithm 1.

The change to the PCM instance is diplayed in Figure 5.6: The two basic components UserMgmt and DBAdapter are connected in a component assembly that directly links their provided and required roles that are of the interface type IUserDB. The change scenario is a standard scenario that is included in the example workspace of the PCM bench: A database caching component DBCache is inserted between the user management component and the database. Even this small change leads to quite a high number of 16 atomic changes, as displayed in the table of Figure 5.6: First, the connector between the roles of the user management and the database, respectively, is deleted (1.). Then, a new assembly context is created, given a name, and connected to the already existing DBCache component (2.–4.). After this, the new connectors between user management and cache (5.–10.) and between cache and database (11.–16.) are created, named, and connected to the appropriate roles.

The example shows that meaningful complex changes are dependent on the semantics of the metamodel: In this case, a direct connection to an assembly was replaced by an intermediate component in a new assembly context. This modification can be described by a single complex operation, if this case represents a frequent modification type in component modelling. The complex change would only need the information of the connector that has to be removed and the component that has to be inserted. Of course, additional constraints have to guarantee that the component to be inserted has each a required and provided role of the compatible type as the ones of the connector that it replaces. This can easily be modelled in OCL for each complex change type. An analysis of meaningful change types for PCM has, however, not been conducted yet and is subject to future work.

5.3. A Change Impact Classification for Metamodel Evolution and Reuse

In this section, we will present a change impact classification for Ecore-based metamodels. This classification can be used in two ways: First, to determine if co-evolution efforts are necessary for existing instances of a metamodel, and second, to determine whether existing metamodels can be re-used in scenarios where metamodels are generated automatically. We will first introduce change severities for Ecore-based metamodels, which will then be used for a difference-based conformance checking that can be used on any two versions of a metamodel, independently of the way in which the metamodel has been modified.

5.3.1. Severities of Changes to Ecore-based Metamodels

Changes to Ecore-based metamodels have an impact on existing models that are instances of these metamodels: Changes to the metamodel may break the instance-of-relation between existing models and the metamodels, so that existing instances contain features that are no longer present in the new version of the metamodel, or do not possess values for mandatory features that have been added, or violate other constraints of the metamodel. Since the metamodel developer who is responsible for the evolution of the metamodel usually does not know all existing instances of a metamodel, the impact of a metamodel change has to be estimated as a worst-case assumption, which is not limited to an actual set of instances, but describes the possible impact in an instance-independent way. In our previous work [27], we have described changes to metamodels based on MOF 1.4 [118] using a *change metamodel*, similar to the one presented in section 5.2. We

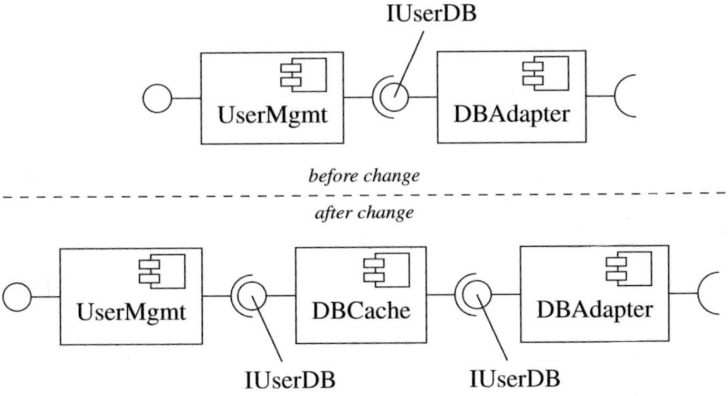

#	Change	type	affected el.	value
1.	Assembly-ConnectorChange	DELETE		
2.	AssemblyContextChange	CREATE		
3.	NameChange	CHANGE	(new el.)	DBCache
4.	EncapsulatedComponent_-AssemblyContextChange	CHANGE	DBCache	DBCache
5.	Assembly-ConnectorChange	CREATE		
6.	NameChange	CREATE	(new el.)	Mgmt_DBCache
7.	RequiringAssemblyContext_-AssemblyConnectorChange	CHANGE	Mgmt_DBCache	DBCache
8.	ProvidingAssemblyContext_-AssemblyConnectorChange	CHANGE	Mgmt_DBCache	DBCache
9.	RequiredRole_-AssemblyConnectorChange	CHANGE	Mgmt_DBCache	(req. role of User-Mgmt)
10.	ProvidedRole_-AssemblyConnectorChange	CHANGE	Mgmt_DBCache	(prov. role of DB-Cache)
11.	Assembly-ConnectorChange	CREATE		
12.	NameChange	CREATE	(new el.)	DBCache_Adpt
13.	RequiringAssemblyContext_-AssemblyConnectorChange	CHANGE	DBCache_Adpt	DBCache
14.	ProvidingAssemblyContext_-AssemblyConnectorChange	CHANGE	DBCache_Adpt	DBCache
15.	RequiredRole_-AssemblyConnectorChange	CHANGE	DBCache_Adpt	(req. role of DB-Cache)
16.	ProvidedRole_-AssemblyConnectorChange	CHANGE	DBCache_Adpt	(prov. role of DBAd-apter)

Figure 5.6.: Example for a Change in an Instance of the Palladio Component Model

have categorised the effects of metamodel changes into three general *change severities*, which are not specific to the MOF 1.4 meta-metamodel; thus, these severities can also be applied for the impact analysis of changes to Ecore-based metamodels.

Definition 15 (Change Severities). *The* severity *of metamodel changes describes the possible impact on instances of the metamodel. We specify the following three severity levels:*

- ***Non-breaking (NB)*** *changes do not change metamodels in a way that existing models become invalid instances of the metamodel. Most additive changes have this change severity.*
- ***Breaking and Resolvable (BR)*** *changes may invalidate existing instances, but a co-evolution operation can be derived automatically from the change, so that existing instances can be migrated to a state where they are valid instances of the new version of the metamodel.*
- ***Breaking and not Resolvable (BN)*** *changes may invalidate existing instances. If instances are invalidated, manual interaction is necessary to migrate them.*

The severities are ordered in the following way:

$$NB < BR < BN$$

For every change description $\underline{d} \in I(D)$ *at the instance level, there exists a function that determines the change severity:*

$$severity : I(D) \rightarrow \{NB, BR, BN\}$$

Breaking changes do not necessarily invalidate any possible instances of metamodels, but only those that actually contain instances of the elements that are changed. The change severities express that, in the case of breaking

Herrmannsdörfer et al. [72]	Burger et al. [27]
model preserving	non-breaking
safely model-migration	breaking and resolvable
unsafely model-migration	breaking and not resolvable

Table 5.4.: Change Severities

changes, there are possible instances that may be affected, or in the case of non-breaking changes, that there cannot be any instances that are affected by the change.

Herrmannsdörfer et al. [72] have also defined three categories for metamodels changes (see Table 5.4), which are however not identical to the change severities of Definition 15, since the purpose of the change representation ist not the impact analysis, but the generation of co-evolution migration scripts. While *model-preserving* changes are identical to non-breaking changes, the difference between *safely* and *unsafely model-migration* changes is determined by the information loss in the models during a co-evolution step. While safely migrating changes do not lead to loss of information, unsafely migrating changes may do so. Thus, the semantics of *breaking* and *model-migration* are not identical.

5.3.2. Severity of Change Sequences

The notion of severity for changes to metamodels describes the effect of single change operations to a metamodel. The three severities presented in subsection 5.3.1 can also be applied to sequence of changes to describe their effect on metamodels. The severity of a sequence is, of course, dependent upon the severities of the change operations that it contains. A change sequence that contains only non-breaking change operations is also a non-breaking change sequence itself. If a change sequence contains breaking changes, however, the severity of the sequence may be breaking or non-breaking. We express this fact in the following corollary:

Corollary 2. *The severity of change sequence* $\underline{D} \subseteq I(D)$ *is at most as high as the highest severity in the elements that the sequence contains:*

$$severity(\underline{D}) \leq \max(severity(\underline{d}) \mid \underline{d} \in \underline{D})$$

An example for a change sequence that contains a breaking change, but has a non-breaking severity, can easily be constructed: Let $\underline{D} = \{\underline{d}_1, \underline{d}_2\}$ be a change sequence that consist of an operation $\underline{d}_1$ that creates a mandatory reference in class, and an operation $\underline{d}_2$ that deletes this same reference: $\underline{d}_1, \underline{d}_2 \in I(ExistenceChange)$, $\underline{d}_1.type = CREATE$, $\underline{d}_2.type = DELETE$, $\underline{d}_1.affectedElement = \underline{d}_2.affectedElement$. The change sequence $\underline{D}$ does not change the metamodel at all, since $\underline{d}_1$ is reverted by $\underline{d}_2$, and thus $eval_{\underline{D}}(M) = M$ for all metamodels $M \in \mathscr{M}$. The severity of $\underline{D}$ is, trivially, non-breaking, even although the creation of a mandatory reference in $\underline{d}_1$ as a single operation may invalidate existing instances, and would thus be classified as *breaking and not resolvable*, following the classification of changes to Ecore-based metamodels (see Appendix B).

To correctly determine the severity of a change sequence, the inequality of Corollary 2 is not precise enough, since it only offers a worst-case estimation. For the purposes of co-evolution and metamodel re-use, an overestimation of the severity of changes is undesirable, since it would classify changes as breaking that do not actually lead to the invalidation of instances. Thus, we have developed a method to refactor change sequences, so that the inequality can still be used to estimate the overall severity of a change sequence, but which respects a number of cases where the change severity is non-breaking. The refactoring of change sequences does not change the semantics of the sequence, so that after a refactoring of change sequence $\underline{D}$ into a sequence $\underline{D}'$, equivalence between these sequences holds: $\underline{D} \sim \underline{D}'$. The refactoring operations are divided into two groups, which will be presented in the following subsections.

5.3.2.1. Removal of Redundant Operations

As demonstrated in the example above, later change operations can modify the outcome of earlier change operations. We have identified three cases of combinations of changes that affect each other:

- **Deletion after Change**: If an element is deleted (expressed by ExistenceChange(DELETE)), all modifications to features of the element that occur before its deletion do not have any effect, neither on the new version of the metamodel, nor on existing instances.
- **Transitive Changes**: Subsequent FeatureChanges of type CHANGE on the same feature can be subsumed by the last change. For example, if an element is renamed twice, only the name of the last change is relevant for the outcome of the change sequence.
- **Inverses**: Pairs of changes that are classified as inverses of each other following the change catalogue of Herrmannsdörfer, [72], can be deleted without modifying the effect of the change sequence.

The refactoring of this changes removes all but the respective last change (in the first two cases), or removes the pairs of changes (in the inverse case).

5.3.2.2. Replacing Atomic Changes with Complex Changes

As a consequence of the observation in Corollary 2, a ComplexChange always has the same or a lower severity than the ModelElementChange elements that it contains. Thus, the semantic lift [83] from a series of atomic changes to a complex change can lead to an improvement in the estimation of the change impact, since a lower change severity is a desired property of a change sequence.

Cases where a sequence of changes has a truly lower total severity than the maximum of its single change severities occur frequently in the change operators of Appendix B. As shown in the example of Figure 5.5, the operation *Pull up Feature* extracts a feature that is present in all subclasses and moves it to a superclass. In the example, Person is an abstract class with the two subclasses User and Actor. The two attributes in the two subclasses with the equal name name, type String, and multiplicities $(1, 1)$ are pulled up to the superclass Person. The complex change sequence that represents the pull up operation contains a change operation (10.) of the type EContainingClassChange, which adds the attribute name to the contained features of class Person. Since name is a mandatory feature, this addition, as a single operation, would be a breaking change, since there may be instances of this class that do not possess a value for this feature, and would thus not be valid instances. Since Person is, however, abstract, there can be no direct instances of this class; since the name attribute was present in all subclasses (User, Actor) in the previous version of the metamodel, all indirect instances of the class Person also possess a value for the feature, and will not become invalid. This information is encoded into the complex change operation *Pull up Feature*, and thus, the change severity of the complex operation is non-breaking.

5.3.3. State-based Analysis of Change Impact

As shown in the preciding sections, delta-based descriptions are superior to the state-based descriptions of changes since they contain more semantic information on the nature and provenance of the changes. To use delta-based analyses, such as the change severities in the change metamodel, the description of changes between to versions of a metamodel have to be expressed in a delta-based format. In this section, we present a method for the estimation of the impact of changes to metamodels that is independent of the way that these changes are applied. The goal of the impact analysis is the re-use of metamodels with existing tools and instances that require a specific metamodel as the target.

5.3.3.1. Metamodel Conformity

While co-evolution methods such as Edapt are focussed on the migration of existing instances, the impact analysis of metamodel changes is used to assist the metamodel developer to plan modifications to metamodels in such a way that the migration effort that is caused by these modifications is as minimal as possible. This is why the change severities presented in in Definition 15 are focussed on the impact on existing instances, so that metamodel developers can estimate the migration efforts, and possibly improve the planned changes. In the ideal case, no co-adaptations are necessary, and the set of possible instances of the new version of the metamodel is a superset of the set of instances of the old version. In this case, we say that the old metamodel *conforms* to the new version.

Definition 16 (Metamodel Conformity). *Let* $M_1, M_2 \in \mathscr{M}$ *be metamodels and* $I(M_1), I(M_2)$ *the sets of all possible instances of* M_1 *and* M_2*. Metamodel conformity is defined as*

$$conforms = \{\langle M_1, M_2 \rangle \in \mathscr{M}^2 \mid I(M_1) \subseteq I(M_2)\}$$

The conformance relation between metamodels is a special case of model typing [145], where M_1 is a subtype of M_2. It does not require full type substitutability, which also concerns operations and return types of metamodels. Instead, the conformance relation poses weaker restrictions on the relation between the two metamodels, which is only affected by the possible instances of the metamodels.

By definition, non-breaking/model-preserving changes alter the metamodel in such a way that all possible existing instances will still be valid instances after the change. Thus, metamodel conformity follows from the existence of a non-breaking change sequence between the two metamodels.

Corollary 3. *If there exists a series $\underline{D}$ of non-breaking changes that can be applied to obtain M_2 from M_1, then M_1 conforms to M_2:*

$$\exists \underline{D}\big(severity(\underline{D}) = NB \wedge eval_{\underline{D}}(M_1) = M_2\big) \Rightarrow conforms(M_1, M_2)$$

Thus, to show that two metamodels conform to each other, it is sufficient to find a non-breaking change sequence between these metamodels.

5.3.3.2. State-based Analysis of Metamodel Conformity

In this subsection, we will present a state-based method for determining the conformance of two metamodels by direct comparison. This method has been developed in the course of the diploma thesis of Aleksandar Toshovski [150], and is contained in a joint publication with the author of this dissertation [30].

As we have shown in subsection 5.2.5, the diff model of EMF Compare can be mapped to our Change Metamodel, so that the engine of EMF Compare can be used to extract a change sequence that describes the difference between two Ecore-based metamodels. As listed in Table 5.1, the state-based comparison has the advantage that the change sequence is minimal and does not contain any redundant operations, since the difference algorithm of EMF Compare yields a minimal sequence of atomic changes. Thus, the removal of operations is unnecessary. The change sequence contains, however, only atomic change operations. To correctly estimate if a change sequence is non-breaking, and, as a consequence of this, the metamodels conform to each other, it has to be refactored with the method presented in subsection 5.3.2.

The process for the state-based analysis of the metamodel change impact is displayed in Figure 5.7. Two metamodels are analysed with EMF Compare, which computes a description of the difference between them. This description is converted into instances of the atomic Ecore change metamodel. This refactoring of atomic changes to complex changes is performed by a rule-based engine, which extracts the complex changes types

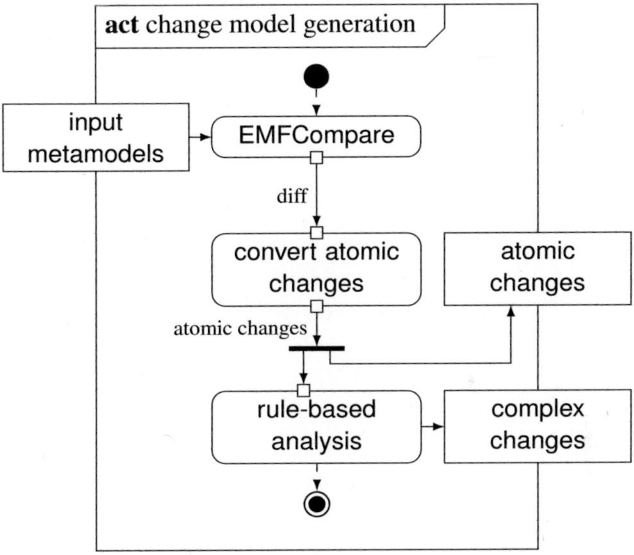

Figure 5.7.: State-based Impact Analysis Process

(see Appendix B), for which the change severities have been analysed by Burger [27] and Herrmannsdörfer [70], and can be looked up in Appendix B.

Since the aim of the conformity analysis is the checking of metamodel conformance, we have implemented rules to check the cases of non-breaking changes. In total, 24 rules have been defined, which cover the non-breaking complex change types. In the protoypical implementation of the analysis, the Java-based *Drools* framework[2] has been used to realise the rules. An example for such a rule can be seen in Listing 2. The shown rule covers the case where the deletion of a structural feature from an EClass element was performed in the course of a *Pull Up Feature* complex change, as in the example of subsection 5.3.2. The IDiff element describes the delta between the two elements of the respective metamodels. The Java helper function `isPullUpFeature()` and `isParentAbstract()` have been implemented by us in the `DroolsUtils` library, and check for the border conditions that have to hold, so that the change can be classified as non-breaking. If the conditions are fulfilled, the rule fires and the change is classified. (The `then`-clause in the rule is empty since we use a listener-base approach to detect rule application.)

```
rule "ReferenceChange␣EClass␣remove␣Attribute/Reference"
   when diff: IDiff( operationType == OperationType.DELETE,
        differenceType == DiffType.REFERENCE, parameter=="
        eStructuralFeatures", DroolsUtils.isPullUpFeature(
        oldValue,newValue,newParent)
   then
end
```

Listing 2: Drools Rule for Deletion of an Attribute/Reference (from [30])

If an IDiff element cannot be classified as non-breaking, we assume that its application can lead to the invalidation of existing instances, and thus, the metamodels do not conform to each other.

[2] `http://www.jboss.org/drools/`, retrieved 26 May 2014

6. Flexible View Type Definitions

In this chapter, we will present the concept of flexible view types, which offers the compact and rapid definition of user-specific view types and views on model-based data. Since flexible views are a general concept for view-based model-driven development, we will first describe the concepts independently of the VITRUVIUS approach. Then, we will discuss the role of these concepts and the integration of tools into the VITRUVIUS approach.

We will introduce the abstract concept of flexible views in section 6.1. For the declarative definition of flexible views, the domain-specific language *ModelJoin* has been developed and implemented, which will be presented in section 6.2. Finally, we describe the usage of flexible views and ModelJoin in the context of VITRUVIUS in section 6.3.

6.1. Concept

In this section, we will describe the concept of flexible views in a technology-independent way. We will first motivate the concept, then introduce the definition of flexible views, and finally, we will define the different notions of editability for flexible views.

6.1.1. Motivation

In software development processes, metamodels and models are used for various purposes; even in processes not labelled as model-based nor model-driven, models are often used in various stages of development, such as specificition, design, or analysis of non-functional properties. In addition, models are used for domain modelling in the specific area for which the software is developed, such as hardware models for embedded design, automotive architecture models, energy topology models, traffic models, and so on. Although often a combination of these models is used, the correspondences between them is rarely made explicit, since every metamodel is usually implemented with a specific modelling tool of its own, and thus the semantic interdependencies between the various models are not specified and cannot be expressed at the instance level due to the lack of an appropriate formalism. The integration of information from heterogeneous models suffers from the problems of fragmentation, redundancy, inconsistency, and complexity, as described in subsection 1.2.3.

To tackle the complexity of the usage of multiple models, view-based approaches offer developers specialised view types that reduce the amount of information and combine elements and properties from several models into integrated views. The definition of these view types requires a metamodel that specifies the elements that can be part of a view that instantiates the view type, and transformations that generate the views and that synchronise them with the models that they represent. Since the specification and maintenance of these metamodels and transformations requires high effort, view-based modelling approaches usually only contain a fixed number of pre-defined view types. In some approaches, special developer roles, such as the methodologist in the Orthographic Software Modeling approach [7], are responsible for the a priori definition of view types, so that they can later be used by developers. If a developer who uses these view-based approaches would like to fulfil a kind of information need that has not been foreseen by the methodologist, or another role who is responsible for the definition of view types, the developer has to resort to a standard model transformation language, which means that he or she has to define the view type metamodel and the bi-directional transformations manually. Since this is a heavy-weight process that requires the definition of several interconnected artefacts, it is not possible to define custom views rapidly, and the evolution of views and viewtypes requires the effort of adapting these artefacts. Furthermore, the definition of view types at the metamodel level is not sufficient to define views that depend on properties at the instance level. Of course, the result of a model transformations (which is defined at the metamodel level) contains elements at the instance level whose properties depend on the source instances; the rules for the creation of these elements do, however, apply to all possible instances that can be used as a source of the model transformation.

As a scenario, we consider the running example of software development with the Palladio Component Model, used for software architecture modelling, and UML, used for the modelling of the object-oriented design. A customised view in the UML-Palladio scenario could display only the classes that implement the component comp_1, and that are responsible for a certain execution time in the performance simulation of Palladio, with an annotation that displays this execution time. To create such a view manually, a developer would first have to create an appropriate metamodel for the view type, in this case a subset or extension of UML; then, the transformation from the metamodels UML, PCM, and Sensor model to the view type metamodel, and back if editability of the view is desired; finally, constraints for the view type metamodel to disallow certain kinds of changes, such as the deletion of a class, or renaming that would violate naming conventions.

This scenario is representative for modern software development, where more and more of the artefacts that are created during the development process, are formalised and thus adhere to a certain metamodel or description language. Metamodels are an appropriate format for the description of these formalisms, since they are suited for any kind of structured information. Even all-purpose programming languages such as Java can be represented in a metamodel-based format, using approaches such as JaMoPP [66]. Thus, view-based modelling can be used for the combination of any kinds of data, system descriptions, documentation, and source code.

6.1.2. Flexible View Types for the Rapid Creation of Views

As a solution to the problem of defining custom, user-specific views on instances of heterogeneous metamodels, we present the concept of *flexible view types*. Flexible view types are defined declaratively and contain a compact definition of the meta level (view type), instance level (view), and information on the editability of elements. The approach is applicable to *projective* view-based approaches (see section 2.1), where the information is persisted in one or multiple base models, so that the views only contain transient information that has been extracted from the base models. The concept of flexible view types has been published by the author of this dissertation in [26] and [25].

6.1.2.1. Definition

The following definition of flexible view types makes use of the *view type scope* notion as introduced in Definition 8 and Definition 11 on page 88.

Definition 17 (Flexible View Type). *A* flexible view type *over a set of models contains:*

- *the definition of the* view type metamodel *and its* projectional scope. *The view type may have a single- or multi-metamodel projectional scope;*
- *the definition of the* selectional scope, *i.e., the selection of elements that are contained in the flexible view. This selection is based on instance properties;*
- *a set of rules for editability of the view and for the back propagation to the source models.*

In Figure 6.1, the abstract concept of flexible view types is shown: Two metamodels M_1 and M_2 and their respective instances $\underline{M}_1$ and $\underline{M}_2$ share a semantic overlap, i.e., different elements of M_1 and M_2 represent the same

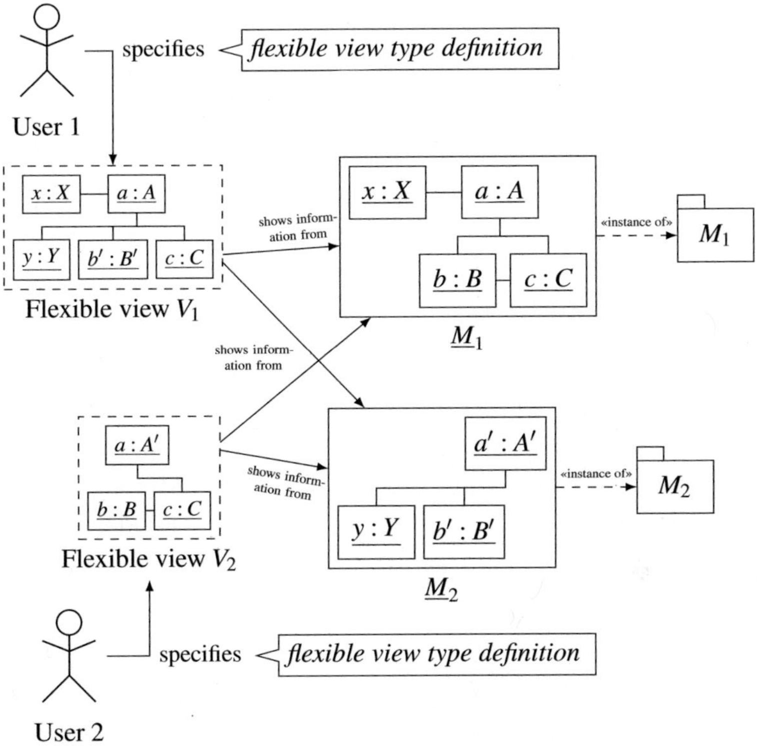

Figure 6.1.: Abstract Concept of Flexible Views Showing Merged Instances of Different Metamodels

entitity type in the system of interest. In the example, this is indicated by similar naming of the elements at the metamodel level (A corresponds to A', etc.) and at the model level (a corresponds to a', etc.). Each of the models carry additional information that is not available in the respective other model, i.e., the elements x, y and the references to these elements. *User 1* wants to create a view that aggregates all information from $\underline{M}_1$ and $\underline{M}_2$, while at the same displaying overlapping elements as one element. The resulting *flexible view* V_1 integrates information from both models and identifies the overlapping elements by a naming convention. *User 2* creates the view V_2, which shows only the overlapping elements, but always the elements of type C. The views in this example are read-only.

6.1.2.2. Proposed Advantages of Flexible View Types

With a flexible view type definition facility, users of view-based approaches can create a merged view of elements from $\underline{M}_1$ and $\underline{M}_2$, based on, e.g., naming of elements or other semantic connections that can be described declaratively based on instance properties. It is not necessary to modify the metamodels M_1 and M_2, for example, by creating explicit references between these metamodels, to define the flexible view type. The correspondences between the instances of M_1 and M_2 are defined in the flexible view type definition. This way of defining views and view type using a single declarative definition has multiple advantages:

- **Compactness**: The definition of the three parts – projectional scope, selectional scope, and editability – in a single, declarative definition, using a domain-specific language, offers a compact way for the complete definition of all properties that have to be defined for a view type and the actual view instance.

- **Non-intrusiveness**: In comparison to other approaches that require the explicit modelling of semantic links that represent the overlaps between models, e.g., EMF-INCQUERY [65], the source metamodels and instances do not have to be modified in any way, since the correspondences are expressed declaratively, and a custom view type and view instance is created from this declarative definition.

- **Rapid Definition**: As a consequence of the compact definition, flexible view type definitions offer a rapid way of defining and modifying view types. Flexible views have a transient nature and can change rapidly as the developer modifies the declarative definitions and experiments with different variants. If the textual definition of a flexible view evolves, the resulting view type and transformations co-evolve automatically, since they are generated from the declarative definition. Therefore, users can develop different versions of flexible views without having to keep metamodel and transformation consistent manually.

6.1.3. Editability in Flexible View Types

Flexible views can be used to display information from heterogeneous models for the purpose of analysis, or to facilitate the navigation in large systems that are described in several formalisms. For the usage in view-based development processes, it is however necessary that the views contain concepts for editability, since views are the only means of modifying information in view-based approaches.

The editability of views is a persisting problem in research of databases ([9, 106], see section 3.7) and metamodelling ([146, 73], see section 3.5). Thus, we do not claim to provide a general solution to this problem in this dissertation. Instead, we follow the principle of the *Lenses* approach by Foster et al. [50]: The flexible view definition contains not only information on how the information of the base models is represented in the views, but also offers means for the definition of editability, from which an automatic update behaviour can be derived where applicable, and which requires the user to define this behaviour manually in the other cases. We deem this semi-automic solution to be superior, since the view developer keeps control over the behaviour of the edit operation while being able to use automatic solutions for recurring cases of editability. This is an approach that is also taken in architectural description frameworks (e.g., [63]).

The specification of the editability of a view consists of two parts: The *editability scope* (see Definition 12 on page 93), which describes which elements can be modified, and rules for the synchronisation with the source models.

6.1.3.1. Editability Scope

The editability scope of a flexible view type is defined at the metamodel level as well as at the instance level. At the metamodel level, the editability scope specifies the elements in the view types for which the instances are modifiable. In addition, the scope can be refined at the instance level to include or exclude instance elements in a view from editability.

Metamodel Level Since a view type is a special kind of metamodel, editability permissions have to be specified for all the elements of this metamodel that can be instantiated, and whose instances can be changed after instantiation.

In this dissertation, we use *Ecore* as the meta-meta-model. Without loss of generality, we will define the notion of editability in view types as edit operations on Ecore-based metamodels. We will apply the considerations of section 3.4, which describe changes to models and metamodels, to define a notion of editability. In Ecore, the following elements have a potency of 2, which means that they can be instantiated twice: A non-abstract EClass can be instantiated as an object, a non-derived attribute can be instantiated as an attribute value, and a non-derived reference can be instantiated as a link. Ecore metamodels also contain elements that cannot be instantiated, such as derived features, abstract classes, or inheritance information. In Ecore metamodels, features of classes (i.e., attributes and references) can furthermore be restricted in their editability by the properties changeable and unsettable: While the changeable property describes whether an feature may be changed after instantiation, the unsettable property describes whether it can be returned to the unset state, which is a special state for features in Ecore that is not equivalent to filling the feature value with the null value. If a feature is not changeable, the value of an attribute or reference can only be set once, usually during construction of the element, but cannot be changed afterwards.

These properties specify the *inherent editability* of a view type, which is defined by the set of valid instances that can be created for the view type metamodel. It can, however, be desired by the methodologist or the developer to specifiy restrictions that cannot be expressed just by the restrictions of Ecore metamodels. For example, with the formalisms of Ecore, a metamodel cannot be specified in a way that instances of a class may not be deleted from a model. It is thus especially not possible to restrict the deletion of elements to certain conditions, for example to only allow the deletion of objects if there are no links pointing to this object.

Thus, the editability scope of flexible views can be further refined by *editability specifications*. These specification, like constraints, are defined at the metamodel level, but affect instances. In contrast to constraints, they do, however, not influence the validity of static instances of a metamodel, but do describe the allowed operations on these instances. For the elements in the view types that can be instantiated and whose elements are changeable, i.e., which are inherently editable, the editability scope can be further refined for all edit operations that are possible on these instances. These operations are specific for the view type metamodel and are exactly covered by the metamodel-specific change metamodel presented in section 5.2. Thus, we can use the categorization of change operations of this metamodel to define editability by allowing or disallowing operations, which are described by instances of the metamodel.

ExistenceChange	**Cr**	**Del**		
ClassChange	✗	✗		
FeatureChange	**Add**	**Rem**	**Chg**	**Uns**
ClassNameChange	–	–	✗	✗
ImplementsChange	✓	✓	✓	✗

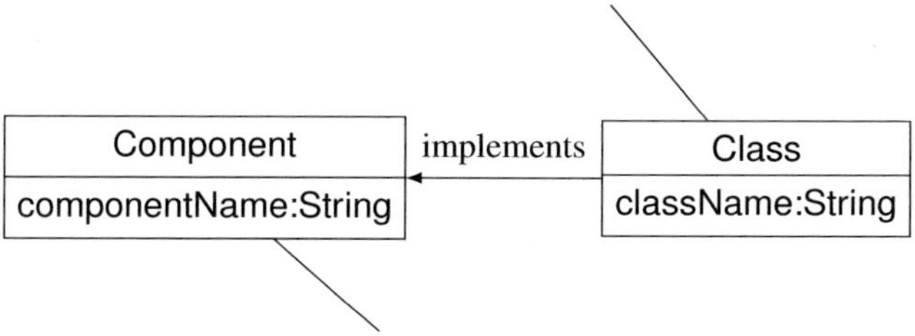

ExistenceChange	**Cr**	**Del**		
ComponentChange	✗	✗		
FeatureChange	**Add**	**Rem**	**Chg**	**Uns**
ComponentNameChange	–	–	✗	✗

Figure 6.2.: Class-Component Implementation View Type with Metamodel-level Editability Scopes (Cr=Create, Del=Delete, Rem=Remove, Chg=Change, Uns=Unset)

For example, the class-component implementation view type of the running example contains components, classes, and an implementation relation between these elements (see Figure 6.2). Thus, the view type metamodel contains the two classes Class and Component, and the reference implements, which is directed from the class element to the component, and thus contained in the Eclass Class. To describe the changes that are possible to this view type, a metamodel-specific change metamodel for this view type has to be created using the methods described in section 5.2. In this example, the existence change classes ComponentChange and ClassChange, and the feature change classes ComponentNameChange, ClassNameChange, and ImplementsChange can be extracted automatically using the change metamodel generation algorithm. The algorithm respects the inherent editability of the metamodel, since change classes are not created for abstract classes and derived features in the metamodel for which the changes are described.

The operations in the change metamodel can now be allowed (✓) or disallowed (✗) to define the editability scope of the view type. In the example of the class-component implementation view, the addition or deletion of classes and components should be disallowed, as well as the modification of the element names. Thus, the only allowed change operation in this view tpye is the ImplementsChange operation, which sets the implements-relation between classes and components. The editability operations that can be restricted by these definitions are defined by the edit types of the change metamodel: For classes, `ADD` and `REMOVE` operations can be allowed or disallowed, while for features, depending on the cardinality of the feature, the operation types `ADD`, `REMOVE` (for multi-valued features), `CHANGE` (single-valued features), and `UNSET` (both cardinalities) operations can be allowed or disallowed. In the example of Figure 6.2, change operations that do not apply are marked with a "–" symbol. For example, to enforce that each class has to implement a component, the UNSET operation can be disallowed, so that the relation can only be changed by assigning the class to a new component. The change metamodel can now be amended with additional constraints in the form of OCL expressions, which further limit the way in which the changes to the implements-relation can be applied. The enforcement of these rules can be handled in several ways in an actual editor that implements the flexible views concept. It is possible that the action is actually forbidden, so the user cannot execute the operation at all, and receives a warning immediately when trying to, e.g., delete the reference. It is also possible that the operation is recorded and the evaluation whether the operation is allowed is deferred until the point where the view is saved and synchronised with the source models, so that the user can work with temporary inconsistencies, but has to revert forbidden operations before a save operation is possible.

If all possible edit operations are disallowed in a view type, it is a read-only view type, and the views that are instances of this view type cannot be modified at all. If these operations are allowed on all elements, no restrictions in editability apply, except those that are defined by the inherent editability of the view type metamodel.

Model Level The modification operation create, delete, and update are also defined at the instance level for actual views. In flexible views, it is also possible to allow or disallow these operation kinds for actual instances. For example, a user-specific component-diagram view of the system in the running example may allow the editing of the comp_1 component, but not of the comp_2 component. The editability of the components can be defined in the the same granularity as it is possible for the elements in the metamodel: Edit operations can be allowed or disallowed for every ClassChange and FeatureChange element in the metamodel-specific change metamodel; the change operations for restrictions at the model level are the same ones that are used to describe restrictions at the metamodel level. The only difference is that they do not accompany a class of the view type, but actual instances in the view. In the example, the comp_1 in Figure 6.3 component may be

ExistenceChange	**Cr**	**Del**		
BasicComponentChange	✓	✓		
FeatureChange	**Add**	**Rem**	**Chg**	**Uns**
EntityNameChange	–	–	✓	✗
ComponentTypeChange	–	–	✓	✗

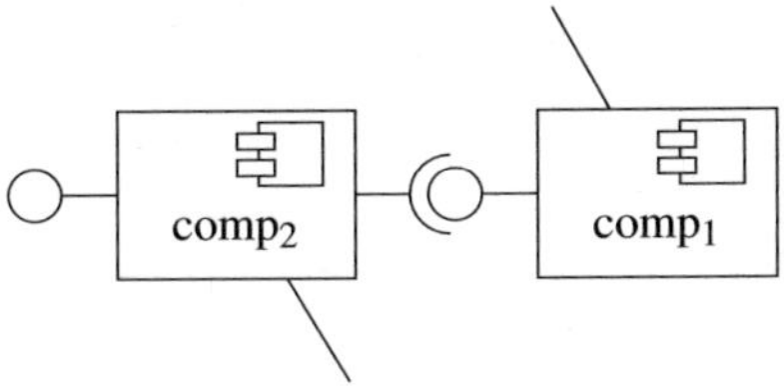

ExistenceChange	**Cr**	**Del**		
BasicComponentChange	✗	✗		
FeatureChange	**Add**	**Rem**	**Chg**	**Uns**
EntityNameChange	–	–	✗	✗
ComponentTypeChange	–	–	✗	✗

Figure 6.3.: Component Diagram View with Instance-level Editability Scopes

edited with FeatureChange elements, such as EntityNameChange, but this is disallowed for the $comp_2$ component.

This instance-specific restriction of editability and update behaviour can be used for collaborative processes, where certain developers are only allowed to change parts of the system, but may browse also the parts of the system that they cannot change.

6.1.3.2. Synchronisation Rules

For the synchronisation of modifications in views, two parts have to be defined: First, changes have to be detected and expressed in a well-defined format, and second, the response to this changes has to be defined.

Change Detection and Description In projective view-based approaches, which are supported by flexible view types, the views are special models that are extracted from base models. Thus, a view is per se only a model, which can be displayed and modified by any kind of textual or visual editor, transformation, or further tool that exports model-based data. Modifications to the view have to be detected so that they can be persisted in the source models of the view. Therefore, the problem of detecting and describing changes in a view can be reduced to the problem of change detection in models.

There are two basic approaches to describe changes in a model (see section 3.5): While in the *state-based* approach, two versions of a model are compared to each other to determine the difference, the *delta-based* approach uses atomic edit operations to describe the differences. As shown by Stevens et al. [146] and discussed in subsection 5.2.5, delta-based approaches are superior to state-based approaches since the edit operations in delta-based descriptions may carry information that cannot be determined by calculating the difference between two versions of a model. For example, if an element in a model can only identified by its name, and not by another universal identifier, then the renaming of the element will lead to a change that, in the state-based approach, is indistinguishable from the deletion and creation of a new element with the new name. In the delta-based approach, this change can be described as an atomic rename operation. To determine the change operations, editing tools that are used to manipulate the model can record the changes to the model. In the Edapt tool by Herrmannsdörfer et al. [72], for example, developers can choose from a set of refactoring operation to explicitly specify the intent of changes to a model. It is possible to convert a delta-based change description into a state-based description by applying the deltas to a model. During this process, the additional information in the deltas is lost. A conversion from state-based to delta-based descriptions is also possible by using a diff algorithm (such as EMFCompare [22]) on the different versions of the model. Since these algorithms use heuristics to recreate the change operations from the state-based difference, the resulting

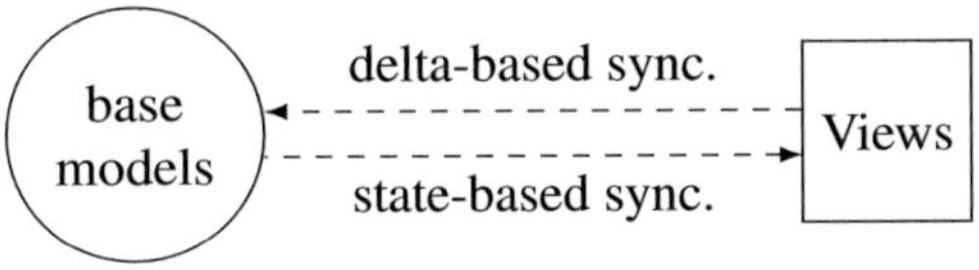

Figure 6.4.: State-based and Delta-based Synchronisation of Base Models and View Types

delta-based description contains less information than a set of deltas that has been recorded during the actual editing by the user (see section 5.3.)

As a consequence of this, the synchronisation rules in flexible view types are defined for delta-based change descriptions. It is not relevant how these descriptions are determined: They can either be determined by recording editing steps or by a state-based comparison of two versions of a view. Since the possible edit operations are specific to the view type, we also use the change metamodel from section 5.2 and require that the editing operations are described as instances of the view type-specific change metamodels. Thus, we can use a unified description formalism for editability and actual changes in a view.

Since the flexible view type approach is based on projective views, views on a system can always be extracted from the information in the base models of the system. These automatically generated views do not contain original information, as it would be the case in synthetic views. Only when views are edited do they contain information that is not in the base models. In this case, the view is called *dirty*, until the modifications have been translated back to the base models. Thus, it is sufficient that only the changes in the views have to be described in a delta-based format; changes in the base models do not have to be propagated to the views, since a re-creation of the views is always possible from the information in the base models. In Figure 6.4, this is depicted at the example of views that synchronise with a single underlying model.

Response Action Once a modification to a view has been detected, a *response action* is triggered that propagates the changes back to the base models. The semantics of changes to a view are encoded in these response actions. Since our approach of flexible views gives the user the possibility to define the views declaratively, the user expresses the intent for the displaying and combining of information with this declarative definition. Thus, the provenance of elements in a view is explicitely specified and can be used to automatically determine the synchronisation behaviour in the form of response actions.

The response action defines the behaviour of an editing operation to a view. Due to the complexity of the view-update problem, there is no universal strategy of how an edit operation in a view should be translated to the underlying base models. This is a persistent problem in database research [40, 59] and has also been applied to other abstract data structures; Foster[50] demands that an update to a view should be translated in a "reasonable" way, which is a general principle to which the flexible view types should also adhere. The rationale behind the flexible view concept is to assume that the user, e.g., a developer who defines a flexible view type, is aware of the complexity of the view-update problem and does not expect the framework that implements the flexible view type concept to be able to handle all update scenarios automatically. The approach of the flexible view type concept is to reduce the accidental complexity of the problem by offering the user means to distinguish the cases where automatic synchronisation is possible from those where manual interaction is necessary, and to provide means to describe this "reasonable" interaction.

As mentioned above, the synchronisation behaviour can not be determined automatically for all kinds of flexible view types definitions. To distinguish between the cases where the synchronisation behaviour can unambiguously be determined, i.e., there is a unique response action for an actual change to the view, and the cases where manual interaction is necessary, we introduce the following *synchronisation modes*, which can be chosen by the user for each element e_{vt} of a view type vt. These modes depend on the provenance of elements, which is expressed in the is-represented-by relation rep between the elements in the base models and those in the view, as well as on the type of the change that triggered the response action. For an element e_{vt} in a view type, one of these three synchronisation modes can be chosen:

- **Automatic**: The edit operation is propagated automatically to the source elements. The default behaviour for changes to this element is executed.
- **Select Policy**: The developer of the view type can choose from a set of update policies.
- **Manual**: The developer has to define the synchronisation behaviour manually in the form of a transformation from the view type to the source models.

Depending on the way in which the view type e_{vt} and the mapping of SUM elements to the view type $rep(e_{sum}, e_{vt})$ (see Definition 6 on page 86) are defined, not all synchronisation modes may be available for every combination of elements and triggering edit operations. Of course, a *manual* synchronisation behaviour can always be defined, but it may be impossible to prove any properties of this synchronisation behaviour, if it is specified in a general-purpose language (due to the possible indecidability of runtime properties). The manual behaviour is intended as a fallback mechanism if none of the other methods is available.

The *select policy* behaviour lets the user or developer who defines the view type choose from a set of synchronisation behaviours, which are offered by the framework that implements the flexible view type concept. This solution has the advantage that the view type developer stays in control of the behaviour of the view type and can select a synchronisation mechanism for which certain properties, such as well-behavedness and hippocraticness, are known, and can be taken into respect for the selection of the appropriate behaviour.

The *automatic* mode is only possible if the relation *rep* is invertible. This does not necessarily mean that the relation is bijective: For example, if two elements of different metamodels represent the same concept, a view type could combine these elements into one element of the view type. A change of properties on this element, e.g. the name of the element, can unambiguously be written back to both source elements, although the relation *rep* is not even injective in this case. The invertability of *rep* is thus dependent on the semantics of the base models and the intent of the developer of the view type.

6.1.4. Discussion

The definition of editability in flexible view types does not require a full bi-directional synchronisation of models. As explained in the preceding subsection, the difference between bi-directional synchronisation of arbitrary models and the synchronisation of views with base models lies in two areas:

1. **Information Asymmetry**: In projective approaches, the views can always be extracted from the information in the base models. Thus, a state-based synchronisation from the models to the views is sufficient and does not have to deal with differences beween the model and the view. These would have to be regarded in a real-time editing scenario, where the base models are subject to change while a view is in the dirty state. At the moment, however, we do not support real-time concurrent modifications of base models.

2. **Well-Defined Edit Operations**: The editability scope of flexible view types limits the edit operations that can be applied to a view to those cases that can be translated back to the base models. For other cases, the synchronisation does not have to be taken into account, since those cases are not allowed in the flexible view types.

This strategy of allowing editability only if there exists a translation operation for persisting the changes back into the base models is also pursued in the lenses approach [50] (see section 3.5). To describe the behaviour of flexible views, we can use the properties *invertibility*, *well-behavedness*, and *hippocraticness*, which have been defined for lenses. We assume that the "concrete" domain consists of the base models, whereas the "abtract" domain consists of views.

6.1.4.1. Invertibility

The automatic generation of a response action for a an element of a view is always possible if the represents relation at the instance level (rep) between the element in the base models and the element in the view is injective. This is the case for *projectional* views. In projectional views, every edit operation can be translated unambiguously to an element in the base models. In the case of *combining* views, the automatic synchronisation behaviour can only offer one default behaviour of many possible translations that fulfil the definition of the view. If the view is not automatically invertible, the user can be prompted by the select policy behaviour to choose between one of the valid inversions of the view definition to persist an edit operation, or define a manual update behaviour.

6.1.4.2. Well-behavedness

Well-behavedness in views is given if two laws are fulfilled:

The GETPUT law states that the generation of a view and an immediate consequent save operation, without changes to the view, must not change the base models. This property is always fulfilled in flexible views, since the response action (which is equivalent to the PUT action) is delta-based, and thus only triggered if a change is detected in a view. Given that the deltas are determined correctly, a save operation without prior change to the view will not cause any response action; thus, flexible views always adhere to the GETPUT law.

The PUTGET law, on the other hand, states that saving and re-generatiing a view from the base model yields a view that is identical to the one that has been saved. The declarative definition of views are, however, useful for generating the transformations that create a view together with those response actions that execute the changes to a view. If an automatic strategy exists, the designer of the view type has to ensure that the automatic response action adheres to the PUTGET law. The same is true for the available operations in the select policy strategy. For manually defined resonse actions, the user who defines the action has to ensure that the PUTGET law is obeyed. Thus, the well-behavedness of views depends entirely on the adherence to the PUTGET law.

6.1.4.3. Hippocraticness

The hippocraticness property in the context of views describes that a combination of model and view that satisfies the declarative view definition are not modified by the view generation engine; thus, if a view already fulfils the view type definition, it must not be re-generated by the view generation mechanism. If an automatic synchronisation mode exists for a certain edit operation, the methodologist has to ensure that the synchronisation fulfils the hippocraticness property. If the user is able to select a policy, the pre-defined policies have to contain a declaration about whether they fulfil hippocraticness or not. For manual response actions, it is in general unknown whether they fulfil hippocraticness or not; the user who specifies the response action has to check manually whether the action fulfils hippocraticness. If a general-purpose programming or model transformation language can be used to specify the response actions, it is in general not possible to prove whether such an action fulfils the property.

6.2. Definition of Flexible Views at Run-Time Using ModelJoin

A definition language for flexible views has to fulfil two contradicting goals: First, the language must be expressive enough to provide means for the properties of flexible views, which have been listed in Definition 17. Second, the language should be as simple as possible and should allow short development cycles, so that developers can write and modify flexible views rapidly. With these goals in mind, we have developed the *ModelJoin* language. ModelJoin is a declarative domain-specific language for the definition of flexible view types, which has a human-readable textual concrete syntax that bears similarities to that of the Structured Query Language (SQL). The language focusses on the information needs of the developer, and is used to describe the desired properties of a view. It abstracts from the technical details of how the view types and views are created. Since the language is designed to be written and understood by developers, the textual ModelJoin definitions can also serve as a documentation of the purpose of a view type.

The concepts and the language definition, which are presented in this section, have been published previously in [29], and are extended in the following subsections. The prototypical implementation of ModelJoin and its technical details are described in the ModelJoin technical report [28].

6.2.1. Concept

6.2.1.1. Analogy to Relational Databases

For the compact definition of flexible view specifications, we exploit the analogy to views in relational databases (see section 3.7). Views in relational detabases can be defined with queries. Such a query determines the schema of the result (which corresponds to the metamodel/view type in the model-driven scenario), and the result set itself (which corresponds to instances/a view). Just as a query can be written and interpreted dynamically, or stored and used as a database view, flexible views can be pre-defined and persisted,

relational concept	Ecore concept
database schema	metamodel
table	model
table row (tuple)	object/instance
column	feature (attribute/reference)
query	model transformation

Table 6.1.: Analogy between Relational Concepts and MDD Concepts (from [28])

or defined at runtime (of the development framework). Different flexible views can be instantiated from an existing view type. A flexible view is defined by rules that determine its contents and behaviour; these rules can be altered for specific modelling purposes by developers themselves or by an additional developer role.

This is an approach that is also followed by other query languages for model-based data, such as EMFQuery.[1] In Table 6.1, we have listed the corresponding constructs of metamodel-based structures and relational structures, which we have identified. If we assume that a metamodel corresponds to a database schema, and a model corresponds to a database table, then a query corresponds to a model transformation. The target metamodel of the transformation, is, however, not defined a priori, but is part of the the query itself: When a query on a relational database is executed, the result set consists of relations that instantiate a new relation schema. For example, in SQL, the table schema of the result of a query is dependent on the columns chosen in the `SELECT` clauses, renaming statements (`AS`), `JOIN` statements, and other constructs. In the model-driven world, this would mean that a query would have to contain a definition of a result metamodel of its own. The result set of this query would combine information from heterogeneous models into a single result model, which instantiates this new result metamodel.

[1] `http://www.eclipse.org/modeling/emf/?project=query`, retrieved 26 May 2014

Existing query languages for Ecore-based models offer, however, only projectional operations on instances of a single metamodels (e.g., EMFQuery), thus making queries on instances of multiple metamodels impossible. This is, however, required to create flexible views with a multi-metamodel projectional scope. Model transformation languages (such as QVT [116], ATL [79]) allow the transformation of information from heterogeneous models, but require a fixed pre-defined result metamodel. ModelJoin overcomes these limitations, and offers developers statements that are similar to the operators of SQL, so that selection, projection and joining of elements from heterogeneous models is possible. Like SQL, ModelJoin is a declarative language, so ModelJoin expressions describe the desired properties of the result set and its metamodel.

The principle for the construction of the result set in ModelJoin is different from that in relational algebra: While the join in relational algebra constructs the cross product of the base relations and reduces these relations via projection, ModelJoin uses a constructive approach that only includes the elements that are specificly defined. Thus, if an operator degenerates to the case where none of the conditions are fulfilled, the execution of the ModelJoin query delivers an empty result set, in contrast to relational algebra, where the complete cross product would be contained in the result set.

6.2.1.2. Example

An example ModelJoin query is displayed in Listing 3. (The metamodels on which the example is based are depicted in Figure C.2 and Figure C.3 in the appendix.) The query selects elements from a library model and an online movie database model.

The library and movie database metamodel contain elements that represent similar concepts, such as persons, films, and the information on which person belongs to the cast of a movie. An integrated view on these two metamodels should thus combine the information from both of the metamodels and

```
import "platform:/resource/edu.kit.ipd.sdq.mdsd.mj.example/models/imdb.ecore"
import "platform:/resource/edu.kit.ipd.sdq.mdsd.mj.example/models/extlibrary.ecore"
target "http://mdsd.sdq.ipd.kit.edu/modeljoin#joinexample"

THETA JOIN imdb.Actor WITH library.Person
      WHERE "Actor.name␣=␣Person.firstName.concat('␣').concat(Person.lastName)"
      AS jointarget.Person {
            KEEP ATTRIBUTES imdb.Person.firstName
            KEEP ATTRIBUTES imdb.Person.lastName
            KEEP SUBTYPE library.Borrower AS TYPE jointarget.Customer
}

LEFT OUTER JOIN imdb.Film WITH library.VideoCassette AS jointarget.Movie {
      KEEP ATTRIBUTES imdb.Film.year
      KEEP CALCULATED ATTRIBUTE "AudioVisualItem.title.concat('␣(').concat(Film.year).concat(')')" AS jointarget.Movie.extTitle
      KEEP OUTGOING imdb.Film.votes AS TYPE jointarget.Vote {
            KEEP ATTRIBUTES imdb.Vote.score
            }
      KEEP SUPERTYPE library.AudioVisualItem AS type jointarget.MediaItem {
            KEEP ATTRIBUTES library.AudioVisualItem.minutesLength
            }
      KEEP OUTGOING imdb.Film.figures AS TYPE jointarget.Figure {
            KEEP ATTRIBUTES imdb.Figure.name
            KEEP OUTGOING imdb.Figure.playedBy AS TYPE jointarget.Person
      }
      KEEP INCOMING library.Borrower.borrowed AS TYPE jointarget.Customer {
      }
}
```

Listing 3: Movie Database ModelJoin Example

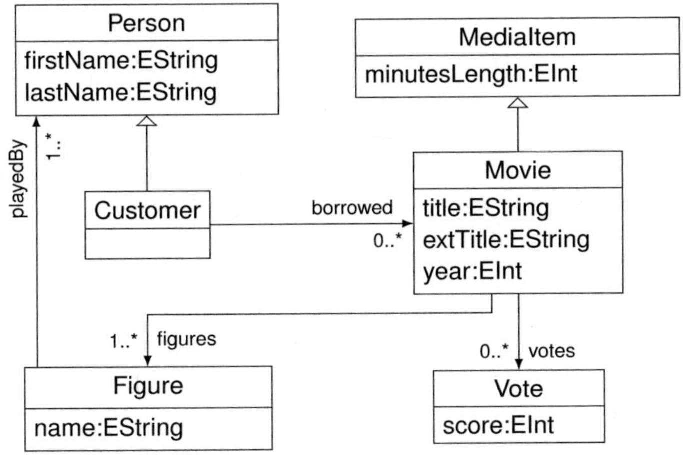

Figure 6.5.: Target Metamodel for the ModelJoin Query in Listing 3

remove redundancies. Since the metamodels are not linked with each other in any way, the instances of these metamodels are also independent of each other, so that the semantic connection between the instances can only be established by structural similarities and naming conventions. Similar to SQL, ModelJoin contains concepts to express these semantic relations at a low level; it is the responsability of the view designer to determine the semantic or structural similarities. ModelJoin is not a data integration framework and does not offer heuristics to determine the similarities between heterogeneous metamodels.

In the example of Listing 3, the elements from the two metamodels are combined by `JOIN` expressions, which, similar to relational algebra, merge two classes into one class in the result set metamodel. The `THETA JOIN` (line 5) expression merges the class Actor from the movie database with the class Person from the library metamodel. The condition of the join is expressed in the `WHERE`-clause using a logical expression written in OCL. Since the two metamodels are not connected in any way, the join operates on name equality of the two classes. Since Actor has a single name attribute, while

Person has two attributes for first and last name, a string concatenation operation is necessary to compare the names.

The `LEFT OUTER JOIN` (line 13) expression selects instances of Film and Videocassette based on equally named attributes (like in SQL), in our case the attribute `name`. The target class name is defined as Movie. Only the attribute name of the target metamodel is generated automatically, since it is part of the join condition. All other parts that should be created in the target metamodel have to be specified by `KEEP` statements. Here, the attribute year has to be added manually with the `KEEP ATTRIBUTES` statement, which creates the attribute in the target class and sets it to the value of the instances of imdb.Film. Likewise, the outgoing references votes and figures as well as a supertype are included via the respective statements. The attribute extTitle of the class Movie is calculated by an OCL expression from properties of the source elements.

The semantics of natural and outer join is inspired by relational algebra, as well as the `THETA JOIN`, which can have an arbitrary condition for the joining of elements. In the current implementation, OCL expressions can be used to reduce the set of instances to a subset that fulfills the OCL constraint in the `WHERE` condition.

The target metamodel, that is defined by the query in Listing 3, is depicted in Figure 6.5. The target metamodel of a ModelJoin query can be derived entirely from the information in the query and the structure of the source metamodels. The structure of the metamodel is independent from the actual instances that are joined during the execution of a query. The relation of source models, metamodels, query, execution, target models, and target metamodels is depicted in Figure 6.6: While the ModelJoin query is aware of the source metamodels, the source metamodels themselves do not have to be in any relation to each other, e.g., by cross-metamodel references. The execution of the query yields a result set that conforms to a target metamodel, which can be derived from the query and the source metamodels.

This example serves as a motivation of the concept of ModelJoin and is written in the textual concrete syntax of ModelJoin, which will be explained in detail in subsection 6.2.3. Before, we will define the abstract syntax of ModelJoin and give a formal definition of the semantics of the ModelJoin statements.

6.2.2. Abstract Syntax

In this section, we will present the abstract syntax of the *ModelJoin* DSL, which realises the flexible view concept presented in section 6.1. In the following subsections, we will define the abstract syntax of ModelJoin, which contains statements that are semantically similar, but not equivalent, to *Selection*, *Projection* and *Join* of relational algebra.

A ModelJoin expression takes at least two models as input, called *source models* in the following, which conform to the *source metamodels*. The evaluation of a ModelJoin expression returns a result set, called the *target model*, which conforms to the *target metamodel* (see Figure 6.6).

To distinguish between the elements at the metamodel level and at the model level, we will refer to the elements of the metamodel as *classes*, *attributes*, and *references*. The elements at the model level, i.e. the instances, will be denominated as *objects*, *attribute values* and *links* respectively.

We use the set notation of Ecore metamodels from subsection 2.3.2 in the following definitions. To distinguish between source and target metamodels, we will write $\mathcal{M}_{source} = \{M_{source_1} \cup M_{source_2} \cup \ldots\}$ for the set of source metamodels, and $\mathcal{M}_{target}$ for the set of target metamodels, with the respective sets CLASS_{source}, CLASS_{target}, ATT_{source}, ATT_{target}, and so on, which together form the sets of named elements $\mathcal{N}_{source}$ and $\mathcal{N}_{target}$.

The ModelJoin language is declarative, so the ModelJoin expressions describe the desired properties of source and target elements after the execution of the query. In the formal definition, we express this as relations between the source and target sets. Since it is possible that an element in

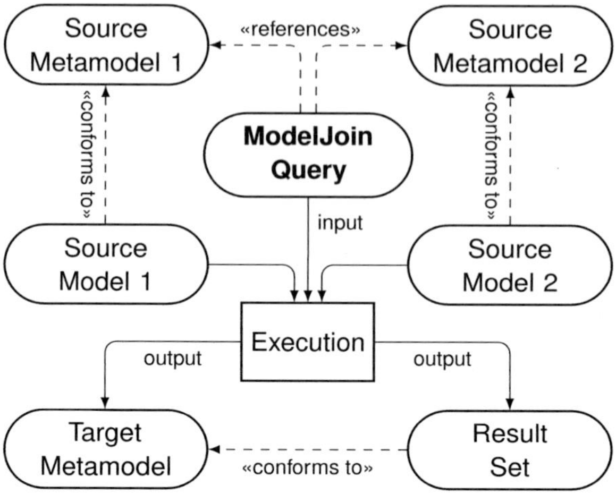

Figure 6.6.: ModelJoin Target and Source Models

a source metamodel is represented by several elements in the target metamodel, this relation is in general not functional. Thus, we cannot formalise the ModelJoin statements as functions in the mathematical sense, although the target metamodel and instances in the result set can always be computed from the elements in the source metamodels. Thus, the following definitions of the statements are not expressed with functions on the source metamodels, but with relations that may not be right-unique.

A ModelJoin expression q is a relation between a tuple of n source metamodels and one target metamodel:

$$q \in \mathscr{Q} = \langle M_{source_1}, M_{source_2}, \dots, M_{source_n}, M_{target} \rangle \in \mathscr{M}^{n+1}$$

Since the result of the execution of a ModelJoin query contains not only the metamodel, but also instances, the relation is twofold. The ModelJoin expressions will be described as such in the following: First, the signature of the expressions and the properties of the elements of the target metamodel are defined; second, the properties of the system state (i.e., the instances) are defined. We will define the effects on the system state as boundary conditions of the target metamodel. The properties of the target metamodel only depend on the source metamodel, but not on its instances, so the target metamodel can always be computed via static analysis of a ModelJoin expression and the source metamodels. Thus, the same ModelJoin expression can be used with different instances, using the same target metamodel.

For each operator, we will use an example in the textual concrete syntax of the prototypical ModelJoin implementation, which has already been used in the example of Listing 3, and which will be explained in detail in subsection 6.2.3.

There are four kinds of ModelJoin expressions:

- *join* expressions $\bowtie \in \mathscr{J}$
- *keep* expressions $\kappa \in \mathscr{K}$
- *selection* expression $\varsigma \in \mathscr{S}$
- *rename* expressions $\rho \in \mathscr{R}$

Thus, the set of ModelJoin queries is the union of these expressions: $\mathscr{Q} = \mathscr{J} \cup \mathscr{K} \cup \mathscr{R} \cup \mathscr{S}$. The single expressions are described in detail in the following subsections. In the relations that are used for the definition of the expressions, the element of the target class represents the "return value" of the expression. To describe the semantic correspondence between elements in the result set and elements from the source set, we introduce a mapping relation at the metamodel and at the instance level.

Definition 18 (Mapping relation)**.** *The target metamodel and the result set contain elements that* represent *elements in the source metamodels and models (cf. Figure 2.1). To express this, we introduce a* mapping relation *both at the metamodel and at the model level. A named element $e \in \mathscr{N}$ is* mapped *to a named element $e' \in \mathscr{N}$ with the relation*

$$\sim_{\bowtie} = \{\langle e, e' \rangle \in \mathscr{N} \times \mathscr{N} \mid e \text{ is mapped to } e'\}$$

The elements in $\mathscr{N}$ are at the metamodel level. Thus, the mapping relation $\sim_{\bowtie}$ expresses the mapping at the metamodel level. To describe the mapping between possible instances $I(c), I(c')$ of classes $c, c' \in$ CLASS, we define an instance mapping relation *at the model level as*

$$\sim_{\underline{\bowtie}} = \{\langle \underline{c}, \underline{c}' \rangle \in I(c) \times I(c') \mid \underline{c} \text{ is mapped to } \underline{c}'\}$$

6.2.2.1. Join Expressions

The core concept of the ModelJoin language is the joining of model elements from heterogeneous models. This may be used for elements that represent the same concept in two different metamodels (cf. the example in Listing 3). The *join statements* are defined over two metamodel classes as input and return a target class, which is newly created in the target metamodel with a specified name. Join operations are ternary relations over two source metamodels and one target metamodel. It is however also possible to join more than two source metamodels by cascading join operations, so that the target metamodel of one join operation serves as the source metamodel of another join operation.

In analogy to relational algebra, we define a *natural join* operator, which joins classes based on identically named attributes that have a compatible type. We call these attributes *join-conforming*. If two classes are joined with a natural join, join-conforming attributes in both of the classes are added to the resulting class in the target metamodel, similar to the columns of the result table of a relational join operation. At the instance level, two objects are joined if they have the same values in the join-conforming attributes, and a corresponding object is created in the target model.

Definition 19 (Join Conformity). *Let $a_1 \in \text{ATT}_{c_1} : t_{c_1} \rightarrow t_1$ and $a_2 \in \text{ATT}_{c_2} : t_{c_2} \rightarrow t_2$ be attributes of classes $c_1, c_2 \in \text{CLASS}$.* Join conformity *is a property at the metamodel level. It is given if two attributes have the same name, type and multiplicities:*

$$\begin{aligned}\cong_{\text{ATT}} = \{\langle a_1, a_2\rangle \in \text{ATT}_{c_1} \times \text{ATT}_{c_2} \mid (a_1 = a_2) \wedge (t_1 = t_2) \\ \wedge\ (\textit{multiplicities}(a_1) = \textit{multiplicities}(a_2))\}\end{aligned}$$

For two classes c_1 and c_2, all possibly joinable attributes are contained in the set of join-conforming attribute pairs*:*

$$A^{\bowtie}_{c_1,c_2} = \{\langle a_1, a_2\rangle \in \text{ATT}^*_{c_1} \times \text{ATT}^*_{c_2} \mid a_1 \cong_{\text{ATT}} a_2\}.$$

At the instance level, two objects $c_1 \in I(c_1)$, $c_2 \in I(c_2)$ fulfil *instance-conformity* if they carry equal values in their join-conforming attributes:

$$\begin{aligned}\cong_I = \{\langle \underline{c}_1, \underline{c}_2\rangle \in I(c_1) \times I(c_2) \mid \\ \forall \langle a_1, a_2\rangle \in A^{\bowtie}_{c_1,c_2} (\sigma_{\text{ATT}}(a_1)(\underline{c}_1) = \sigma_{\text{ATT}}(a_2)(\underline{c}_2))\}\end{aligned}$$

With these helper sets and relations, we will now define the join operations.

Definition 20 (Natural join). *For two classes $c_1 \in \text{CLASS}_{source_1}$, $c_2 \in \text{CLASS}_{source_2}$ and a target class $c' \in \text{CLASS}_{target}$, the* natural join *is defined as*

$$\bowtie = \langle c_1, c_2, c'\rangle \in \text{CLASS}_{source_1} \times \text{CLASS}_{source_2} \times \text{CLASS}_{target}$$

where the target class and its instances have the following properties:

- *The the mapping relation holds for each of the source classes and the target class:*

$$(c_1 \sim_{\bowtie} c') \wedge (c_2 \sim_{\bowtie} c')$$

- *For each of the join-conforming attribute pairs in the source classes, an attribute of the same name and type exists in the target class:*

$$\forall \langle a_1, a_2 \rangle \in A^{\bowtie}_{c_1,c_2} \exists\, a' \in \text{ATT}_{c'} (\\ (a' : t_{c'} \to t_1) \wedge (a_1 = a') \wedge (a_1 \sim_{\bowtie} a') \wedge (a_2 \sim_{\bowtie} a'))$$

- *For all instance-conforming pairs in the source models, an instance that has the same attribute values in the join-conforming attributes exists in the target model:*

$$\forall \langle \underline{c}_1, \underline{c}_2 \rangle \in \sigma_{\text{CLASS}}(c_1) \times \sigma_{\text{CLASS}}(c_2) (\\ \underline{c}_1 \cong_I \underline{c}_2 \Rightarrow \exists\, \underline{c}' \in \sigma_{\text{CLASS}}(c')(\underline{c}' \cong_I \underline{c}_1))$$

When executing a natural join expression, the target class c' is always created and contains only the common attributes. If no common attributes exist, the target class is generated without attributes. This is different to the natural join in relational algebra in two ways: Firstly, the natural join in ModelJoin does not add the other non-join-conforming attributes to the target class; secondly, it does not degenerate to the cartesian product if no common attributes exist. To add attributes to a class in the target metamodel, the *keep attributes* expression is used (see subsubsection 6.2.2.2). In contrast to the projectional approach in relational algebra, we use a constructive way of building the target metamodel. The name of the target class is by default set to c_1 and can be changed with the *rename* expression.

Example In the running example, the classes Film from the IMDB metamodel and AudioVisualItem from the library metamodel represent the same concept of a motion picture. Thus, these classes can be joined into a newly created class Movie in the target metamodel. The classes Film and AudioVisualItem contain the join-conforming attributes title, which is of the type EString in both classes and has the same upper cardinality 1. Thus, the `NATURAL JOIN` expression can be used to create the target class. The necessary ModelJoin expression is depicted in Listing 4.

```
NATURAL JOIN imdb.Film WITH library.AudioVisualItem AS jointarget.
    Movie {
}
```

Listing 4: ModelJoin Natural Join Example

Although the class Film contains the further attribute year, and the class AudioVisualItem contains the attributes minutesLength and damaged, these attributes are not created in the target class by the `NATURAL JOIN` operator. At this point, the semantics of the natural join in ModelJoin deviates from that of the natural join in relational algebra, which would include all columns from the source tables of a natural join into the result set. The class Movie is created in the target metamodel regardless of the existence of instances that fulfil the join condition (identical values in the attribute title). At the instance level, an element in the result set is created if there are two instances of Film and AudioVisualItem respectively that have identical values in the attribute title. The target instance then also carries this value.

ModelJoin furthermore provides an *outer join* operator, which also creates instances of the target metamodel for unmatched instances of elements in one of the metamodels CLASS_{source}.

Definition 21 (Outer join). *The* outer join *operator is equivalent to the* natural join *operator in its type signature and the constraints on the target metamodel. Deviating from the natural join, the result set $\{\underline{c}'_1, \underline{c}'_2, \ldots\}$ contains a respective instance for each instance in the source model, regardless of instance-conformity:*

$$\forall \underline{c}_1 \in \sigma_{\text{CLASS}}(c_1) \exists\, \underline{c}' \in \sigma_{\text{CLASS}}(c') (\underline{c}' \cong_I \underline{c}_1) \wedge$$
$$\forall \underline{c}_2 \in \sigma_{\text{CLASS}}(c_2) \exists\, \underline{c}' \in \sigma_{\text{CLASS}}(c') (\underline{c}' \cong_I \underline{c}_2)$$

In addition to the general outer join, there is a left outer join *and* right outer join *operator, which only creates instances for the left class (c_1) and right class (c_2) respectively.*

Example If we modify the natural join example from Listing 4 to an right outer join, the element Movie in the target metamodel is not affected at all. It is also created independently of matching instances and will contain the join-compatible common attribute title. The difference of the outer join statement to the natural join statement is only in the generation of the instances. In the example of Listing 5, if a film is present in the library but not in the movie database, an instance of the class Movie would still be created in the result set.

```
RIGHT OUTER JOIN imdb.Film WITH library.AudioVisualItem AS jointarget.
    Movie {
}
```

Listing 5: ModelJoin Outer Join Example

The outer join thus may create elements in the target result set that are only mapped with the relation $\sim_{\underline{\bowtie}}$ to one instance of the source instances. If the example contained a keep statement for attributes or references of the class Film, these target instances do not have an instance of the Film from which these values are taken. This could lead to invalid instances of the target model if the lower bound of the multiplicity of these features is 1. Thus, if attributes or references from the left class are are included in a keep statement of a right outer join and vice versa, their lower multiplicity is set to zero in the target metamodel. For instances that have no corresponding element in the source models, the features are initialised with a null value ($\perp$) in the target model.

The natural and outer joins are specialised statements for the most common cases of attribute equality in heterogeneous classes, when attributes have the same name and a compatible type. The join condition can, however, be generalised from join conformity to arbitrary logical conditions (depending on the actual language used in the implementation) on the instances of the source metamodels. In analogy to relational algebra, we call this operator *theta join*.

Definition 22 (Theta join). *For source classes* $c_1 \in \text{CLASS}_{source_1}$, $c_2 \in \text{CLASS}_{source_2}$, *a target class* $c' \in \text{CLASS}_{target}$, *and a logical expression* $\theta = I(c_1) \cup I(c_2) \rightarrow$ *true,false, the* theta join *is defined as*

$$\bowtie_\theta = \langle c_1, c_2, c' \rangle \in \text{CLASS}_{source_1} \times \text{CLASS}_{source_2} \times \text{CLASS}_{target}$$

where the target class c' *has the following properties:*

- *The the mapping relation holds from the source classes to the target class:*
$$(c_1 \sim_\bowtie c') \wedge (c_2 \sim_\bowtie c')$$
- *For all pairs in the source models for which the join condition* θ *holds, an instance exists in the target model:*

$$\forall \langle \underline{c}_1, \underline{c}_2 \rangle \in \sigma_{\text{CLASS}}(c_1) \times \sigma_{\text{CLASS}}(c_2)($$
$$\theta(\underline{c}_1, \underline{c}_2) \Rightarrow \exists\, \underline{c}' \in \sigma_{\text{CLASS}}(c')((\underline{c}_1 \sim_{\underline{\bowtie}} \underline{c}') \wedge (\underline{c}_2 \sim_{\underline{\bowtie}} \underline{c}')))$$

The target class c' does not have to contain any attributes from the source classes; if desired, they have to be added manually by a *keep attributes* statement. (This behaviour is different to the theta join of relational algebra, where all columns are added to the result table.)

The *theta join* is the most general of join statements, since it can contain an arbitrary join condition. In the prototypical implementation, these conditions can be expressed in OCL. Natural and outer joins can be expressed by a theta join operator, where the θ-expression contains the join conformity constraints, and where appropriate *keep attribute* expressions add the join-conforming attributes.

Example The natural and outer join statements are only applicable when a join-conforming attribute is present in both of the classes that are joined. In the library example, the classes Actor and Person represent similar concepts, but do not have such a common attribute. Although they can be identified by their names, the name is stored in a single attribute in the class Actor, while first name and last name are stored separately in the class Person. This simple circumstance cannot be expressed with the natural join operator.

```
THETA JOIN imdb.Actor WITH library.Person WHERE "Actor.name␣=␣Person.
    firstName.concat('␣').concat(Person.lastName)" AS jointarget.
    Person {
}
```

Listing 6: ModelJoin Theta Join Example

In Listing 6, a theta join is displayed, which creates the class Person in the target metamodel. The join condition is expressed using OCL. The names of the classes (Actor, Person) act as variables in the OCL expression. The theta join operator does not add an attribute to the class Person in the target metamodel, not even if this attribute is part of the join-condition. At the instance level, the execution of the theta join operator will create an instance of the target class Person only if the join condition is fulfilled for the source instances. In this example, it is of course quite impractical that no attribute is added to the target class; to acquire a meaningful result, the attribute name should be included using a `KEEP ATTRIBUTE` statement.

6.2.2.2. Keep Expressions

The *keep* operator defines additional structural features (i.e., attributes and references) and supertype relations of the target model that are not defined by the join statements. It serves a purpose that is similar to the projection operator in relational algebra, but unlike projection, the keep operator is constructive: if there is no explicit keep statement, no attributes (apart from those that are added because they are part of a natural join condition) or references are included in the target metamodel. The rationale behind this behaviour is to avoid the potentially high number of attributes and references inherited from superclasses. Keep statements can be applied to classes that have been mapped by join statements or other keep statements.

There are different statements for the inclusion of attributes, references, and supertype relations. For the definition of references in set notation, we assume the existence of functions *associates*() and *multiplicities*() that express the respective properties of a reference as described in [123].

Definition 23 (Keep attributes). *Let* $a : t_c \rightarrow t \in \textsc{Att}_c^*$ *be an attribute of class* $c \in \textsc{Class}_{source}$ *(directly defined or in one of its superclasses) and* $c' \in \textsc{Class}_{target}$ *a class in the target metamodel with* $c \sim_{\bowtie} c'$. *The* keep attributes *operator is then defined as*

$$\kappa_{att} = \langle a, a' \rangle \in \textsc{Att}_c \times \textsc{Att}_{c'}$$

where the target attribute a' *has the following properties:*

- a' *is an attribute of the target class* c'*:*

$$a' : t_{c'} \rightarrow t \in \textsc{Att}_{c'}$$

- a' *has the same name and multiplicity as the attribute* a *in the source class* c*. In case the target class* c' *was created by an outer join, it is necessary to allow empty values for the attribute, so the lower boundary of the multiplicity of* a' *must always be* 0*:*

$$(a \sim_{\bowtie} a') \wedge (a = a') \wedge (multiplicities(a') = multiplicities(a) \cup \{0\})$$

- *The instances of* c' *carry the same attribute values as those instances of* c *that they are mapped to. For unmapped instances, the attribute value is null (⊥):*

$$\forall \underline{c}' \in \sigma_{\text{CLASS}}(c') : \sigma_{\text{ATT}}(a')(\underline{c}') = \begin{cases} \sigma_{\text{ATT}}(a)(\underline{c}) & \textit{if } \exists \underline{c} \in \sigma_{\text{CLASS}}(c) \mid \underline{c} \sim_{\underline{\bowtie}} \underline{c}' \\ \bot & \textit{else} \end{cases}$$

Example Keep statements can only be used in the context of join statements or other keep statements. For the keep attributes operator, this context determines the class in which the attribute is contained in the target metamodel; thus, it can only be used in the context of joins, keep references, and keep super-/subtype statements. In Listing 7, there are three keep attributes statements inside a join, a keep references operator, and a keep supertype operator.

```
LEFT OUTER JOIN imdb.Film WITH library.VideoCassette AS jointarget.
    Movie {
     KEEP ATTRIBUTES imdb.Film.year
     KEEP OUTGOING imdb.Film.votes AS TYPE jointarget.Vote {
          KEEP ATTRIBUTES imdb.Vote.score
          }
     KEEP SUPERTYPE library.AudioVisualItem AS type jointarget.
         MediaItem {
          KEEP ATTRIBUTES library.AudioVisualItem.minutesLength
          }
}
```

Listing 7: ModelJoin Keep Attributes Example

The keep attributes operator can be invoked for attributes that are contained in the source classes directly, and for attributes that are inherited from a superclass. The attribute minutesLength, for example, could also be contained directly in the class Movie of the target metamodel by moving the `KEEP ATTRIBUTES` statement so that it is a direct child of the outer join operator in the ModelJoin statement of Listing 7.

Attributes can also be defined as an *aggregation* of values in the source model, similar to the SQL feature `GROUP BY`.

Definition 24 (Aggregation function). *An aggregation function is defined as* $f_\alpha : S \rightarrow \mathbb{R}, S \in \mathbb{R}^n$

ModelJoin supports the following arithmetic aggregation functions for $s_1, \ldots, s_n \in S$:

- sum: $f_{sum}(s_1, \ldots, s_n) = \sum_{i=1}^{n} s_i$
- average: $f_{avg}(s_1, \ldots, s_n) = \frac{1}{n} \sum_{i=1}^{n} s_i$
- maximum: $f_{max}(s_1, \ldots, s_n) = max(s_1, \ldots, s_n)$
- minimum: $f_{min}(s_1, \ldots, s_n) = min(s_1, \ldots, s_n)$

In addition to these arithmetic functions, a size function $f_{size} : S \rightarrow \mathbb{R}, S \in \mathcal{T}_B$ is defined, which can also operate on non-numerical attributes.

- size: $f_{size}(s_1, \ldots, s_n) = n$

The aggregation operator groups elements by a certain reference through which they are linked to the source class. The result of the aggregation is then persisted as a new attribute in the target class.

Definition 25 (Aggregation). *Let* $r \in \text{REF}_{source}$ *be a reference between classes* $c, \hat{c} \in \text{CLASS}_{source}$*, i.e., the reference signature is* $associates(r) = \langle c, \hat{c} \rangle$*, and let* $\hat{a} : t_{\hat{c}} \rightarrow t \in \text{ATT}^*_{\hat{c}}$ *be an attribute of class* $\hat{c}$ *that is of a numeral type* $t \in \{UnlimitedNatural, Integer, Real\}$*, and* $c' \in \text{CLASS}_{target}$ *a class in the target metamodel with* $c \sim_{\bowtie} c'$*, and let* f_α *be an aggregation function. The* aggregation *operator is then defined as*

$$\alpha = \langle r, \hat{a}, a' \rangle \in \text{REF}_c \times \text{ATT}_{\hat{c}} \times \text{ATT}_{c'}$$

where the aggregate result a' has the following properties:

- *a' is an attribute of the target class c' with type t:*

$$a' : t_{c'} \rightarrow t \in \mathrm{ATT}_{c'}$$

- *The instances of c' carry an attribute value in a' that is determined by an aggregation function f_α those instances of c that they are mapped to. For unmapped instances, the attribute value is null ($\perp$):*

$$\forall \underline{c}' \in \sigma_{\mathrm{CLASS}}(c') : \sigma_{\mathrm{ATT}}(a')(\underline{c}') =$$
$$\begin{cases} f_\alpha\left(\bigcup\limits_{\underline{\hat{c}} \in L(r)(\underline{c})} \sigma_{\mathrm{ATT}}(\hat{a})(\underline{\hat{c}})\right) & \text{if } \exists \underline{c} \in \sigma_{\mathrm{CLASS}}(c) \mid \underline{c} \sim_{\underline{\bowtie}} \underline{c}' \\ \perp & \text{else} \end{cases}$$

Depending on the type of the aggregation function, the aggregation operator is written as α_{sum}, α_{avg}, α_{max}, α_{min}, or α_{size}. In the case of α_{size}, the attribute $\hat{a}$ can also be of a non-numeral type.

Example The aggregation operator groups features of a set of elements that are linked to a certain instance. They are grouped as an attribute that is calculated by one of the aggregation functions. In the library example, the votes for a movie by members of the movie database platform are represented as instances of the class Vote in the IMDB metamodel. This class contains the numerical attribute score.

With the aggregation operator, it is possible to define a flexible view that does not contain all the vote elements, but only the average of all votes. In Listing 8, such a flexible view is defined using the `KEEP AGGREGATE` operator.

The instances that are in the result set contain only the aggregated value for the attribute avgScore. This way, the result set is a small model even if the source models contain a large number of instances of the class Vote.

```
LEFT OUTER JOIN imdb.Film WITH library.VideoCassette AS jointarget.
    Movie {
      KEEP AGGREGATE avg(imdb.Vote.score) OVER idmb.Film.votes AS
           jointarget.Movie.avgScore
}
```

Listing 8: ModelJoin Aggregation Example

To generalise the aggregation operation, ModelJoin also allows generic calculated attributes in the target model. The values of these attributes are derived from arbitrary values of source instances. These attribute are, however, called *calculated* and not *derived* in ModelJoin, since the term *derived attribute* is defined in EMF as an attribute that is derived from other properties of the same instance. A calculated attribute in ModelJoin depends on properties of source instances that are not linked to the target instance in any way. The process of calculating the values of the attributes is part of the query execution, in contrast to the on-access computation of derived attributes in EMF, which is called the *volatile* property of attributes. Furthermore, the values are persisted in the result set, so they are not *transient* like derived values in EMF.

Definition 26 (Calculate attribute). *Let $a' : t_{c'} \rightarrow t \in \text{ATT}^*_{c'}$ be an attribute of type t in a target class $c' \in \text{CLASS}_{target}$ and $\phi = \mathcal{N}^n \rightarrow t$ a function over arbitrary elements with the return type t. The* calculate attribute *operator is defined as*

$$\delta_\phi = \langle e_1, \ldots, e_n, a' \rangle \in \mathcal{N}^n_{source} \times \text{ATT}_{c'}$$

where the attribute values of a' are defined by the function ϕ over instances $\underline{e_1}, \ldots, \underline{e_n} \subseteq \{\sigma_{\text{CLASS}} \cup \sigma_{\text{ATT}} \cup \sigma_{\text{REF}}\}$:

$$\forall \underline{c}' \in \sigma_{\text{CLASS}}(c') : \sigma_{\text{ATT}}(a')(c') = \phi(\underline{e_1}, \ldots, \underline{e_n})$$

The operator for calculated attributes is the most general way of defining attributes in the target model. The keep attributes operator and the aggregations of Definition 25 can also be expressed by calculated attributes. In actual use cases, the function ϕ will very likely (but not necessarily) be over classes c_1, c_2 with $c_1 \sim_{\bowtie} c'$, so that the calculation is based on instances instances $\underline{c}_1, \underline{c}_2$ that have been mapped to the target instance by another operator. In the prototypical implementation, we use the general purpose language OCL [123] for the definition of calculated attributes.

Example The calculate attribute operator exposes the full expressivity of OCL in ModelJoin. Similar to the theta join operator, the class names of the keep statements context can be used as variables, which are replaced by the actual instances of the classes. In Listing 9, the target class Movie contains an extended title attribute extTitle, which contains the title of the movie and its year to distinguish movies with the same title. (For example, "Star Trek (1979)" and "Star Trek (2009)").

```
LEFT OUTER JOIN imdb.Film WITH library.VideoCassette AS jointarget.
    Movie {
      KEEP CALCULATED ATTRIBUTE "AudioVisualItem.title.concat('(').
          concat(Film.year).concat(')')" AS jointarget.Movie.extTitle
}
```

Listing 9: ModelJoin Aggregation Example

The preceding three keep statements have the identical effect on the target metamodel and the instances: They create attributes and attribute values.

The *keep references* operator, on the other hand, defines which references exist in the target metamodel. It can only be applied to classes that have already been mapped, e.g., by a join operator or another keep references operator. The keep references operator is realised in two directions, *keep incoming* and *keep outgoing*. These variants only differ in the end of the reference, which already has to be mapped: either the start point of the reference (*keep outgoing*) or the end point of the reference (*keep incoming*). If the class at the respective other side of the reference has not been mapped yet by another join or keep operator, it is generated in the target metamodel. The differentiation between incoming and outgoing references is, however, only relevant for the concrete syntax and the prototypical implementation, but not for the formal definition; thus, this differentiation is not made in the following definition.

Definition 27 (Keep references). *Let $r \in \text{REF}_{source}$ be a reference between classes $c, \hat{c} \in \text{CLASS}_{source}$, i.e., the reference signature is $associates(r) = \langle c, \hat{c} \rangle$, and $c' \in \text{CLASS}_{target}$ a class in the target metamodel with $c \sim_{\bowtie} c'$. The* keep references *operator is defined as:*

$$\kappa_{ref} = \langle r, r' \rangle \in \text{REF}_{source} \times \text{REF}_{target}$$

where the target reference r' has the following properties:

- *r' is defined between the classes that are mapping targets of the classes of r.*

$$associates(r') = \langle c', \hat{c}' \rangle \wedge (\hat{c} \sim_{\bowtie} \hat{c}'); \hat{c}' \in \text{CLASS}_{target}$$

- *Since there may be target instances where the reference is not set, the multiplicity of r' is extended by 0:*

$$multiplicities(r') = multiplicities(r) \cup \{0\}$$

- *For every instance pair of c and $\hat{c}$ that is linked by r, a mapped instance pair of c' and $\hat{c}'$ also exists that is linked by r':*

$$\forall \langle \underline{c}, \underline{\hat{c}} \rangle \in \sigma_{\text{CLASS}}(c) \times L(r)(\underline{c}):$$
$$\exists \langle \underline{c}', \underline{\hat{c}}' \rangle \in \sigma_{\text{CLASS}}(c') \times L(r')(\underline{c}') \mid \underline{c} \sim_{\underline{\bowtie}} \underline{c}' \wedge \underline{\ddot{c}} \sim_{\underline{\bowtie}} \underline{\ddot{c}}'$$

The evaluation of κ_{ref} creates the class $\hat{c}'$, if it does not exist in the target metamodel, and creates the reference r' between c' and $\hat{c}'$.

Example The keep references operator can be used to construct the metamodel along the references between classes in a star-shaped manner. The join statements at the root of ModelJoin expressions serve as the starting point for the creation of the target metamodel. Since the direction of references plays an important role in EMF, the ModelJoin concrete syntax contains two seperate statements for the keeping of outgoing and incoming references. The keep references statements can cause the creation of classes in the target metamodel, if they have not been created by another join or keep operation.

```
LEFT OUTER JOIN imdb.Film WITH library.VideoCassette AS jointarget.
     Movie {
      KEEP OUTGOING imdb.Film.votes AS TYPE jointarget.Vote {
             }
      KEEP INCOMING library.Borrower.borrowed AS TYPE jointarget.
            Customer {
      }
}
```

Listing 10: ModelJoin Keep Reference Example

In Listing 10, the classes Vote and Customer are created in the target metamodel by the `KEEP INCOMING` and `KEEP OUTGOING` statements. If there are any other statements that also map the source classes at the respective other ends of the source references to a target class of the same name as that in the keep references operator, the classes in the target metamodel will be identical.

If several classes are created in the target metamodel that have a common superclass in the source model, common attributes or references have to be created in each of the single classes if they should be included in the target metamodel. To avoid this redundancy, it is also possible to include super- or subtype relations of the source metamodels in the target metamodel with the *keep supertype* and *keep subtype* statements. Again, ModelJoin does not automatically create any of these inheritance relationships. They have to be made explicit by the author of the ModelJoin expressions. If the respective super- or subclass is not present in the target metamodel, it is created during the execution of the ModelJoin expression.

Definition 28 (Keep supertype). *Let* $c, \hat{c} \in \text{CLASS}_{source}, c' \in \text{CLASS}_{target}$ *be classes with* $c \prec \hat{c}$ *and* $c \sim_{\bowtie} c'$. *The* keep supertype *operator is defined as:*

$$\kappa_{super} = \langle c, c' \rangle \in \text{CLASS}_{source} \times \text{CLASS}_{target}$$

with $\exists \hat{c}' \in \text{CLASS}_{target} \mid (c' \prec \hat{c}') \wedge (\hat{c} \sim_{\bowtie} \hat{c}')$

Example The keep supertype operator is only responsible for the creation of the class and the generalization link in the target metamodel. It does not have a direct influence on instances in the result set, although instances are influenced indirectly since additional features, which are inherited from the superclass, can now be contained in the instances. These features, however, have to be included explicitely by a keep attributes or keep reference statement.

In the example of Listing 11, the superclass AudioVisualItem of the class VideoCassette in the source models is added as the superclass MediaItem to the target class Movie. The attribute minutesLength has to be included explicitely in this keep supertype statement. If this statement were included right below the join statement, the attribute would be contained in Movie rather than in MediaItem in the target metamodel.

Definition 29 (Keep subtype). *Let* $c, \hat{c} \in \text{CLASS}_{source}, c' \in \text{CLASS}_{target}$ *be classes with* $c \succ \hat{c}$ *and* $c \sim_{\bowtie} c'$. *The* keep subtype *operator is defined as:*

$$\kappa_{sub} = \langle c, c' \rangle \in \text{CLASS}_{source} \times \text{CLASS}_{target}$$

```
LEFT OUTER JOIN imdb.Film WITH library.VideoCassette AS jointarget.
    Movie {
     KEEP SUPERTYPE library.AudioVisualItem AS type jointarget.
         MediaItem {
          KEEP ATTRIBUTES library.AudioVisualItem.minutesLength
          }
}
```

Listing 11: ModelJoin Keep Supertype Example

with $\exists \hat{c}' \in \text{CLASS}_{target} \mid (c' \succ \hat{c}') \wedge (\hat{c} \sim_{\bowtie} \hat{c}')$.

It should be noted that the κ_{super} / κ_{sub} statements do not automatically alter the signature of attributes or references, i.e., they do not move attributes or references to a superclass. This has to be made explicit in the respective κ_{att} and κ_{ref} statements. The keep super-/subtypes statements have no effect on the system state of the target metamodel.

Example The keep subtype operator is useful if instances of the result set shall be distinguishable by the type that the corresponding source instances have. When the query is executed, instances are transformed into the most special class of the target metamodel that is applicable. In the example of Listing 11, the class Borrower is added to the target metamodel. This way, it is visible if the element that was joined with an Actor element belonged to the class Borrower in the source model.

```
THETA JOIN imdb.Actor WITH library.Person WHERE "Actor.name␣=␣Person.
    firstName.concat('␣').concat(Person.lastName)" AS jointarget.
    Person {
          KEEP SUBTYPE library.Borrower
}
```

Listing 12: ModelJoin Keep Subtype Example

The keep subtype operator can lead to ambiguities if more than one operator is applied to a joined class: If the example of Listing 12 contained another statement that included a subclass of Actor, such as TVActor (which does not exist in our example metamodel), the evaluation of such an expression would be ambiguous: If an instance of Borrower were joined with an instance of TVActor, it would be unclear whether the joined instance should be of type Borrower or TVActor. For this reason, keep subtype statements as children of join statements are only allowed for either the left or the right source class of the join. This limitation of the keep subtype operator is described in detail in the ModelJoin technical report [28, section 3.2.2.6].

6.2.2.3. Select

The selection operator restricts the result set to a subset of elements for which a logical predicate is fulfilled. Since only the set of instances is reduced by this operator, selection does not have any impact on the generated metamodel.

Definition 30 (Selection). *Let $I(c)$ be a set of instances of a class $c \in$ CLASS and $\varphi = J \rightarrow \{true, false\}, J \in I(c)^n$ be a logical expression over instances $\underline{c} \in I(c)$. The* selection *operator is defined as an unary operator*

$$\varsigma_\varphi(I(c)) = \{\underline{c} \in I(c) \mid \varphi(\underline{c})\}$$

Our prototypical implementation uses OCL statements for the logical expressions, since it is based on QVT. In general, any other language could be used.

6.2.2.4. Rename

Since the *join* and *keep* operations take the entity names from the first of the source elements as the name of the target element, a *rename* operator is needed to specify the entity names in the target metamodel.

Definition 31 (Rename). *Let $e, e' \in \mathcal{N}$ be a names.* Rename *is an unary operation $\rho_{e'}(e) = e'$.*

The rename operator is realised as part of the keep and join statements in the `AS`-statements.

6.2.3. Implementation

The prototypical implementation of the ModelJoin approach is joint work of the authors of the ModelJoin Tech Report [28] and [29]. The project is being developed as open source and can be obtained via the ModelJoin Homepage[2]. We will not describe the technical details of the implementation here, but instead highlight crucial design decisions that had major influences on the way the protoype has been implemented.

6.2.3.1. Concrete Syntax

The ModelJoin statements, whose semantics has been defined in subsection 6.2.2, are implemented in the ModelJoin prototype with the textual concrete syntax that has already been used in the examples of the preceding subsections.

The keywords of the language have been chosen in analogy to those of the Standardized Query language (SQL). The root of every ModelJoin expression consists of a join expression, which is either a `NATURAL JOIN`, `OUTER JOIN` or a `THETA JOIN` statement. Based on these expressions, further `KEEP` statements can be added as children. The `KEEP REFERENCE` statements can have further children of their own. This hierarchical structure is noted in curly brackets in the textual syntax. The correspondence of the statements in formal notation to the concrete textual syntax can be seen in Table 6.2.

In the protoypical implementation, the textual syntax of ModelJoin has been implemented using the Xtext[3] framework. The complete Xtext grammar definition is displayed in Listing 16 on page 279 of the appendix. The implementation prototype features a textual editor with syntax highlighting,

[2] `https://sdqweb.ipd.kit.edu/wiki/ModelJoin`, retrieved 26 May 2014
[3] `http://www.eclipse.org/Xtext`, retrieved 9 May 2014

operator	keyword
$\bowtie$	NATURAL JOIN
$\bowtie_{lo}$	LEFT OUTER JOIN
$\bowtie_{ro}$	RIGHT OUTER JOIN
$\bowtie_{\theta}$	THETA JOIN
κ_{att}	KEEP ATTRIBUTE
α	KEEP AGGREGATE
δ_{ϕ}	KEEP CALCULATED ATTRIBUTE
κ_{ref}	KEEP REFERENCE
κ_{super}	KEEP SUPERTYPE
κ_{sub}	KEEP SUBTYPE
ς_{φ}	WHERE
ρ	AS

Table 6.2.: Textual Syntax of ModelJoin statements

autocompletion and automatic triggering of the generation workflow when a query is saved. Furthermore, the generation workflow also validates whether the ModelJoin query leads to the creation of a valid metamodel and diplays error markers in the textual editor if this is not the case. A parsed query is converted into a model-based representation by Xtext automatically, which eases further processing of the information with model-based technologies.

6.2.3.2. Query Execution Workflow

The execution of a ModelJoin query yields a target metamodel and a result set (see Figure 6.6). In the protoypical implementation, this process that realises query execution consists of three parts:

1. generation of the target metamodel, which contains the elements that have been declared in the query;

2. generation of a QVT-O transformation, which realises the logic of the query;

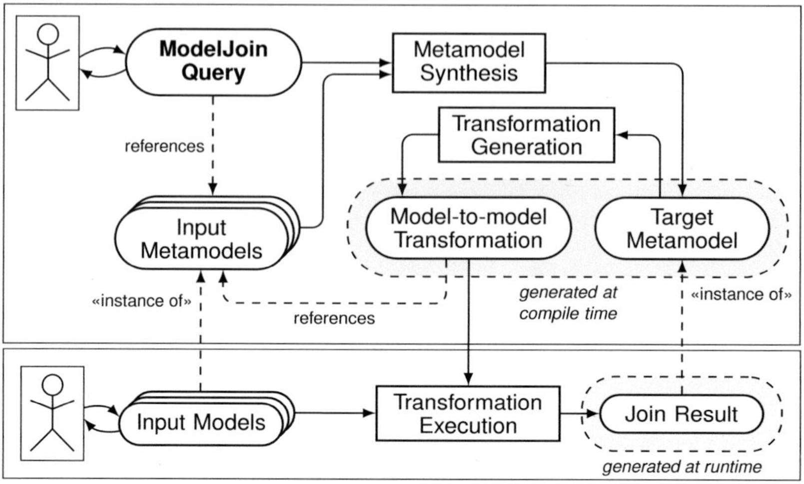

Figure 6.7.: ModelJoin Query Execution Workflow (in FMC notation, from [29])

3. execution of the transformation, which yields the result set.

The process is depicted in Figure 6.7: While the upper section contains the first and second step of the query execution, which produces the target metamodel and the transformation, the lower section contains the third step of transformation execution, which produces the join result. The elements in the structural variance blocks ◌ represent generated artefacts, which vary with the input query and metamodels (in the upper section), or the input models (lower section). The generation of target metamodel and the model-to-model transformation is denoted as a *compile-time* generation, since these artefacts can be re-used on varying input models. If the query itself is not modified, the execution of the query on actual input models does not require the re-generation of these artefacts. The execution of the query itself at *runtime* is performed by executing the generated transformation code with the given input models.

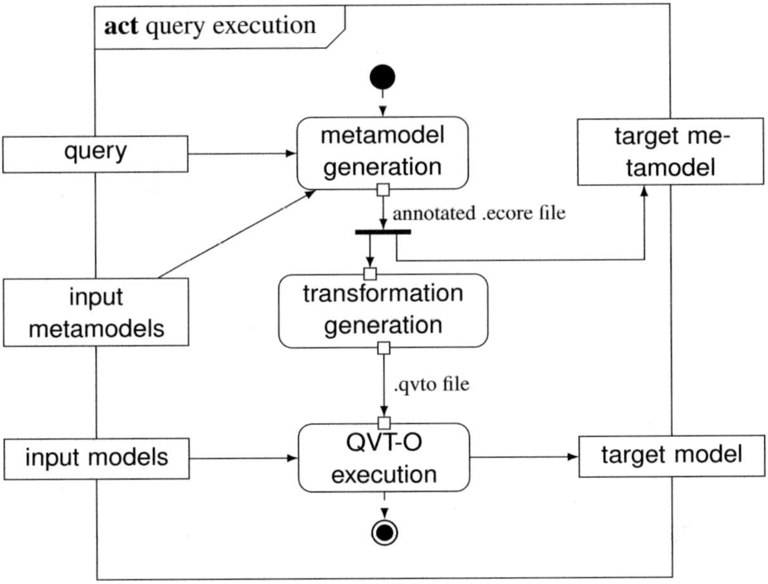

Figure 6.8.: Steps of ModelJoin Query Execution

In the prototypical implementation, the *metamodel generation* component has been realised in plain Java, while the *transformation generation* is implemented as a model-to-text transformation in Xtend.[4]

6.2.3.3. Annotated Target Metamodel

The transformation generator needs to be aware of the layout of the target metamodel, but also requires information about how the elements in the target metamodel were created during the metamodel synthesis. For example, the creation of a class in the target metamodel can be caused by a `JOIN`, a `KEEP SUPERTYPE/SUPTYPE` or a `KEEP REFERENCE` operation. The behaviour of the transformation differs for each of these cases. The information on how a class is created is available during metamodel synthesis, but is not

[4] `http://www.eclipse.org/xtend/`, retrieved 26 May 2014

directly necessary for the creation of the metamodel. Thus, we are using the EAnnotation element of Ecore to encode the information on which kind of statements lead to the creation of the element. The information in the annotation is sufficient for the transformation generator to calculate the transformation statements without having to analyse the input query at all. This strategy avoids a double analysis of the parsed ModelJoin query, which would lead to duplicate code and would increase the execution time for a query.

A detailed description of the functionality of the metamodel generator and the algorithm that is used to calculate the target metamodel is found in [28] and will not be included here. During the generation process, the generator determines which elements of the source metamodel were joined to an element of the target metamodel, which was the attribute for the join condition, etc. The information is stored in the target metamodel using EAnnotation elements, which reference the elements in the source metamodels directly.

This is possible since the EAnnotation element in Ecore contains a reference named references, which is typed with the reflective element EObject, which is the superclass of all classes in the EMF framework. Since there is no linguistic supertype of all metamodel classes in Ecore, this would not be possible in a strict MOF-compliant metamodel, since it would violate the metamodel levels. The EAnnotation class is an EMF-specific element that relates to the reflective class EObject. The generated target metamodel will thus contain references to the source metamodels, but only inside these EAnnotation elements. EAnnotations have a name (called source in EMF), an element that they refer to (reference), and can contain additional information details in key/value pairs. Since EAnnotations cannot be differentiated through subtypes, we have introduced naming conventions for the different annotation types.

As displayed in Figure 6.8, the annotated Ecore metamodel serves as an input for the transformation generation step, and is also part of the produced artefacts of the query execution. This strict decoupling of the metamodel generator and the transformation generator increases the modularity of the prototype and simplifies a possible re-implementation of one of the components using a different technology, such as a model transformation for the metamodel generator instead of the existing plain Java implementation, or the generation of transformations using a higher-order transformation instead of the textual generation of QVT-O code with templates. Future modifications to the ModelJoin prototype have been outlined in the future work section of [28].

6.2.3.4. Transformation Generation

A ModelJoin query is executed as a model-to-model transformation taking the input models and resulting in a model that conforms to the generated joint metamodel. In order to generate the transformation, we used a model-to-text (M2T) approach based on Xtend2, which generates the transformation directly using templates.

We chose QVT-O [116] as the transformation language, into which the Xtend templates generate the textual queries, because of the stability of the transformation engine, debugging support and Eclipse integration.

The following steps are necessary when automatically generating the transformation in the transformation generation step of Figure 6.7.

1. Create the OCL expression to filter joinable elements. In accordance with Definition 19, "joinable" means that they have the same name and are type-compatible.

2. Convert the (optional) *where*-clause to an OCL selection on the joined elements.

3. Create mappings to transfer attributes from source to target model (only those marked as "keep").

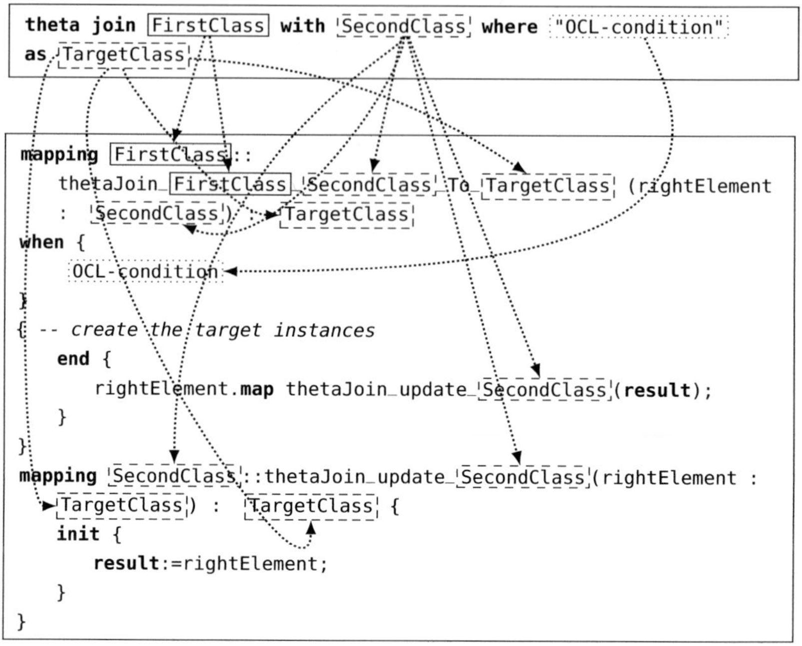

Figure 6.9.: The QVT Template for a Theta Join (from [29])

4. Create mappings to transfer references from source to target model (only those marked as “keep”). Note that this usually includes setting values to the newly created meta classes in the target model.

5. Combine the single fragments generated in 1.-4. to one transformation.

Let us consider the exemplary template shown in Figure 6.9. The theta join of FirstClass and SecondClass means that the model elements are joined using a condition expressed as an OCL constraint. The resulting QVT-O script will have two mappings for realising the join, as QVT-O has no support for n-to-1 mappings. While the first mapping is used for checking the condition of the theta join and instantiating the TargetClass, the second mapping is used solely for storing tracing information. The tracing information is later on required for resolving the source instances of a target instance. To be more specific, they are put to use in the mappings created for transferring attributes and references.

In addition to the shown code, the `main` method of the QVT-O script is extended to call the generated mappings for the cartesian product of the sets of instances of FirstClass and SecondClass. Mappings for natural joins are created in a similar manner by using the joinable features, identified during synthesis, as join criteria. For realising the left outer join functionality, the sets of instances that the mappings are called with are adjusted accordingly.

As an alternative, the transformation generator could create a mapping from a *set of* Firstclass elements and a *set of* SecondClass elements to TargetClass elements (i.e. building the Cartesian product). This would, however, have negative effects on performance, since a potentially large number of objects would be loaded into memory. The selection criteria would be ignored until checked in the mapping. Therefore, we decided to filter on the left element side first.

6.2.3.5. Transformation Execution

As last step of the ModelJoin query evaluation process, the generated QVT-O transformation is executed to automatically create instances for the synthesised metamodel (step Model-to-model transformation in Figure 6.7). Currently, our workflow uses the QVT-O engine that is part of the Eclipse M2M project. For every source metamodel, a corresponding model can be defined in the workflow all of which are then used as input models for the transformation engine. After the transformation workflow has been executed, the resulting model can be visualised using the standard EMF editors.

Transformation execution can be repeated for multiple instances of the source metamodels without having to create the target metamodel and transformations again, thus creating new views for the generated view type.

6.2.4. Re-Use of Target Metamodels

Since the target metamodel of a ModelJoin query can be completely derived from the statements in the query itself, it is possible to generate an appropriate metamodel for each ModelJoin query automatically. In the ModelJoin prototype, this is realised by metamodel generator component. The automatic generation has the advantage that the generated metamodel and the generated transformations are always compatible to each other, since they are generated in pairs. The automatic generation of the target metamodel is, however, also a disadvantage since it limits the further usage of the results of a ModelJoin query.

In model-based processes, models are the primary artefacts that are created and modified at runtime. Metamodels usually stay stable for a longer period of time, since the modification of a metamodel causes further adaptation activities, such as co-evolution of existing instances, and adaptation of existing editors, concrete syntaxes, and transformations that are based on the metamodels. This problem does not occur if ModelJoin is used for the ad-hoc definition of views [25] to satisfy particular information needs of a developer. If the ModelJoin view is, however, persisted and re-used frequently, the target metamodel may be used for the aforementioned purposes, so the compatibility to this specific metamodel has to be preserved. If a change is applied to the ModelJoin query, a new target metamodel is generated, and the compatibility may be violated.

```
NATURAL JOIN imdb.Film WITH library.VideoCassette AS jointarget.Movie
    {
      KEEP ATTRIBUTES library.AudioVisualItem.minutesLength
}
```

Listing 13: ModelJoin Query for the Movie Database Example

As an example, let us consider the movie database query in Listing 3. Let us assume that the target metamodel of this query (Figure 6.5) is already in use, so the compatibility to the metamodel would be beneficial, since a visualization or further transformation can be used. A further ModelJoin query on the movie databases is displayed in Listing 13. Similarly to the query in Listing 3, it joins the classes Film and VideoCassette, but in a natural join rather than in an outer join. Furthermore, the attribute minutesLength, which is an attribute of the superclass AudioVisualItem in the source metamodel, is included directly in the class Movie in the target metamodel, rather than in a superclass, like in the previous query. The resulting metamodel for this query consists only of the class Movie with the attributes name (from the natural join) and minutesLength. Its instances are however also valid instances of the target metamodel of the query in Listing 3, since the class Movie also exists in this metamodel, contains the attribute name, and inherits the attribute minutesLength from the superclass MediaItem. Thus, we can re-use this target metamodel for the current query.

We use the *metamodel conformity* relation of Definition 16 (see page 147) to check whether a metamodel can be re-used for a ModelJoin query. In the example, the difference between the classes Movie in the different target metamodels is detected as an *extract superclass* operation (cf. Appendix B), which is a non-breaking operation, and thus, the target metamodel of this query conforms to the target metamodel of the query in Listing 3.

The prototypical implementation of the conformance check [30] contains a simple file-based metamodel repository, which makes it possible to discover if there are conforming metamodels that can be used for a given ModelJoin query. The process is displayed in Figure 6.10: The conformance check is performed between the generation of the target metamodel and the usage of the target metamodel. It can replace the generated target metamodel with a compatible metamodel from a repository. During the checking, the generated metamodel is compared with the metamodels in the repository. If a conforming metamodel is found, the repository metamodel is used instead of the generated target metamodel. If no conforming metamodel is found, the generated metamodel is used and added to the repository for further

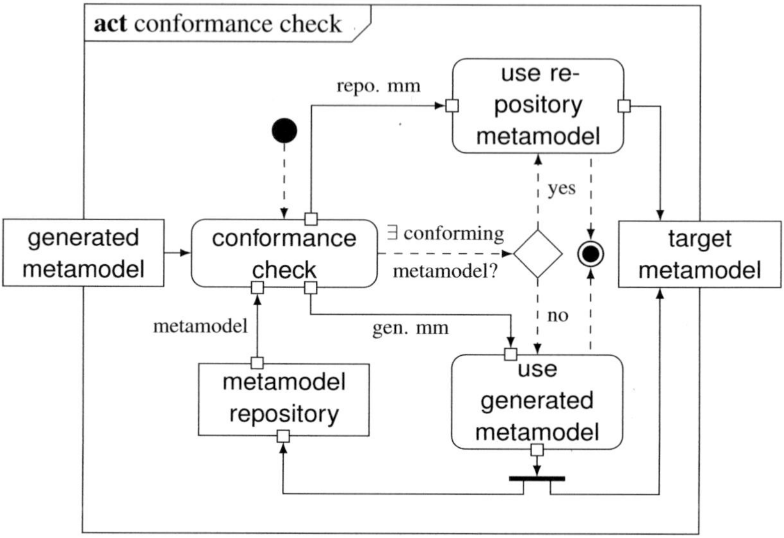

Figure 6.10.: Re-Use of Target Metamodels in ModelJoin

usage, so that ModelJoin queries that are created later can possibly use the metamodel. In the UI of the prototypical implementation, the user has the possibility to choose whether the generated or the repository model shall be used.

The conformance checker can also be used to formulate a ModelJoin query whose target metamodel conforms to a pre-existing metamodel: The UI of the conformance check presents two metamodel metrics to the user, which indicate the number of conflicts that prevent the conformity of a ModelJoin query with an existing metamodel. This information can be used by the editor of the ModelJoin query to modify it in such a way that the target metamodel conforms to the desired existing metamodel.

Since the conformance checker acts as a proxy between metamodel generation and metamodel usage, it can be integrated into the ModelJoin query execution process (see Figure 6.7) between metamodel synthesis and transformation execution. The transformation generator has to be adapted to always take the generated metamodel as input, since it contains the necessary annotations for the generation of the model-to-model transformation, but to take the repository metamodel as the target of the transformation. The transformation execution will then generate instances of the repository metamodel.

6.2.5. Assumptions/Limitations

In this subsection, we will discuss the current assumptions and limitations of the ModelJoin language. These limitations concern the language itself; limitations that concern the prototypical implementation will not be discussed here. We refer the reader to the technical report of ModelJoin [28] instead.

6.2.5.1. Joining over References

The natural and outer join statements are based on the definition of join-conformity, which is given if the classes to be joined contain join-conforming attributes. The join statements could be extended to support joins over common references. This is, however, currently not supported in ModelJoin, since the semantics of such a join are complex, and several preconditions would have to be fulfilled. The join condition of natural and outer joins demands that attributes with equal name, type, and cardinality have the same values. A join over a reference would have the join condition that the same element is linked via a reference with equal name and cardinality. The problem with this condition is the fact that the definition of identity of two elements is not possible as easily as with primitive-typed attribute values. If the join is over two classes from heterogeneous metamodels with no common classes, it is impossible to have references with an identical type. Thus, the type-compatiblity and identity can only be derived from the fact that the respective classes at the end of the references are also joined by another join expression in the same query. This is shown in an example

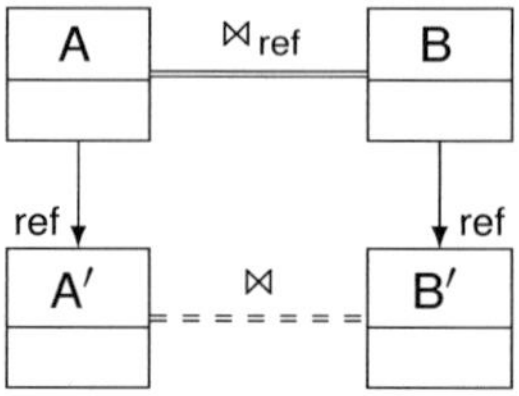

Figure 6.11.: Example for Joining over References

in Figure 6.11: If class A and B are joined over the reference ref, it would require that there are identical instances linked to instances of A and B. Since A and B can be part of distinct source models, the classes at the end of ref may also be distinct, like the classes A′ and B′ in the example.

Thus, a join over a reference would require that the classes at the end of the references are either identical or have also been joined, so that the identity of the instances can be determined. This is, however, a serious restriction to the ModelJoin language, since the validity of one join statement would depend on the existence of another join statement (in the example, a join over classes A′ and B′). For this reason, there is no specific operator to join over references. The behaviour of such an operator can, however, be expressed with a `THETA JOIN` with an appropriate OCL statement, and additional join and keep operations.

6.2.5.2. Purpose of the ModelJoin Language

The ModelJoin language does not contain constructs for identifying structural similarities of different metamodels. It is not meant as a data integration framework, but for the creation of views. Thus, it assists the developer in the rapid definition and execution of a view, but not in finding the semantic overlap of two heterogeneous models. It should also be noted that we did not aim at creating a complete query or transformation language. ModelJoin is a domain-specific language for the rapid creation of views. Hence, it cannot be used for any kind of fixed, pre-existing target metamodels. It is however possible to align ModelJoin queries with pre-existing metamodels using the conformance checking mechanism.

6.3. Flexible View Types in VITRUVIUS

The flexible view types concept is applicable to any view-based model-driven scenario, where view types on heterogeneous metamodels are required or can be useful. In this section, we will describe the integration of the flexible view concept in the VITRUVIUS approach. We will first describe the way in which the flexible view concept can be applied in VITRUVIUS-based development scenarios (subsection 6.3.1). The integration of the ModelJoin language and implementation is the subject of subsection 6.3.2. Finally, we will investigate how the synchronisation policies of VITRUVIUS affect the properties of flexible view types in subsection 6.3.3.

6.3.1. Applicability

VITRUVIUS is a view-centric approach and extends the Orthographic Software Modeling concept [7]. One of the core prinicples of OSM is the dynamic generation of views, at the instance level, from the single underlying model. The definition of view types, at the metamodel level, and of the transformations that synchronise the views with the SUM is in the responsibility of the *methodologist* role. Thus, for the developer who uses an OSM-based development framework, the view types are fixed and are usually not meant to be changed by the developers themselves. The flexible view concept in VITRUVIUS overcomes this limitation by offering the developers means to define user-specific view types, or, to put it differently, to create views that fulfil a specific information need for which no view type has been pre-defined by the methodologist. This specific information can also be created by restricting or re-organizing an existing view type.

The concept of flexible view types can be used in VITRUVIUS for the definition of view types. Flexible view types are used by the methodologist

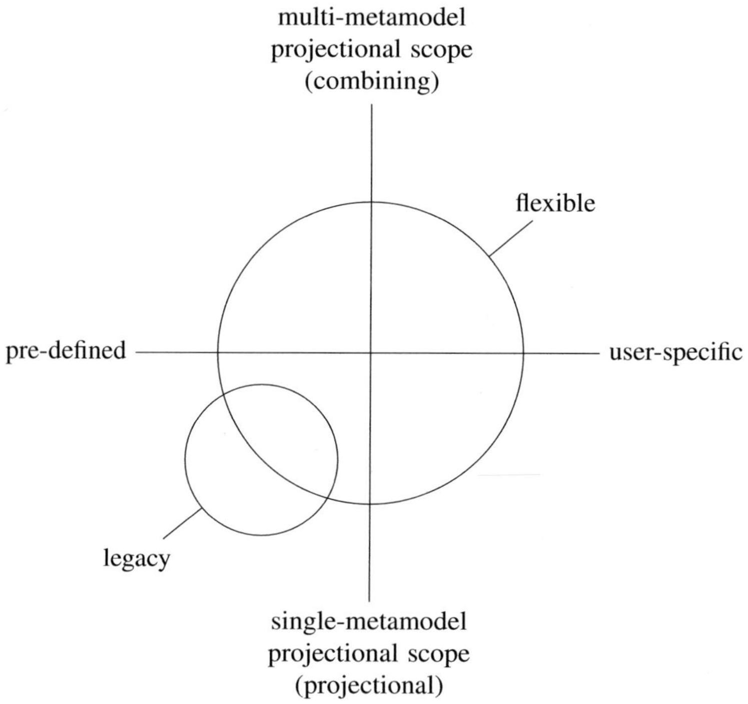

Figure 6.12.: View Type Categories

as well as the developers to specify view types, views and editability properties. In the prototypical implementation of VITRUVIUS, the ModelJoin DSL is used as a compact language for the definition of flexible view types.

Flexible views can be applied at several points of the development process and by different developer roles. We will explain this with the view type categories *pre-defined* and *user-specific*, as introduced in subsection 4.4.2. The connection between the view type terms *specificity* (pre-defined/user-specific), *projectional scope* (single-/multi-metamodel), *legacy*, and *flexible* is displayed in Figure 6.12: Specificity and and projectional scope are orthogonal categories. All of these kinds can be defined with flexible views, or with other view definition methods. Legacy metamodels are a special case of pre-defined view types with a single-metamodel projectional scope. They can be defined as flexible view types or by other means.

In the following, we will describe the application fields of the flexible views concept and the ModelJoin DSL in the context of VITRUVIUS.

6.3.1.1. Pre-defined View Types

The ModelJoin DSL can be used by the methodologist role to define view types that combine information from several sub-metamodels of the modular SUM metamodel. In this case, the source metamodels for a ModelJoin expression are a subset of the metamodels in the modular SUM metamodel. These metamodels can be legacy metamodels that have been included by the methodologist during the creation of the modular SUM metamodel, or additional metamodels that express semantic relations between these metamodels, or metamodels that express further additional information. The artefacts that are automatically generated by ModelJoin, i.e., target metamodel and model-to-model transformations, can be used to create custom views at the instance level. If the methodologist wishes to further customize the view types with functionality that cannot be expressed with ModelJoin, the generated artefacts can be further refined by the methodologist by editing them manually. Similar to code generation in model-driven software development, these manual modifications may, however, be overwritten if the artefacts are re-generated from the ModelJoin expression. The state-based metamodel conformance checking of section 5.3 can be used to check if the manual modifications to the target metamodel preserve the compatibility to the generated metamodel, so that the transformations are still compatible to the metamodel.

In the case that the flexible view type is used exactly as defined in the ModelJoin expression, the ModelJoin code then also serves as a specification for the view type and can be used as documentation of what is contained in the view type.

6.3.1.2. Legacy View Types

Legacy view types are a special case of pre-defined view types, which have a single-metamodel projectional scope. They are specified to offer compatibility to existing tools and transformations that are based on a specific sub-metamodel of the modular SUM metamodel. Legacy view types may be total view types if the legacy metamodel is partitioned in to sub-metamodel in the same way as the legacy view types are partitioned. It is possible to define legacy view types with a flexible view definition that conforms to a fixed view type metamodel, for example, UML class diagrams. The flexible view definition can pose restrictions on the selectional scope of elements and restrict the editability. Thus, the compatibility of the flexible view type with the legacy view type is preserved, since the projectional scope and the represents-relation are not modified, but the restrictions in selectional scope and editability can be used to integrate these view types in the VITRUVIUS-based development process.

6.3.1.3. User-specific view types

In addition to the pre-defined view types that are specified by the methodologist, developers in a VITRUVIUS-based development process also have the possibility to define user-specific view types. The flexible views concept and the ModelJoin DSL offer the developer a method for the declarative, rapid definition of additional view types that have not been pre-defined by the methodologist. Compared to the methodologist, the developer is however limited in accessing information in the SUM, since the developer is not supposed to change the structure of the modular SUM metamodel (which includes the pre-defined view types and the transformations). Thus, user-specific flexible views can only access information that is exposed in other, pre-defined view types (see Figure 4.9 on page 98) and must comply with the editing restrictions that have been defined on them. Thus, the SUM metamodel still remains a black-box for the developer. Nevertheless, a developer can combine information from those sub-metamodels by legacy or other view types; existing view types can serve as a starting point for the definition of user-specific view types, which may restrict the set of instances; for example, they may only show the abstract classes of a class diagram or only show specific kinds of elements, such as interfaces of a Palladio component diagram.

If total legacy view types expose the complete sub-metamodels with full editability, the developer can specify new view types in the same way that a methodologist can.

6.3.1.4. Projectional Scope

The typical case for flexible view types that are defined with ModelJoin are combining view types, which integrate information from several other view types or sub-metamodels. It is, however, also possible to join classes from just one metamodel, or to use self-joins to re-arrange the information at the instance level. Although this is not the main purpose of ModelJoin, it is thus also possible to create projectional views.

6.3.2. ModelJoin as a View Specification Language in VITRUVIUS

The usage of a textual DSL, as provided by ModelJoin, offers the developers the possibility to rapidly define views on a SUM, which combine information in a different way than the existing view types do. The view types that are created in this way have a transient nature, since the metamodels are generated on-the-fly by the implementation of ModelJoin. If the ModelJoin expression is modified, the metamodel is generated anew. It is of course possible to persist such a view type and the transformations, so that they become part of the SUM metamodel. In this case, the methodologist can integrate a user-specific view type that has been defined by a developer into the SUM metamodel, so that it becomes a pre-defined view type.

Since ModelJoin offers the declarative specification of view types based on equality of attributes or other features, it is suited for cases where the metamodels, on which the view type shall be defined, are completely heterogeneous. Thus, it can be helpful in the construction of the modular SUM. Semantic overlaps can be expressed in ModelJoin, and the resulting view type can be reused as part of the interface that the SUM offers. The consistency relations in the SUM can also be derived from ModelJoin expressions, since they represent semantic relations that the author of the expression has already identified.

6.3.2.1. ModelJoin Queries as Flexible View Type Definitions

The definition of flexible view types in VITRUVIUS with the ModelJoin language is performed with a ModelJoin expression

$$q \in \mathscr{M}_{sum} \times \text{VIEWTYPE}$$

The target metamodel of the query q is the view type metamodel $VT \in$ VIEWTYPE. The elements in VT are related to elements in $\mathcal{M}_{sum}$ by the mapping relations $\sim_{\bowtie}, \sim_{\underline{\bowtie}}$ of ModelJoin. These mappings realise the is-represented-by relations *rep* and $\underline{rep}$ of VITRUVIUS. In the prototypical implementation of ModelJoin, the relation $\sim_{\bowtie}$ is expressed in the EAnnotation elements of the generated target metamodel, which contain the information about the provenance of a view type element. At the instance level, the relation $\sim_{\underline{\bowtie}}$ is persisted in the trace model that is created by the QVT-O engine during the execution of the generated model-to-model transformation.

This tracing information at the metamodel level as well as at the instance level is necessary for the delta-based synchronisation mechanism of VITRUVIUS. The effects of changes to elements in a view are expressed as change operations to the corresponding elements in the SUM.

6.3.2.2. Editability

The ModelJoin language does not contain language constructs to define editabilty of the view types and views that can be specified with a ModelJoin query. The specification of editability scopes and response behaviour in VITRUVIUS is very fine-grained, since editability can be described for each class and feature in a view type, and additionally for single elements at the instance level. Thus, the ModelJoin language would have to be extended by a great number of language elements to support the definition of editability scopes.

Including editability into the ModelJoin DSL would thus introduce new advantages as well as disadvantages: On the one hand, a consistent definition of the three parts of a flexible view type (view type, view, and editability) is beneficial for the evolution of such a view type, since the generated parts evolve together when the textual definition is changed. On the other hand, the specification language would gain additional complexity, which is opposed to the aim of ModelJoin to offer a compact language for the definition of view types. In the current state of ModelJoin, we have thus not included language elements for the specification of editability. This functionality may, however, be included in future version of ModelJoin (see section 8.2).

The consideration of the trade-off between these factors should be based on the purpose for which ModelJoin is used. For the ad-hoc definition of user-specific view types, editability is not a central factor, since the primary purpose of such a view type is to fulfil a specific information need of the developer. Thus, it is acceptable if such a view type is not editable, as it is the case for view types defined with ModelJoin. If ModelJoin is used by the methodologist to specify pre-defined view types for a SUM metamodel, editability must, however, be specified for these view types. Since ModelJoin does not offer means for the specification of editability, these specification has to be expressed for the generated artefacts of the a ModelJoin query execution (view type metamodel, instances) by the means of VITRUVIUS. Since pre-defined view types have a longer evolution cycle than user-specific view types, the problem of co-evolution of these view type specifications and the adjacent editability specifications does not arise as frequently as in the user-specific case. If a methodologist modifies a ModelJoin specification of a pre-defined view, he or she has to adapt the editability specification manually.

6.3.3. Synchronisation

In this subsection, we will describe how the flexible view types concept interacts with the synchronisation mechanisms of VITRUVIUS.

6.3.3.1. Description of Edit Operations

The synchronisation of views with a SUM in VITRUVIUS requires that the edit operations in the views are expressed as a series of atomic edit operations [95] to trigger the synchronisation mechanisms. Such a series of editing operations can be determined in different ways, as discussed in subsection 5.2.5. The advantages and disadvantages of recording editing operations compared with the delta-based determination of a change sequence also apply to edit operation in flexible views. Depending on the frequency in which the views are synchronised with the SUM, an operation-based description that has been gained by recording manual editing steps in an editor can be minimised using the method presented in subsection 5.3.2, to avoid unnecessary synchronisation operations from the view to the SUM. This has to be determined based on a trade-off of the execution time of the minimizing operation for change sequences in comparison to the synchronisation operation with the SUM.

The VITRUVIUS approach allows developers to work with temporary inconsistencies in a view. If every atomic action were immediately synchronised with the SUM, the developer would have to react to a great number of requests for manual interaction, if an edit operation cannot be synchronised automatically. For this reason, the synchronisation of views with the SUM should be triggered at points of time that are specified by the user of a flexible view type, e.g., when a saving operation is invoked by the user. If a view is to be synchronised with the SUM, it must contain a valid instance of the view type. It is, however, still possible to create invalid instances of the view type, just as it is possible to create invalid instances of any metamodel. The validity of a view itself is precondition for the synchronisation with the SUM, so only valid instances can trigger a consistency conservation operation in the SUM (see Figure 4.8 on page 95).

Before the synchronisation operation, the validity of the view type can only be checked with respect to the rules and restrictions that are defined in the view type itself. The consistency with the base models in the selectional scope of the view, and the consistency with the rest of the SUM, can only be checked through the synchronisation operation. Depending on the execution time of such a consistency check, a framework that implements the flexible view type concept should give the developer the possibility to distinguish between a *local* consistency check, which only determines the consistency of the view with its base models, and a *global* consistency check, which determines the total consistency of the SUM. In flexible views with a multi-metamodel projectional scope, the local consistency check also includes the correspondences that are defined between the sub-metamodel of the SUM metamodel that are in the projectional scope of view. If the view type is defined thoroughly, the constraints of the view type should already respect these correspondences, as mentioned in subsection 4.3.4.

The separation of local and global consistency checks can be compared to code-based development scenarios, where users can check the validity of their working copy by executing a local build of the software, and use a continuous integration server or nightly builds to determine the conformity of the project parts on which they are working (which can be seen as a partial textual view of the system under development).

6.3.3.2. Well-behavedness of Flexible Views in VITRUVIUS

In section 6.1, we have evaluated the properties *invertibility*, *well-behavedness*, and *hippocraticness* for flexible views. In the context of the VITRUVIUS approach, the well-behavedness property is affected by the synchronisation mechanisms of the modular SUM, because the PUTGET law is not always adhered to: The PUTGET states that a modification to a view, which is written back to the base model, followed by a re-generation of the view from the base model, leads to an identical view. In VITRUVIUS, this property cannot be guaranteed, since the propagation of a change in a view to the SUM can lead to further consistency-preserving operations in the SUM, which may also alter the part of the SUM by which the contents of the view is affected. This is not a property of the view type itself, but rather of the whole view-based development framework; even if the view type itself is well-behaved, the PUTGET property is affected by the automatic synchronisation mechanism in VITRUVIUS.

As an example, let us consider a possible edit operation in a UML class diagram view of the CBSE scenario (see Figure 6.13). The PCM component model may contain a constraint that component names in an the instance $\underline{M}_{PCM}$ have to be unique. If such a naming collision is caused by the synchronisation of the component model with other models, such as UML class models that are linked to the component metamodel with correspondence links, a response action has been specified that renames the conflicting component. For example, if a synchronisation operation causes two components with the name comp_1 to be created, they are renamed into comp_1 and comp'_1 to avoid the name conflict. Let us furthermore assume that the SUM contains a mapping by which every component is implemented by exactly one class in the UML model, and a response action that creates new classes or components if an element is created in the respective other sub-model. The UML model, however, does not contain a constraint that requires name uniqueness for classes, since uniqueness is preserved by other features, such as a unique identifier. If a class with the name comp_1 already exists, and a developer adds a second class with the name comp_1 in a UML class diagram view, this modification will thus violate neither the inner consistency of the class diagram view, nor that of the UML instances in the SUM, so no conflict is detected and displayed fo the user. The save operation will however cause the creation of the class comp_1 in the UML sub-model of the SUM (indicated by the plus symbol $\oplus$ in Figure 6.13), which will cause a response action that creates a PCM component of the same name in the PCM sub-model. Because of the name uniqueness constraint in PCM, this component is renamed into comp'_1 by the consistency preservation response. (The rename operation, which is created by this response, is depicted as (AB) in the figure.) Since the component is mapped to the class comp'_1 with a correspondence link, this change will be propagated back to to the UML model, where the class is also renamed to comp'_1. The update operation on

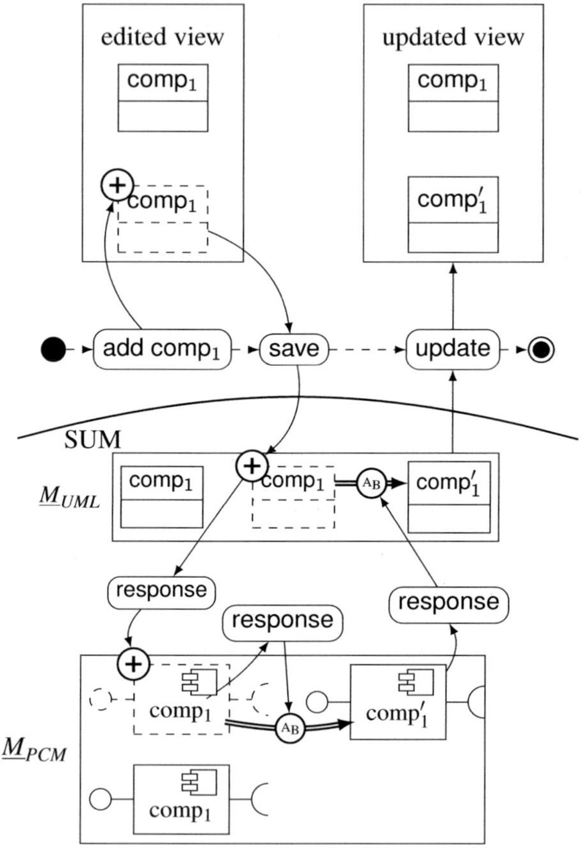

Figure 6.13.: The PutGet Property of a View is Affected By The Vitruvius Synchronisation Mechanism

the view will then also rename the class in the view into comp'_1. Although the developer did not create the class with this name, the save operation has altered the contents of the view, and thus the PUTGET law was not adhered to.

It could of course be argued that in such a case, the UML metamodel should also contain a constraint that requires name uniqueness in classes. This would, however, violate the principle of modularity in VITRUVIUS. If every one of the sub-metamodels would be required to contain constraints that respect all other sub-metamodels in the SUM metamodel, each of the sub-metamodels would carry the total complexity of the SUM in its constraints. This would severely impede evolution to the sub-metamodels, since every change to a single element would cause the investigation and possible modification of all other elements in all sub-metamodels of the SUM metamodel. To prevent this case, the VITRUVIUS approach is built on a modular SUM and explicit correspondence information with rules for the re-establishing of consistency in case of a rule violation.

7. Evaluation

In this section, we will evaluate the two main contributions of this dissertation:

In section 7.1, we will evaluate the flexible view type concept and its protoypical implementation, the ModelJoin language. We will demonstrate that the expressivity of the ModelJoin language is sufficient to specify user-specific views on heterogeneous models, and that it reduces the complexity of this task in comparison with manual definitions.

In section 7.2, the view-based VITRUVIUS approach will be evaluated. Since the VITRUVIUS prototype is not fully functional at the point of writing of this dissertation, we will focus the potential benefits of the flexible view types approach within VITRUVIUS using two case studies: one from the field of component-based software development, and one from the field of systems engineering in the automotive domain.

7.1. Expressivity of ModelJoin

In this subsection, we will evaluate the completeness of the ModelJoin language for the definition of flexible view types. ModelJoin implements the concept of flexible view types in a textual DSL that is suited for the definition of the projectional and selectional scope of view types. The rationale behind ModelJoin was not to create a full-fledged model transformation language (see subsection 6.2.5), but rather a specialised DSL for the rapid definition of view types and views. Thus, we do not intend to demonstrate that ModelJoin has the same expressivity as common model transformation languages, such as QVT [116], ATL [79], or Xtend,[1] or even general-purpose programming languages such as Java, which can also be used for model transformations. Nevertheless, methodologists and developers should be able to cover all kinds of modelling elements with a ModelJoin expression.

Instead, we will analyse the expressivity of ModelJoin using the following two categories: The *projectional expressivity* describes which kinds of metamodels can be defined with ModelJoin, while the *selectional expressivity* defines the sets of elements at the model level that can be defined with ModelJoin.

7.1.1. Projectional Expressivity

The projectional expressivity of the ModelJoin language is determined by the kinds of elements in the target metamodels that can be created with ModelJoin expressions. Since ModelJoin is neither a metamodel definition language nor a model transformation language, the properties of elements in the target metamodel always depend on the properties of the elements in the source metamodels of a ModelJoin query. It is not possible to freely create classes, attributes, references, etc., which are not in a relation to elements in the source metamodels. For example, it is not possible to specify a reference between two classes in the target model if there is no reference between the classes in the source models that they represent.

Thus, the notion of projectional expressivity in the context of ModelJoin describes that all parts of a metamodel are reached by the ModelJoin operators. In VITRUVIUS and ModelJoin, without loss of generality, we assume that Ecore is used as the meta-metamodel for the definition of metamodels. Since the Ecore model only contains a finite number of elements, it is possible to check whether these elements are reachable by ModelJoin. The Ecore model contains, however, also elements that are only relevant for the generation of Java code from the metamodels, but not for the cre-

[1] `http://www.eclipse.org/xtend/`, retrieved 26 May 2014

ation of view types, such as the EFactory or the EOperation class. This is why we will not analyse for every element in the Ecore model if it can be reached with a ModelJoin query. Instead, we use the change operator catalogue by Herrmannsdörfer [72], which has already been used in chapter 5 to describe the evolution of Ecore-based metamodels. The operators of the catalogue already exclude those classes that are not relevant for non-programmatic instantiation of models. In Appendix B, we have further categorised these operators into atomic and complex operators. Complex operators can be expressed with a sequence of atomic operators. Since the operators of Herrmannsdörfer cover all practical cases of changes to Ecore-based metamodels, we assume that it is sufficient to show that every element that can be created with such an operator can also be created with an operator of ModelJoin. For the complete coverage, it is furthermore sufficient to only regard the atomic operators, since all other operators can be expressed by them.

In Table 7.1, we have listed the atomic operators and their coverage by the ModelJoin operators. We have only listed these change operators that are responsible for the creation of elements, and excluded those that are reponsible for the deletion of elements, since the evaluation of ModelJoin should cover the generation of metamodels rather than the modification or destruction. For example, the operator catalogue contains the operators *Create Class* and *Delete Class*; of such pairs, we only regard the respective "create" operators. The table shows that the basic elements of Ecore Metamodels (Packages, Classes, Attributes), whose creation is covered in the *structural primitives* of the catalogue, are created by several of the ModelJoin operators. Classes are created implicitely by join ($\bowtie$) and keep (κ) operators, and can only be created by these operators; it is impossible to construct a class that is not a result of these operators. Attributes are created by natural and outer joins and by the keep operators for attribute (κ_{att}), calculated attributes (δ_{ϕ}), and aggregations (α). Data Types, enumerations and enumeration literals are automatically created in the target metamodel if an attribute of this type is

	$\bowtie$	$\kappa_{super/sub}$	κ_{ref}	κ_{att}, δ_{ϕ}, α	ρ
Structural Primitives					
Create Package	✓	✓	✓	-	-
Create Class	✓	✓	✓	-	-
Create Attribute	✓	-	-	✓	-
Create Reference	-	-	✓	-	-
Create Data Type	✓	-	-	✓	-
Create Enum	✓	-	-	✓	-
Create Literal	✓	-	-	✓	-
Non-structural Primitives					
Rename	-	-	-	-	✓
Add Super Type	-	✓	-	-	-
Make Class Abstract	-	✓	-	-	-
Make Attr. Identifier	-	-	-	✓	-
Make Ref. Composite	-	-	✓	-	-
Make Ref. Opposite	-	-	-	-	-

Table 7.1.: Structural Primitives for Metamodel Generation Covered by ModelJoin Operators (adapted from [29])

created with a keep operator. References can only be created with the keep reference operator (κ_{ref}), since joining over references is not possible with ModelJoin (see subsection 6.2.5). The *non-structural primitives* concern those parts of the metamodels that do not lead to an instantiation (of an M3 class at the M2 level), but only change an attribute value at the M2 level.

The *rename* operator ρ offers the renaming of every element that has been created with one of the other four operator types. In the concrete textual syntax of ModelJoin, this is realised with the keyword AS, which can be appended to the join and keep operators. The supertype hierarchy can be specified in the target metamodel by keeping supertype relations of the source metamodel with the keep supertype operator. The last four entries in Table 7.1 concern properties of classes and features. Although these properties are not directly influenced by the ModelJoin operators, the operators copy these properties from the source metamodels to the target metamodel, where possible. For example, an abstract class that is joined with another class will be non-abstract in the target metamodel, since the view generation may create instances of this class. If an abstract superclass of a class is processed by the keep supertype operator, the abstractness property will be preserved, since there is at least one non-abstract subclass in the target metamodel. The abstractness property can thus not be changed directly by the author of the ModelJoin query; it is set automatically based on properties of the source metamodel and depending on the ModelJoin operator with which the class in the target metamodel is created. The same is true for the identifier and composite property: they cannot be actively set by ModelJoin, but are respected by the metamodel generation if the property is set in the source models. The last property in the table, the opposite field of references, is not supported by ModelJoin.

As a conclusion from this analysis, we estimate that the ModelJoin language is sufficient to specify the view type part of flexible view types, since all constructs that can be created in Ecore metamodels can be reached. For some properties, this is only possible if the respective property has been defined in the source metamodel. We do, however, not see this as a serious limitation, since the semantics of changing these properties for individual elements in a view type are not evident, and would have to be respected with a high number of special language constructs. Since this would reduce the comprehensibility of the ModelJoin language, we have refrained from including these concepts into the language. If a developer whishes to include them, they will have to be modified in the target metamodels manually. Such a modified target metamodel can still be used with the ModelJoin query if it fulfils the metamodel conformance relation (see section 5.3).

7.1.2. Selectional Expressivity

The selection of elements that are contained in the actual views, and that are created by the execution of a ModelJoin query, are mainly determined by the *join* statements in the query. While natural and outer join statements match elements in the source models based on equality of common attributes, the theta join operator offers arbitrary join conditions, which can be formulated in the Object Constraint Language (OCL) [123]. Since the join operators are the starting point of any ModelJoin query, the initial set of elements in the generated view is determined by these selections. From these elements, further instances are added to the views with the keep references operator, which adds the instances to the target model for which a link exists in the source model.

The ModelJoin language thus allows selections based on the properties in the source models using the join operators. Since the theta join operator offers the usage of OCL, the selectional expressivity is only limited to that of OCL. Although ModelJoin only offers restrictions that are based on properties of the source instances, the result sets of ModelJoin can always be filtered by additional means, such as evaluation of an OCL constraint on the set of target instances. In contrast to the target metamodel, which should not be changed after its generation, the instance filtering does not have an effect on the compatibility of these instances to the generated view type, so the result set can be restricted by further manual or automatic selection of elements.

7.2. Applicability of the Flexible View Concept in the VITRUVIUS Approach

In this section, we will evaluate the applicability of the Flexible Views concept in the VITRUVIUS approach. To this end, we have conducted two case studies from the field of software and systems development: The first case study is an extension of the running CBSE scenario example that is used throughout this dissertation. The second case study is a systems engineering scenario in the automotive systems engineering domain. We will analyse both of these case studies using the same criteria, which we will now formulate in the form of goals, questions, and metrics.

7.2.1. GQM Plan

The goal-question-metric (GQM) approach [11] is a systematic method of defining and measuring the quality properties of software systems. We will, however, use this method to evaluate the aptitude of the flexible views concept for the scenarios of the case studies, rather than measure the quality of a software system. The goals, questions, and metrics that we define are then applied equally to both of the case studies.

In the introduction chapter of this dissertation, we have identified four problem areas of software development with heterogeneous models (subsection 1.2.3): Fragmentation, redundancy, inconsistency, and complexity. View-based approaches tackle these problem areas by explicit modelling of correspondences between heterogeneous artefacts. Rather than reducing the *essential complexity* (see subsection 2.1.2) of the aforementioned problem fields, the aim of these approaches is to reduce the *accidental complexity* of working with heterogeneous formalisms. The same is true for VITRUVIUS;

thus, we have formulated the following goals for the evaluation of the approach along these problem areas. For each of the goals mentioned above, specific questions have been formulated that refine the goals and enable the quantification of the feedback. To evaluate the questions in the GQM plan, we have formulated generic metrics, which will be refined in the individual case studies.

7.2.1.1. Fragmentation

G1 The VITRUVIUS approach aims to reduce the fragmentation of information across heterogeneous modelling formalisms.

- **Q1.1** Which concepts suffer from fragmentation and are expressed by heterogeneous model elements in the system description?
  - **M1.1.1** How many combining view types are identified by the methodologist that contain information from heterogeneous submetamodels?
- **Q1.2** How is this fragmentation reduced for the modeler?
  - **M1.2.1** How many of such combining view types are specified by the methodologist?

7.2.1.2. Redundancy

G2 The VITRUVIUS approach aims to create a controlled redundancy in information that is modelled about the system under development.

- **Q2.1** Which redundancies in the modelled systems can be indentified?
  - **M2.1.1** How many semantic overlaps between classes in the submetamodels of the modular SUM metamodel are identified by the methodologist?
- **Q2.2** Which of these redundancies are under control by the means of VITRUVIUS?

M2.2.1 How many combining view types are specified by the methodologist that merge information from heterogeneous sub-metamodels?

7.2.1.3. Inconsistency

G3 The purpose of VITRUVIUS is the detection and prevention of inconsistencies between heterogeneous models that are used in the view-based development of software and systems.

Q3.1 Can inconsistencies can be dectected with the flexible view approach?

M3.1.1 How many MIR mappings between classes of heterogeneous sub-metamodels are specified by the methodologist?

Q3.2 Can inconsistencies can be prevented with the flexible view approach?

M3.2.1 How many response actions for violations of consistency are defined by the methodologist?

7.2.1.4. Complexity

G4 The purpose of VITRUVIUS is to reduce the accidental complexity of view-based development for developers in the context of software and systems development.

Q4.1 Does the flexible view concept help to answer information needs of developers?

M4.1.1 How many of the identified integrated view types could be modelled with the flexible views concept?

Q4.2 Does the flexible view concept facilitate the definition of view types and views in comparison with manual modelling?

M4.2.1 How many elements in the metamodel of the view type definition have to be modelled manually without the flexible view concept?

M4.2.2 How much lines-of code are necessary in a common model transformation language in comparison to ModelJoin?

7.2.2. Case Study: Component-based Software Development

In this section, we will use the running example of component-based software development with the Palladio Component Model, UML, and the Sensor Model, which has been introduced in subsection 1.2.2. In this case study, we will integrate these three formalisms into a modular SUM metamodel and evaluate the VITRUVIUS approach using the aforementioned GQM plan. Although the scenario presented in subsection 1.2.2 contains Java as a fourth formalism, we will not regard the support of general purpose programming languages in this case study, since the integration of textual programming languages into the VITRUVIUS approach is subject of ongoing work [103].

7.2.2.1. Modelling Languages

In this section, we will briefly describe those properties of the modelling languages in the scenario that are relevant for the integration into a VITRUVIUS-based development process: the view types that are part of each language's specification, the extension mechanisms that the modelling languages offer, and interdependencies to other modelling languages. For a more detailed description of the models and languages, please refer to chapter 2.

PCM The Palladio Component Model (version 5.00) [134] is a domain-specific metamodel for the description of software architectures with a special focus on extrafunctional properties, such as performance, reliability, and maintainablility. The component model is organised in five diagram types: repository, system, behaviour, deployment, and usage. The Palladio Workbench is an EMF-based tool, which contains an Ecore intance of the Palladio Component Model.

The Palladio Component Model has been amended by a customised version of EMF Profiles [96], which offers an extension mechanism that is similar to profiles and stereotypes in UML [125].

Sensor Model The sensor model is a data model for the storage of measurements of various properties of systems, such as performance, or system state. It is used for the persisting of sensors, experiments, and simulation runs, and stores the results of these experiments. The sensor model is part of the Sensor Framework[2]. Although this framework has been developed in the course of the Palladio Workbench, it can be used for arbitrary measurements of live systems or simulations, and does not depend in any way on the Palladio Component Model. The metamodel of the sensor model is generic and does not contain any references to an actual metamodel of the entities for which the measurements are stored. Its instances can be used for the storage of various data items, which are not limited to software performance data. The sensors in an instance contain a universal identifier, which allows expressing a relation to elements of another model by naming conventions.

UML In its current version 2.4.1 [125], the UML specification contains 14 types of diagrams. Class diagrams are by far the most frequently used diagram type [100]. Although the UML specification also contains concepts for the modelling of components and usage profiles with the component diagram and the use case diagram, we will only use the class diagram type in this scenario, which is used to model the object-oriented design of systems.

[2] `https://sdqweb.ipd.kit.edu/wiki/Palladio_Component_Model/Sensorframework`, retrieved 12 May 2014

7.2.2.2. Process

The languages and metamodels that are used in this scenario are already part of specific software development processes that are built on these formalisms. For example, the component-based Palladio approach defines a process model of its own, and also five developer roles (compent developer, software architect, system deployer, domain expert, and quality-of-service analyst). Existing developer roles are included into the VITRUVIUS-based process as sub-roles of the VITRUVIUS role *developer*. In this section, we will describe how the CBSE scenario has been adapted to use the VITRUVIUS approach. The following process steps realise the development process described in section 4.4.

Selection/Definition of Metamodels In the first step, the metamodels and languages that are used in the scenario are identified by the methodologist, so that they can later be part of the modular SUM metamodel. If an Ecore-based metamodel exists for a particular formalism or language, it is integrated without modification into the modular SUM metamodel; if a metamodel for this particular formalism does not exist yet, the methodologist is responsible of specifying a metamodel for this formalism.

The metamodel of the Palladio Component Model, which is included in the Palladio Workbench, is defined by the Palladio developers with the IBM tool *Rational Software Architect*[3], and exported from there into the Ecore format. The Ecore-based metamodel is included in the deployed versions of the EMF-based Palladio Workbench. Thus, the Ecore Metamodel for Palladio is available for each released version of the Palladio Workbench and can be extracted from there. The current version (5.00) of the Palladio Metamodel contains about 100 classes and about 200 other metamodel elements.

[3] `http://www-03.ibm.com/software/products/en/swarchitect-websphere`, retrieved 14 May 2014

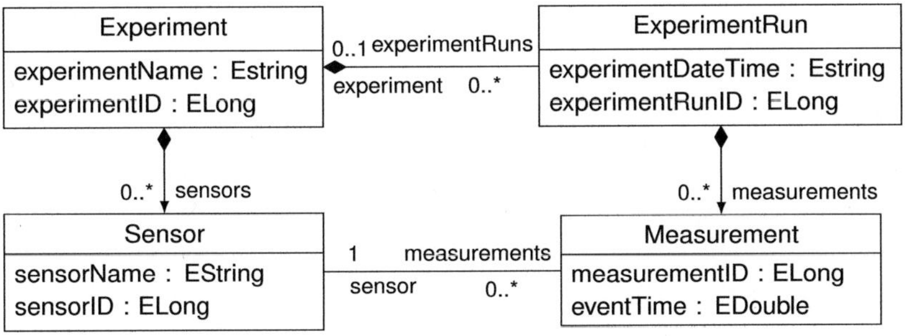

Figure 7.1.: Metamodel of the Sensor Framework (Excerpt Showing the Top-level Classes)

The UML metamodel is available in the Ecore format as part of the UML plug-in provided by the Eclipse Modeling Framework itself. It is the basis of EMF-based UML modelling tools, such as Papyrus.[4]

The Sensor Framework supports several persistence engines; a memory-based and a database store are included in the Sensor Framework implementation. The Java objects that are created in the memory-based store can be serialised and persisted as files using a binary serialization format. In the course of the development of the ModelJoin prototype [29], an Ecore-based metamodel of the Sensor Framework result model and an XMI serialiser for instances of sensor framework data have been developed. If we see the development of the ModelJoin protoype as a part of the process of introducing VITRUVIUS in the component-based scenario, then this development is part of the responsibilities of the methodologist. An excerpt of this resulting metamodel is displayed in Figure 7.1 (only the classes at the top level of the inheritance hierarchy are shown).

Specification of View Types After the metamodels have been determined, the existing and desired view types for the development scenario are

[4] `http://www.eclipse.org/papyrus`, retrieved 14 May 2014

investigated by the methodologist. As mentioned above, PCM contains five diagram types, which are included as legacy view types in the modular SUM metamodel. Since the Palladio metamodel is structured along these diagram types, the view types are projections of the PCM sub-metamodel.

Of the 14 diagram types that the UML metamodel specification contains, only the class diagram is used in this scenario. Thus, it is the only legacy view type for the UML sub-metamodel in the SUM metamodel.

For the sensor model, there is only one legacy view type, which is a *total* view type, since it is identical to the metamodel in Figure 7.1.

In addition to the legacy view types, the methodologist determines which kind of information from the legacy view types and the sub-metamodels can be included into meaningful combined view types. As already mentioned in the description of the running example in section 4.6, the relation between classes and components is of interest in this scenario: In a specialised combining view, the *class-component implementation view*, the implements-relation between components and classes shall be displayed, with the possibility to edit this relation, but not the classes and components themselves. As a further combining view type, the system view of Palladio, which displays the components and their assembly contexts, is combined with the results sensor model to offer the developer an integrated view of components and performance properties. This view type is called *component performance view*.

Specification of Correspondences The correspondences between the sub-metamodels of the SUM metamodel are identified by analyzing the desired combining view types, which have been specified in the preceding step. These combined view types, which have been specified, but not implemented yet, can be understood as requirements on the correlations that have to be supported in the VITRUVIUS-based development process.

The first combining view type that has been identified above is the *class-component implementation view type*, whose projectional scope intersects with the PCM and the UML sub-metamodel. Since there is no connection between the PCM and the UML metamodel at the metamodel-level, the information of which component is implemented by which class was expressed by naming conventions before the introduction of the VITRUVIUS-based process: If a class carries the same name as a component, this indicates that the class is an implementation of the component. In addition, further UML classes can be part of the implementation of the component, which are not named in a particular way, and for which the connection to the component is only expressed in natural language in the documentation of the object-oriented design. For this reason, the correspondence between PCM components and UML classes has to be modelled explicitely in the SUM metamodel, so that it can also be specified manually.

The *component performance view type* combines information from the sensor model and the component model. The correspondence between the respective elements can be determined by exploiting a naming convention. The instances of the Sensor Framework metamodel element Sensor contain the attribute sensorName. A Sensor element describes particular performance properties that are bound to a PCM component in an AssemblyContext element. By convention, the sensor contains the identifier string id of the AssemblyContext element in the attribute sensorName. Thus, the connection between a sensor and an assembly context can be determined by a comparison of these attributes. It is not persisted explicitely in mapping elements.

The Modular SUM Metamodel The modular SUM metamodel for the CBSE scenario contains the three sub-metamodels PCM, UML, and the Sensor Framework Metamodel. Although only the class diagram view type is supported in the VITRUVIUS-based development process, the UML metamodel is included completely into the SUM metamodel, since a reduction to the parts that are relevant to the class diagrams would require a refactoring of the metamodel and its constraints. Thus, the advantage of compatibility to existing instances would be lost. Furthermore, the reduction step would have to be repeated each time that the UML sub-metamodel evolves, for example, when a new version of UML is issued. By integrating the UML metamodel completely, this effort is avoided.

Implementation of Correspondences The information of how PCM components are implemented by UML classes is expressed as a special, PCM-specific UML profile that is applied to the UML classes, and which contains a reference to the respective component which the class implements. This is only one possibility to express the information (see subsection 4.2.3). The alternative methods would have been to apply a profile to PCM, or to define a third linking metamodel, which contains elements that link classes to components with, e.g., an implements and implemented reference. The UML profile approach was chosen over the PCM profile approach since the UML class diagram can be seen as a refinement of the component diagram, and thus the more specific model contains the reference to the more generic metamodel. This is useful if there are multiple object-oriented implementations of a component-based architecture, so that the class-component implementation can always be determined unambiguously for a specific implementation. Furthermore, the profile approach has the advantage that the information can also be included if a UML model is exported, e.g., to be processed by a model transformation.

The second combined view type that has been identified is the *component performance view type*. Since the elements of PCM and the sensor model are implicitely connected with a universal identifier, the correspondence between the elements Sensor and AssemblyContext need not be modelled explicitely in the modular SUM. The methodologist can specify this implicit corresondence in a MIR element to detect changes in the universal identifiers, so that sensor model instances can be co-adapted if the universal identifier in a PCM instance should be modified.

Implementation of View Types The class-component implementation view type is implemented as a manually created metamodel that only contains the necessary elements for components, classes, and the implements-relation. The view types are created by a model-to-model transformation, which takes the UML models with the applied component implementation profile and the PCM instances as an input and produces the view. Thus, the class-component implementation view is realised as a pre-defined view, which is created by the methodologist.

The component performance view type, on the other hand, is described as a flexible view type using a declarative ModelJoin specification. Thus, the component performance view type can either be specified by the methodologist as a pre-defined view type, but can also be specified by the developer as a user-specific view type. The ModelJoin definition thereof is displayed in Listing 14: The element of interest in the sensor model is the class TimeSpanSensor, which represents performance data such as execution times and waiting periods. The implicit correspondence with PCM elements, which is realised by a naming convention, is used in the `THETA JOIN` statement (lines 5–6) to combine the TimeSpanSensor class with the class AssemblyContext from PCM into the identically named target class AssemblyContext. The components in this assembly context are included with the `KEEP OUTGOING` statement in lines 8–12. To distinguish between basic and composite components in the created view, these subtypes are also specified in the target model using the `KEEP SUBTYPE` operator. The experiment data is included into the view type with the `KEEP INCOMING` statement in lines 13–22. The time spans of the measurements are aggregated using the ModelJoin operator `KEEP AGGREGATE` to display size, average, minimum, and maximum of an experiment run. The target metamodel that is specified by this ModelJoin query is displayed in Figure 7.2.

Connection with Existing Tools The legacy view types preserve the compatibility to existing tools and transformations that are based on the

```
import "platform:/plugin/de.uka.ipd.sdq.pcm/model/pcm.ecore"
import "platform:/plugin/edu.kit.ipd.sdq.mdsd.sensormodel/model/Sensor.ecore"
target "http://sdq.ipd.kit.edu/mdsd/ComponentSpeed/0.2"

theta join Entities.TimeSpanSensor with pcm.core.composition.AssemblyContext
where "TimeSpanSensor.sensorName.indexOf(AssemblyContext.id)␣>␣0" as jointarget.AssemblyContext {
  keep attributes pcm.core.entity.NamedElement.entityName, Entities.Sensor.sensorName
  keep outgoing pcm.core.composition.AssemblyContext.encapsulatedComponent__AssemblyContext as type jointarget.Component {
    keep attributes pcm.core.entity.NamedElement.entityName
    keep subtype pcm.repository.BasicComponent as type jointarget.BasicComponent
    keep subtype pcm.repository.CompositeComponent as type jointarget.CompositeComponent
  }
  keep incoming Entities.Experiment.sensors as type jointarget.Experiment {
    keep attributes Entities.Experiment.experimentName, Entities.Experiment.experimentID
    keep outgoing Entities.Experiment.experimentRuns as type jointarget.Run {
      keep attributes Entities.ExperimentRun.experimentRunID, Entities.ExperimentRun.experimentDateTime
      keep aggregate size(Entities.ExperimentRun.measurements) as jointarget.Run.measurementCount,
        avg(Entities.TimeSpanMeasurement.timeSpan) over Entities.ExperimentRun.measurements as jointarget.Run.avgTime,
        min(Entities.TimeSpanMeasurement.timeSpan) over Entities.ExperimentRun.measurements as jointarget.Run.minTime,
        max(Entities.TimeSpanMeasurement.timeSpan) over Entities.ExperimentRun.measurements as jointarget.Run.maxTime
    }
  }
}
```

Listing 14: Response Time ModelJoin Example

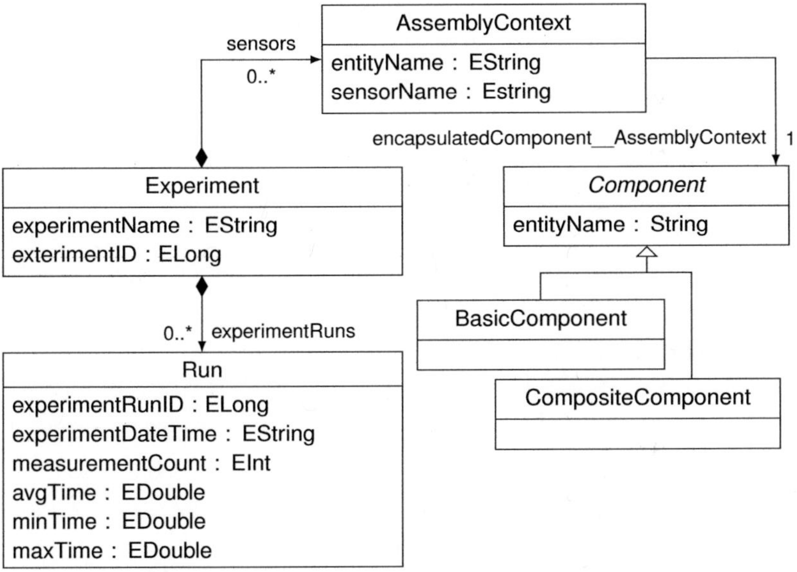

Figure 7.2.: Generated Target Metamodel for the Component Speed Example

metamodels of UML, PCM, and the Sensor Model. The instances that are created as views can be serialised as XMI files, which can be exported and used by other tools. For the sensor model, the Ecore-based representation of results has to be converted by the Sensor Framework implementation in the the binary serialziation format, so that the visualization tools and further statistic analyses can use the data.

If models have to be imported into the SUM, e.g., after an exported model has been edited by an external tool, these models have to be described as a series of atomic editing operations. This can be achieved by using the EMF Compare tool, as described in subsection 5.3.3

7.2.2.3. Empirical Study

To evaluate the usability and benefit of the Flexible View concept and the ModelJoin language, we have conducted an empirical study using the MediaStore example from [13]. The results of this case study have previously been published in [29]; the study has been conducted in cooperation with the authors of this publication.

To adress the question whether flexible view types reduce the complexity of the definition of view types (Q4.2), we have conducted a case study using the Palladio Metamodel and the Sensor Model. Using the MediaStore example from [13], we simulated performance properties of the MediaStore system and persisted them as instances of the Sensor Model.

Test Design The question of whether ModelJoin reduces the complexity of view type definitions was in the focus of the empirical study. To estimate this complexity, the comparison between generated ModelJoin transformation code and manually implemented code was not of interest, since generated code is usually less readable and larger in size than manually optimised code. Instead, we compared the manual creation of a combined view type with a multi-metamodel projectional scope to the definition of such a view type with ModelJoin. Since the ModelJoin prototypes is based

Metric	P_1	P_2	P_3	P_4	*Gen*	*MJ*
Metamodel						
Classes	4	8	5	5	6	
Attributes	4	14	0	5	7	
References	3	6	7	2	2	
Inheritance	1	8	2	2	3	
Transformation						
Source LoC	46	76	53	50	179	18
# Operations	6	10	10	5	24	9

Table 7.2.: Metrics for the Empirical Study of the Component Speed Example (from [30])

on Ecore and the transformation language QVT-O, and due to the stability of the language and the execution support in the Eclipse Modeling Framework, we chose these standards for comparison.

We asked researchers who had two to four years of experience in the design of model transformations, and who were familiar with the Palladio Component model and the model transformation language QVT-O, to implement the *component performance view type* as an Ecore metamodel, and the transformations that create the views from the base models, using QVT-O as the transformation language. Four participants (P_1–P_4) were asked to create the component performance view type manually, based an assignment sheet that contained the task description in natural language, and links to the models in a Subversion repository. The participants did not receive detailed information on where the desired information in the view type can be found in the metamodels, but only the description of the desired contents of the view type. The time to solve the task was not limited. This assignment sheet that was given to the researchers is replicated in Appendix D.

Statistical Evaluation We used the M2M quality measurement framework[5] to apply code metrics to the QVT-O implementations that were created by the participants. The results can be seen in Table 7.2. While the first four columns contain the metrics for the implementations by the participants, the last two columns contain the metrics for a reference implementation of the view type with ModelJoin, against which the participants' implementations where compared. We have applied a statistical analysis to these results, which is displayed in Table 7.3: The column S shows the standard deviation of the sample, while $\bar{P}$ shows the average. The test statistic T was determined by the calculation of $\sqrt{n}(\bar{P} - \mu_{MJ})/S$. The significance level for rejection of the null hypothesis is $1-\alpha$ (one-tailed test) or $1-\alpha/2$ (two-tailed test). The Student's one-sample t-Test [114] was applied to analyse the data.

For the comparison of the manually implemented transformation code with the ModelJoin query, we assumed that the experimental results would be larger than the reference ModelJoin query. Thus, we used the one-tailed t-statistic to to calculate the significance levels. The size of the generated metamdoels was analysed with a two-tailed test, since we did not assume that the size of the manually implemented metamodels would be either larger or smaller than the automatically generated metamodels.

The results in Table 7.3 indicate that the complexity of creating the component speed view on heterogeneous models is high, and that the effort of creating such a view with ModelJoin is lower than the manual implementation. As the null hypothesis H_0, we assumed that the size of the ModelJoin definition of the view type and the implementation in QVT-O were identical. This hypothesis can be rejected at a significance level of 99% The alternative hypothesis H_1 states that the average number of lines of code (LoC) is higher for the manual implementation.

The sizes of the manually implemented model, shown in the rows for number of classes (Cl.), attributes (Attr.), references (Ref.), and inheritance

[5] `http://code.google.com/p/m2m-quality/`, retrieved 26 May 2014

Metric	$S(P_{1..4})$	$\bar{P}$	*Gen/MJ*	T	Sign. Level
Cl.	1.732	5.50	6	-0.577	-
Attr.	5.909	5.75	7	-0.423	-
Ref.	2.380	4.50	2	**2.100**	80%**
Inh.	3.202	3.25	3	0.156	-
LoC	13.475	56.25	18	**5.677**	99%*
# Ops	2.630	7.75	9	-0.951	-

* one-tailed test $(1-\alpha)$
** two-tailed test $(1-\alpha/2)$

Table 7.3.: Statistical Evaluation of the Empirical Results (from [30])

relations (Inh.) in Table 7.3 only produced significant results for the number of references. Here, we assumed as the alternative hypothesis that the number of artefacts in the manually implemented solution is significantly higher than in the automatically generated solution. We conclude from this observation that the participants have over-engineered the solution, i.e., they have implemented more features than those that were demanded in the precisely formulated task specification. Defining the information need of the task specification with ModelJoin was beneficial in this case to create a compact textual definition.

Biases and Threats to Validity In the preparation of the case study, we did not treat the population. The participants served as a reference candidates who implemented a typical problem, and who were selected based on their expertise in model-driven engineering. Since this sample was not randomly chosen, it lead to and overestimation of similarities, and an underestimation of variance, in the population.

Due to the low number of participants, it is unclear whether the results of this case study can be generalised to other metamodelling scenarios. The population of the experiment was very small and not representative. The selection of the task was, however, a typical scenario in model-driven and view-based development, where information from heterogeneous models is combined into custom representations.

7.2.2.4. Evaluation of the Scenario

In this case study, seven legacy view types have been defined by the methodologist, which have been included from the existing formalisms. In addition to these, two desired view types have been identified by analysis of the semantic correlations for these formalisms (M1.1.1). Both have been specified as combining view types and as a part of the modular SUM metamodel (M1.2.1).

The redundancy in this scenario was low, since the metamodels have little semantic overlap and are almost orthogonal to each other. The naming conventions that are used to identify the correspondenc of classes and components as well as assembly contexts and sensors can be seen as a form of redundancy. It is identified by the combining view types for both cases (M2.1.1), but only controlled in the MIR element between components and sensor data (M2.2.1). For the class-component relation, the naming convention states that from name equality follows correspondence, but the opposite is not true in general. Thus, this redundancy is not controlled automatically, but has to be managed manually by the developer in the class-component view type.

This also directly affects the detection and handling of inconsistencies: While inconsistencies can be detected in the class-component view type, they cannot be analysed in the component speed type, since this view type only displays elements for which the naming convention is obeyed. Thus, only one of the inconsistencies can be detected (M3.1.1) and resolved (M3.2.1).

The flexible view approach could only be used in for the component speed type, since the declarative definition of the correspondence between the sub-metamodels on which the view type is based was only possible there (M4.1.1).

The statistic analysis of the ModelJoin example offers an estimation of the reduction of complexity that the flexible view type approach offers: The ModelJoin language reduces the complexity of defining a view type with a multi-metamodel procjectional scope in terms of lines-of-code that have to be written for the transformation (M4.2.2). Regarding the size of the resulting view type metamodel, a significant difference in the size can be identified for the number of references that has been modelled, but not for classes, attributes, or inheritance relations (M4.2.1). Of course, it should be noticed that this comparison disregards the fact that the metamodel still has to be modelled manually, while in the ModelJoin scenario, it is automatically generated by the execution of the query.

7.2.3. Case Study: Automotive Systems Engineering

The construction of automobiles has seen an exponential increase of the usage of software in automobiles during the last 30 years [21]. While more and more software systems are built into automobiles, the construction of these systems suffers from the usage of heterogeneous modelling languages and tooling. Automotive architectural description languages [39] have been proposed as a method to model all relevant information of automotive systems. Domain-specific tools such as MATLAB/Simulink are, however, often required in the development process nevertheless, since they offer specific analyses of the system under development. Model-driven technologies have been used to combine standard languages, such as UML and SysML, with tools such as Simulink [142, 141]. These approaches are, however, limited to a specific combination of two models or languages, and offer only a conversion into one direction instead of full bidirectionality.

To demonstrate the benefits of the VITRUVIUS approach for the automotive systems development, we have applied VITRUVIUS to an automotive system development scenario where three languages are used: SysML, EAST-ADL, and Simulink. Each of these languages incorporates special concepts that are not present in the respective other two. In the following subsections, we will introduce the three languages shortly, describe the VITRUVIUS-based development process, and evaluate the questions of the GQM plan for this scenario.

7.2.3.1. Modelling Languages

SysML The Systems Modeling Language (SysML) [124] is a derivate of the UML2 standard for systems engineering. SysML features a set of nine *diagram types*, which overlaps with the diagram types of UML2: while two diagrams are specific to SysML, five diagrams are identical with those of UML2, and two are modifications of UML2 diagrams. The diagram types cover requirements, structural, and behavioural view points, which can be used for the modelling of hardware, software, and processes.

MATLAB/Simulink Simulink[6] is a graphical programming language for the modelling of dynamic systems. The Simulink tool can be used for analysis and simulation of systems, as well as for code generation. The basic elements in Simulink diagrams are graphical *blocks*, which are connected via ports and signals. Simulink is a proprietary software and is not based on a metamodelling standard. There are, however, several research projects during which a grammar and metamodel for the Simulink file format has been reverse-engineered [68, 143, 3]. These approaches offer a conversion of the Simulink MDT file format into a metamodel-based representation, which can be used for further analysis and transformations.

EAST-ADL The Embedded Architectures and Software Technologies – Architecture Description Language (EAST-ADL) [46] is a language for the automotive domain. The language is organised in four abstraction levels: Vehicle level, analysis level, design level, and implementation level. At each

[6] `http://www.mathworks.com/products/simulink/`, retrieved 12 May 2014

level, the full system is represented at a specific level of detail EAST-ADL integrates concepts from SysML as well as from AUTOSAR. The latter is used to represent the software architecture and implementation details of the hardware. EAST-ADL is supported by a number of tools, including the Eclipse-based demonstrator EATOP,[7] which also contains the EAST-ADL metamodel in Ecore format.

7.2.3.2. Process

Selection/Definition of Metamodels In the first step of the VITRUVIUS process, the methodologist role determines the languages and metamodels that are used in the development of the system and choses or specifies an Ecore-based metamodel for each of these languages. In the automotive scenario, the three modelling languages EAST-ADL, SysML and Simulink are used. Since EAST-ADL and SysML are both model-based concepts, we can use the metamodels of these languages directly. For EAST-ADL, we have used the metamodel defined in conjunction with the EATOP demonstrator. The SysML metamodel has been defined in Ecore format for the TOPCASED tool.[8] Finally, for Simulink, a model-based representation has to be chosen, since the native MDL format of simulink is not based on a metamodel. There are however several efforts in literature to represent Simulink models in a metamodel-based way; in our case study, we have chosen the the approach of [68], which uses the conQAT[9] parser for the conversion of MDL files to instances of a Ecore-based Simulink metamodel, and an Xpand model-to-text transformation for the generation of MDL files from these models.

Specification of View Types After the sub-metamodels of the SUM metamodel have been determined, the methodologist role defines the view types

[7] `https://code.google.com/a/eclipselabs.org/p/eclipse-auto-iwg/wiki/EATOP`, retrieved 12 May 2014

[8] `http://www.topcased.org/`, retrieved 12 May 2014

[9] `https://www.cqse.eu/en/products/conqat/overview/`, retrieved 12 May 2014

that are used to display and modify the modelled system. As a first step, existing diagram types and views are integrated into the SUM metamodel as *legacy view types*. In EAST-ADL, we have identified eight view types, which are defined by the eight top level packages: structure, environment, behaviour, variability, requirements, timing, dependability, and infrastructure. For SysML, the view types are the nine diagram types: block definition diagram, internal block diagram, package diagram, use case diagram, activity diagram, sequence diagram, state machine diagram, requirements diagram, and parametric diagram. Simulink contains only two kinds of structural view types that are relevant for the architectural modelling of systems: block diagrams and state chart diagrams. In total, we have defined 18 legacy view types this way.

In addition to the legacy view types, the methodologist specifies combining view types, which aggregate information from more than one of the metamodels. The existing SysML and Simulink views offer black-box and white-box views of the function blocks: While the SysML block diagram is used to show the connection of blocks, the Simulink view of a block shows the internal definition of control flow. An analysis of the control flow between block requires switching between view types. Thus, a *Grey-box Control Flow View Type*, which combines the assembly information from SysML with the control flow information from Simulink, is desirable.

The EAST-ADL metamodel contains elements for the feature modelling of automotive systems. Similar to SysML, the function blocks are modelled as black-box components. To combine this with the block definitions in Simulink, a customised view has to be created, which combines the information of control flow from the Simulink model with the architectural information from the EAST-ADL model.

Specification of Correspondences After the view types have been specified, concepts in the different metamodels are mapped to each other in MIR (mapping/invariant/response) elements. A MIR mapping definition is defined between each two metamodels, so the methodologist who is responsible for creating the mapping has to be familiar with the concepts in these two metamodels. To gather the semantic correspondences between the metamodels, the methodologist analyses the required combining view types and deducts the necessary mappings in the metamodels of which the view types display information.

In the example scenario, MIR elements have to be defined between Simulink and SysML, and between Simulink and EAST-ADL. These correspondences result from the existing scenarios, where in all cases combinations of two modelling formalisms are used and synchronised by means other than VITRUVIUS, such as the import and export functionalities of the IBM Rational Rhapsody modelling tool[10], which offers a Simulink im- and exporter. Thus, the correspondences are not modelled between each three pairwise combinations of SysML, EAST-ADL and Simulink. Through transitive synchronisation rules, the complete SUM metamodel is covered nevertheless.

The EAST-ADL model of a system also contains concepts for the modelling of functional components, ports, and the connectors between them. Since EAST-ADL is a language specifically designed for the automotive domain, its elements are aligned with the AUTOSAR standard. The relevant part of EAST-ADL that corresponds to the function blocks of SysML and MATLAB/Simulink is the *FunctionModel* sub-package of the EAST-ADL specification. EAST-ADL uses the terminology of AUTOSAR for the functional model. Thus the appearance of a function is called *prototype*, which conforms to a more general *type*. A prototype corresponds to a block in SysML/Simulink. Ports are first-class entities in EAST-ADL: They are bound to prototypes with a *connector* element.

For the functional structure, the classes *FunctionPrototype* with its subclasses *AnalysisFunctionPrototype* and *DesignFunctionPrototype* are of

[10]`http://www-03.ibm.com/software/products/en/ratirhapfami`, retrieved 7 May 2014

Simulink	SysML	EAST-ADL
Block	Block	FunctionType
SimulinkModel	View	
PortBlock	FlowPort	FunctionFlowPort
Line	Connector (UML)	FunctionConnector

Table 7.4.: Mapping of Concepts from SysML, Simulink, and EAST-ADL

relevance. *FunctionFlowPorts* can be connected to these prototypes with *FunctionConnector* elements.

The Modular SUM Metamodel Once the metamodels, view types, and correspondences have been selected or defined by the methodologist, they are combined to form the modular SUM metamodel, which forms a base for development of automotive systems. The three metamodels of SysML, Simulink, and EAST-ADL do not have to be modified in any way to be part of the SUM metamodel. All additional information, such as view type definitions and correspondences, are defined declaratively and do not require invasive changes to the metamodels.

Implementation of Correspondences The correspondences between the elements listed in Table 7.4 have been implemented in the declarative MIR description language [95]. The mapping rules relate the elements via naming conditions. For the Port elements, a special mapping has been defined since the directionality of ports is modelled differently in Simulink than it is modelled in the other two metamodels: While Simulink distinguishes InPortBlock and OutPortBlock model elements, EAST-ADL and SysML contain only concepts for generic port elements with an attribute direction that indicates the nature of the port. The mapping of the concepts is displayed in Figure 7.3. The figure shows the relevant elements from the three metamodels in use, and the mapping of elements as double lines ═.

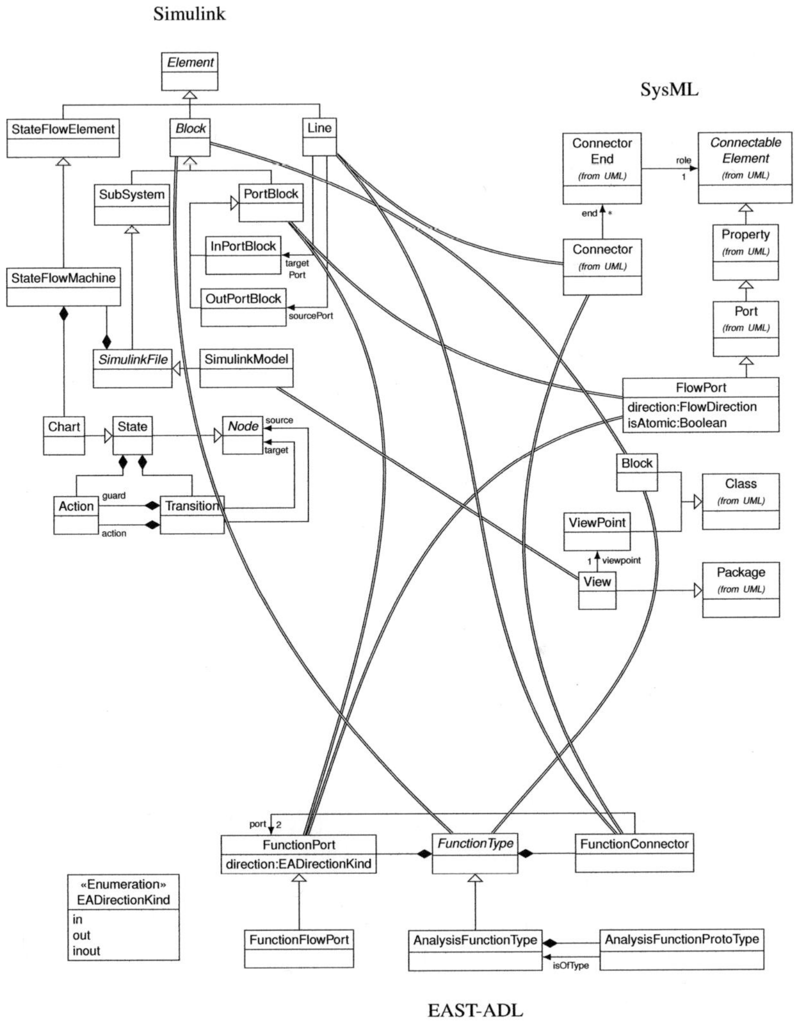

Figure 7.3.: Mapping between the Metamodels of Simulink, SysML, and EAST-ADL (showing relevant excerpts of the metamodels)

Implementation of View Types The 18 legacy view types that have been identified by the methodologist are exposed by the SUM metamodel for compatibility reasons. In addition, two grey-box control flow view types have been specified, which integrate information from Simulink and one of the other sub-metamodels.

The view type that combines information from EAST-ADL and Simulink has been defined with the ModelJoin language. The view type definition is displayed in Listing 15. The methodologist has used the `NATURAL JOIN` feature to establish the connection between the EAST-ADL element FunctionType and the Simulink element SimulinkModel, which represents a special block in the Simulink model that can contain the execution semantics, expressed as a state machine. This element StateFlowMachine is included into the view type, so that the execution semantics of the FunctionType are visible in a grey-box view.

The view types each combine information from two sub-metamodels of the SUM metamodel. A view type that combines more than two elements into a single element cannot be specified in ModelJoin with the current protoype, since joining of more than two elements is not directly possible. In this scenario, however, this limitation does not reduce the expressiveness of the view types, since the information in the SUM is synchronised by the MIR elements between each of the sub-models. Thus, a partial view on, e.g., EAST-ADL and Simulink always contains the updated structure that is synchronised with the SysML sub-model. To integrate information from the SysML sub-model into this view type, it is possible to define a flexible view type that takes the EAST-ADL/Simulink view type and the SysML metamodel (or its block definition diagram view type) as source metamodel. This way, a single view type element can represent information from all three sub-metamodels. Such a view type would reduce fragmentation, but, as mentioned above, would not affect the consistency in the SUM.

```
import "de.uni_paderborn.fujaba.simulink.model"
import "http://east-adl.info/2.1.10/eastadl21/east_adl/structure/
    functionmodeling"

natural join functionmodeling.FunctionType with model.SimulinkModel as
      jointarget.System {
  keep outgoing model.SimulinkFile.stateFlowMachine as type jointarget.
      StateFlowMachine {
    keep outgoing model.stateflow.StateFlowMachine.charts as type
        jointarget.Chart {
      keep supertype model.stateflow.State as type jointarget.State {
        keep attributes model.stateflow.State.name
        keep supertype model.stateflow.Node as type jointarget.Node
        keep outgoing model.stateflow.State.transitions as type
            jointarget.Transitions
          keep outgoing model.stateflow.Transition.source as type
              jointarget.Node
          keep outgoing model.stateflow.Transition.target as type
              jointarget.Node
      }
    }
  }
  keep outgoing functionmodeling.Functionport.Port as type joinTarget.
      Port {
    }
  }
}

theta join functionmodeling.FunctionFlowPort with model.PortBlock
  where "FuncionFlowPort.direction==in␣and␣PortBlock.oclIsKindOf(
      InPortBlock)␣or␣FuncionFlowPort.direction==out␣and␣PortBlock.
      oclIsKindOf(OutPortBlock)"
  as jointarget.FlowPort {
      keep attributes functionmodeling.FunctionFlowPort.direction
      keep attributes model.PortBlock.type
      keep supertype functionmodeling.Flowport as type jointarget.Port
}
```

Listing 15: Grey-Box Control Flow View Type for EAST-ADL and Simulink

Connection with Existing Tools Existing instances that have been modelled in the modelling languages EAST-ADL, SysML, and Simulink, have to be imported into the Ecore-based format to be used in the VITRUVIUS-based process. For EAST-ADL and SysML, this import poses only small effort since the formats are model-based, so that modelling tools either use XMI as the native format or offer an import and export function to XMI. In the case of Simulink, the conversion developed in [142] is used to convert MDT files into the model-based format.

7.2.3.3. Results

In this case study, 18 legacy view types have been defined, which are derived from the diagram types in SysML, the top level packages in EAST-ADL, and the two types block diagram and state chart of Simulink. As mentioned above, each of these three sub-metamodel contains information that cannot be expressed with the respective other two formalisms. In the case study, two combining view types have been specified (M1.1.1) that concern the structural information in the EAST-ADL and SysML sub-metamodel. Although these models also contain formalisms to model the behaviour of systems (*behaviour* view type in EAST-ADL, activity/sequence diagrams in SysML), these formalisms are not used in the scenario in favour of Simulink models. This fragmentation is alleviated by the two grey-box control flow view types (M1.2.1). These view types have been specified with the flexible view type concept.

The three metamodels in the scenario share a high semantic overlap, since they have been designed for very similar purposes in the field of systems modelling. In the scenario, overlaps have only been specified in the parts of the metamodels that describe the structural aspects of the systems, since the functional specification is only modelled in the Simulink part of the models. Thus, the overlapping concepts are those that have been identified in Table 7.4, and which can be seen as the common denominator of systems modelling with blocks, ports, and connectors (M2.1.1). This redundancy is controlled by the MIR elements that have been defined between EAST-ADL and Simulink, and Simulink and SysML (M2.2.1). Since the ModelJoin prototype is at the moment not able to merge more than two source elements into view type elements, it has not been possible to create a view type that contains information from all three of the sub-models with a single ModelJoin query.

Inconsistencies are controlled in the case study between the EAST-ADL submodels and Simulink, as well as between the SysML submodels and the Simulink models. For these purpose, a MIR element has been specfied for each of this cases (M3.1.1). These definition of these MIR elements is defined according to the combining grey-box view types that have been described above. It is in the responsibility of the methodologist to check that the MIR definitions match the semantic overlaps that have been defined for the view types; currently, the VITRUVIUS prototype does not contain any means to check whether they do or do not match. Thus, inconsistencies between the EAST-ADL/SysML model and the Simulink model can be prevented by the MIR elements that result from the combining view types (M3.2.1). Further inconsistencies, which may exist between the EAST-ADL and the SysML model, can be prevented as far as the common Simulink model to which they refer is affected; otherwise, they cannot be prevented.

The reduction of complexity (goal G4) has not been measured in this case study, since a manual implementation of the identified combining view types was not carried out.

7.3. Discussion

The current state of the implementation of the VITRUVIUS and ModelJoin prototypes lack two main features, which have impeded the full validation of the flexible view types concept:

- **Editability:** Currently, the ModelJoin prototype only supports read-only views. Thus, it can only be used to specify the projectional and selectional scopes of flexible view types, but not the editability information.

- **SUM Synchronisation:** The VITRUVIUS prototype is currently being developed and does not yet support the evaluation of MIR elements with automatic synchronisation.

Thus, the validation in this section has focussed on the expressivity of the flexible views concept by showing the coverage of all relevant elements in the Ecore metamodel, as well as the applicability of the approach in software development scenario, and a systems development scenario. The lack of editability in ModelJoin is partly caused by the lacking synchronisation functionality in the VITRUVIUS prototype. Since the synchronisation mechanisms from a view type to a sub-model of the SUM uses the same description concepts for changes in the respective instances, the editability of flexible view types that are defined with ModelJoin have to be aligned with the underlying synchronisation mechanisms.

The case studies show that the flexible views concept as such is appropriate for the definition of views with a multi-metamodel projectional scope, which is a novel concept of the VITRUVIUS approach, and which offers the possibility to integrate information from heterogeneous sub-models into custom view types. Although it is possible to define these view types in a manual way, for example, by creating metamodels and model-to-model transformations by hand, the empirical study in the CBSE scenario has shown that the compact, declarative, and textual definition of flexible view types with the ModelJoin language reduces the complexity of such a definition by a considerable amount. Although the scenarios used real-life metamodels and example systems, the user base for the empirical study was small, so that the results cannot be generalised to all kinds of model-based development scenarios. To investigate the benefits of ModelJoin, further studies should be conducted with a larger user base, and a real-life development scenario with heterogeneous models.

A ModelJoin expression serves as a central point for the definition of a flexible view type. Thus, the potential benefit of ModelJoin is the evolution of view type definitions, either because of external factors such as changes in the source metamodels, or because of internal factors such as desired changes in the semantics of a view type. The investigation of these positive effects in an evolution scenario should be quantified in a larger case study with a realistic evolution scenario. The Palladio Component Model, which has undergone several releases with evolutionary modifications in the past years, could again serve as an example metamodel for such a scenario.

Of the problem areas that have been identified in the introduction of this thesis (subsection 1.2.3), fragmentation and complexity have been adressed most by the case studies in this section. Flexible view types do reduce fragmentation and complexity by integrating information with the novel concept of combining views, so that developers gain an overall view of the system under development. While the problem of controlled redundancy is yet to be fully adressed by the VITRUVIUS prototype in the MIR elements and their implementation, these case studies have shown that the process of first specifying combined view types and then deriving the redundancies in the modular SUM metamodel from them is a viable solution. The problem of inconsistency cannot be solved by flexible view types alone, but depends strongly on the synchronisation mechanisms in the implementation of VITRUVIUS. Nevertheless, flexible views are helpful for the identification of inconsistencies, even if they have to be resolved manually at the current state of the implemenation of VITRUVIUS.

The scenarios in this section have been evaluated against engineering processes where semantic overlaps and interdependencies are not made explicit. We believe that this is a realistic scenario, since existing approaches, to our knowledge, do not offer the possibility to create view types with multi-metamodel projectional scopes, and thus to combine information from heterogeneous sources in a view-based approach. To further evaluate the benefits of VITRUVIUS in general, and the flexible view concept in particular, these scenarios should be extended with realistic instance data from component-based projects and automotive system engineering scenarios, and evaluated against existing approaches (see chapter 3). Although these approaches may only offer parts of the functionality of VITRUVIUS, such as synchronisation between pairs of formalisms, the impacts of existing approaches in the problem fields fragmentation, redundancy, consistency, and complexity should be investigated with larger case studies when a complete VITRUVIUS prototype is available.

8. Future Work

In this chapter, we will identify future work in the development of the Vitruvius approach as well as in the flexible view concept and the ModelJoin language. We will cover potential conceptual advances in these approaches as well as technical developments that have not yet been adressed.

8.1. Vitruvius

8.1.1. Coupling of View Type Definitions with SUM Metamodel Correspondences

During a development process that implements the Vitruvius approach, the methodologist first specifies the desired view types, and then derives the correspondences in the modular SUM metamodel from these specifications; the identification of desired combined view types serves as a requirements document and a starting point for the definition of the correspondences in ←(MIR)→ elements. After the specification of correspondences, the methodologist implements the view types by using either the flexible view concept, or by manual implementation of the view types and the necessary transformations. Although the information about how information is combined is strongly coupled to the way in which elements in the SUM are related to each other, it is, however, not possible with the current methods of Vitruvius to create the correspondences from the view types automatically or vice versa. To derive the correspondences from the view type specification, the methodologist has to implement the MIR manually and respect the information in the view type information while doing so. Since this semantic relation is not formalised in the SUM, it cannot be checked automatically whether a view type definition is compliant with the correspondences that are defined between the sub-metamodels of the modular SUM metamodel. Thus, the conciseness of these definitions has to be determined manually at every change, which can lead to co-evolution problems if one of these definitions is altered independently of the other.

The absence of a connection between view type definitions and MIR elements also leads to problems of editability at runtime: When instances in a view are modified, this can lead to the violation of consistency constraints in the SUM, which may not be resolved automatically. For projectional view types, this behaviour is tolerable since a view type should not have to be aware of all possible consistency violations that may occur. For combining view types, however, modification operations should not violate the consistency constraints between the sub-metamodels from which they combine the information.

The cross-pollination of consistency constraints in the SUM on the one side and in the view types on the other side is thus an important factor in the creation of a modular SUM metamodel. In the process of installing the VITRUVIUS approach, the methodologist first defines the desired view types, then implements the MIR relations, and finally implements the view types. Thus, a method should be developed to derive properties of the combined view types from the MIR definitions and to check whether they conform to each other.

8.1.2. Mapping to Textual General Purpose Programming Languages

The case studies that have been presented in this dissertation deal with the combination of metamodels that mostly describe the structural properties of systems in graphical languages such as PCM, UML, SysML, and EAST-ADL. Recent advances in model-driven engineering offer metamodel-based representations of textual languages, so that model-based tools can be used to deal with textually defined languages. These approaches have been used to define a model-based representation of general-purpose programming languages such as Java. Examples for such projects are the KDM Java metamodel of MoDisCo (Model Discovery) [23], or JaMoPP (Java Model Printer and Parser) [66], which is based on EMFText[1].

The integration of such metamodel-based representations into the VITRUVIUS approach is subject of ongoing research [103]. The support of general purpose programming languages is an important step towards the overall vision of Orthographic Software Modeling, which the VITRUVIUS approach aims to realise, that all the information available on the system under development is represented in a single underlying model. Although the technical representation of program code in a model-based format does not pose a real challenge with the aforementioned tools, the synchronisation of these models with the other sub-models of the SUM is yet to be investigated. Proposed benefits of such a synchronisation could be the automatic checking of architecture rule violations in the implementation of a system, support in the refactoring of systems across several formalisms, and a higher usability of code generators, since the generated code would stay synchronised with the other sub-models in the SUM even after manual adaptations of the code.

8.1.3. Versioning

As mentioned above, the VITRUVIUS approach aims to cover all aspects of a software engineering process. This also includes meta-information of the artefacts that are developed. The support of *versioning* elements in a model is normally achieved by specialised tools that offer the connection between file-based versioning systems, such as Subversion or Git. These systems work very well for the management of text-based documents, and developers are usually familiar with the differencing and merging of textual formats. For model-based data, special differencing and merging tools,

[1] `http://www.emftext.org/index.php/EMFText`, retrieved on 9 May 2014

such as EMFCompare [22] have been developed. The Edapt tool, although developed as a a metamodel co-evolution approach, can also be used as an operator-based versioning tool [71].

With VITRUVIUS, the information about the version history of each element in a SUM can, however, be recorded in a semantically rich way, since all change operations to the instances in a SUM are carried out by atomic change operators, which are propagated between the model elements. Thus, it is possible to encode the information of the history of a model element directly into the SUM, so that the elements are aware of their own version and can also carry a record of how (and why) they have been modified. Since the elements in the SUM can exclusively be modified by the view types that are defined on the modular SUM metamodel, this information can be stored with richer semantic information than in ordinary versioning systems. For example, the cause for a change in a model element can be traced back to a manual change via a view type, a change because of a synchronisation response that was triggered in another part of the SUM metamodel, or to the violation of a specific consistency rule. Since all this context information can be derived automatically from the synchronisation mechanisms in the SUM, the context of a change would less depend on the interactions of developers, which have to describe changes in a meaningful textual description, e.g., in a commit message of the versioning system.

The support for versioning could be realised as a special small metamodel, which is truly orthogonal to every other metamodel in the modular SUM metamodel, and which is supported by default in every implementation of VITRUVIUS.

8.1.4. Metamodel Evolution in the Modular SUM Metamodel

The modular SUM metamodel that is used in a VITRUVIUS-based project is initially defined by a methodologist. The metamodel can be created specifically for a project, or an existing SUM metamodel can be re-used from similar types of projects. In most cases, the modular SUM metamodel will contain legacy metamodels that have to be supported because of external factors, such as compatibility to tools or because of other obligations. Thus, the development cycle of these metamodels is not in the control of the methodologist; if a new version of such a metamodel has to be supported, adaptations are necessary to the modular SUM metamodel. These adaptations may either be applied by defining new view types, which act as a compatibility layer between the SUM metamodel and the new version, or by modifying the sub-metamodels of the SUM metamodel directly. The latter approach has the advantage that migration scripts, which may be provided by the creator of the metamodel that is evolving, can be used to co-evolve existing instances of this sub-metamodel. It has, however, the disadvantage that all adjacent elements of the SUM metamodel, such as MIR definitions and view type definitions, also have to co-evolve. While co-evolution of metamodels and instances [70, 27] as well as the co-evolution of metamodels and transformations [99] have been investigated in related work, the effect of metamodel evolution on the VITRUVIUS-specific artefacts (MIR definitions, flexible view types) has not been investigated yet and is the subject of future work.

8.1.5. VITRUVIUS for Non-Software Engineering Models

The VITRUVIUS approach has its roots in the Orthographic Software Modeling approach and has thus initially been developed for scenarios where software engineering is the central part of development. Metamodels and model-based tools are, however, used in a large number of disciplines where the users of these tools are not software developers, but other engineers, such as electrical engineers, mechanical engineers, and so on. Especially in the development of cyber-physical systems [108], which contain software and non-software parts that are both modelled in specialised languages, inconsistencies and redundancies also lead to problems that could be adressed with the VITRUVIUS approach.

Although the case studies in this dissertation are focussed on software modelling languages, the VITRUVIUS approach as such is a general approach that is not limited to software metamodels. It can be used to model any kind of data that can be represented as instances of an Ecore-based metamodel. Since, in contrast to UML, the Ecore metamodel is not a software-specific meta-metamodel, it is not limited to the software engineering domain. The aptitude of VITRUVIUS for these models would have to be tested with more case studies that cross the borders of software development and the modelling of other systems, such as energy nets, network topologies, traffic simulation, production plant planning, and other systems.

8.2. Flexible View Types

8.2.1. Editability

The ModelJoin language currently only contains constructs for the definition of read-only views. Thus, it can only be used for the definition of the projectional and selectional scope of flexible view types, but not for the definition of the editability of the elements in the generated view types and views. Furthermore, the generated view types and views do not offer any synchronisation mechanism for the propagation of changes that are applied in a view back to the source models.

To support the definition of editability scopes, as defined for flexible view types in subsection 6.1.3, the ModelJoin language must be extended by the following concepts:

- **Inherent Editability and Synchronisation Mode of ModelJoin Operators:** The definition of view types with the ModelJoin language offers the advantage that the purpose of the view type is expressed declaratively with the well-defined operators of the ModelJoin DSL.

The definition of these operators should be extended by a default editability behaviour, so that the effects of an element that has been created by, e.g., a keep reference or a join statement, are clear to the developer, and that an editable view can be generated automatically using the automatic synchronisation mode.

- **Editability Specifications:** In addition to the inherent editability of view type elements that have been created by a specific ModelJoin operator, the user of ModelJoin should have the possibility to specify the editability scope at the metamodel level. Since the operators of ModelJoin describe the elements in the target metamodel, which acts as the view type, additional language elements for the existing keep operators could be introduced, which describe the editability scope of of the target metamodel element. At the instance level, the editability scope description would require that single instances are identified by a universal unique identifier (UUID) or an unambiguous name; although this would also be possible in the ModelJoin DSL, it would restrict a ModelJoin query to a certain set of instances, and hinder its re-use for other instances. Thus, the instance-level editability scope should better be specified in an graphical or tree-based editor that shows the actual instances that are in the result set of an actual execution of a ModelJoin query.

- **Synchronisation Modes:** The synchronisation modes for flexible view types (automatic, select policy, manual, see subsection 6.1.3) should be specifiable within a ModelJoin query. While the automatic synchronisation mode, as mentioned above, should be active by default, the extension of the ModelJoin behaviour by the editability behaviour should include policies that are specific to the respective operation. For example, a modification to an element in a view that was created by a join operator could be propagated to the source models by changing the left element, the right element, or both (if it is allowed at all). These policies can be selected by the user by including additional language constructs to the respective ModelJoin operators.

These extensions mentioned here would amend the ModelJoin DSL at the conceptual level. The prototypical implementation of ModelJoin would of course also have to be extended by new, essential functionality. Although the ModelJoin prototype is a stand-alone tool that can be used independently of VITRUVIUS, an integration of the ModelJoin engine into the VITRUVIUS workbench would profit from the synchronisation mechanisms of VITRUVIUS to realise the editability of view types. The definition of editability in subsection 6.1.3 is compatible with the planned definition of change propagation in the VITRUVIUS approach, so that the synchronisation mechanisms, once implemented, can also be used with ModelJoin.

8.2.2. Metamodel Conformance Checking

The metamodel conformance checking in ModelJoin (see subsection 6.2.4) can be used to find a suiting metamodel from a repository that can be used with a specific query. The current prototype of the conformance checker implements a simple metric that presents to the developer of a view type the number of conflicts that exist between the view type definition in the current ModelJoin query, and the existing metamodels in the repository. These conflicts have to be solved manually by the developer. To assist the developer in adjusting the ModelJoin query in such a way that the conformance to an existing metamodel is given, the ModelJoin editor should offer the developer the information on which statement is responsable for the non-conformance, and also possible hints on corrections (quick-fixes) that would establish conformance.

Although this is mainly a convenience function for the developer of the ModelJoin query, the tracing of view type elements to the actual expression in the textual ModelJoin definition can also be helpful in the development process of a view type in general: Since the ModelJoin definition of a view type can also be seen as a documentation on the purpose of the view type, the traceability between the generated view type and this definition would increase the quality of the documentation of the generated view type. Since the protoype of ModelJoin uses the Xtext[2] framework to define the grammar of ModelJoin, and to generate the textual editors, a model-based representation of the textual queries is available during the process of executing the query. Thus, the traceability information could be encoded into the target metamodel during the metamodel synthesis step by linking it to the Xtext model.

Furthermore, the repository that stores the target metamodels for comparison is currently implemented as a simple, file-based registry of Ecore metamodels [30]. In future versions, the conformance validator can be extended to support other metamodel repositories, such as CDO[3], Teneo[4], or EMFStore.[5] These repositories offer a database backend and are thus suited for large amounts of instances. This is especially important if target metamodels of former ModelJoin queries are persisted frequently, which would lead to a large number of metamodels that have to be persisted and loaded for comparison. A metamodel repository that supports versioning of metamodels is beneficial in this case to record the history of changes to a ModelJoin query and the generated target metamodel. To keep these artefacts consistent, the repository can also save the model-based Xtext representation of the ModelJoin query together with the target metamodel.

[2] `http://www.eclipse.org/Xtext/`, retrieved 9 May 2014
[3] `http://www.eclipse.org/cdo`, retrieved 9 May 2014
[4] `http://wiki.eclipse.org/Teneo`, retrieved 9 May 2014
[5] `http://www.eclipse.org/emfstore`, retrieved 9 May 2014

8.2.3. Performance Properties of the ModelJoin Algorithms and Implementation

The ModelJoin prototype consists of two main components that contain complex execution logic: The *metamodel synthesis* component and the *transformation generation* component (see Figure 6.7 on page 200). The performance of these components in terms of execution time and memory consumption depends on several factors: size of the input metamodels, size of the input models, size of the query, and complexity of the query. To test the runtime behaviour of the ModelJoin prototype, a systematic exploration of these parameters is necessary. The problem with a systematic variation of this parameters is, however, that the metamodels, models, and queries have to conform to each other, and should also produce reasonable results. Thus, an automatic generation of test cases and data requires a sophisticated mechanism for the creation of appropriate models.

To address this problem, a synthetic test framework for ModelJoin is currently under development.[6] The framework incorporates advanced concepts for the parameterised creation of synthetic metamodels, instances and matching queries. Furthermore, it already provides the measurement of execution times for the ModelJoin metamodel synthesizer and transformation generator. To explore the multi-dimensional parameter space of the synthesizer, an adapter for the Software Performance Cockpit (SoPeCo) [155] experimentation tool has been developed.

In future work, the model and query synthesizer can be used to create extensive tests of the ModelJoin implementation. With these test, the interdependencies between the various size dimensions of the input data and runtime behaviour can be measured. At the moment, the performance of the ModelJoin prototype is expected to depend mostly on the metamodel and query size. The size of the input instances only effects the query execution, which is carried out by the QVT-O engine of the Eclipse Modelling

[6]`https://sdqweb.ipd.kit.edu/wiki/ModelJoin/Synthetic_Tests`, retrieved 7 May 2014

Framework. The test framework offers, however, means to measure the execution time of this engine seperately from the components of the ModelJoin prototype. The investigation of the behaviour of ModelJoin with large amounts of data is an important factor for the aptitude of ModelJoin for model-based scenarios such as automotive systems development, which can contain thousands of elements.

9. Conclusion

The view-based VITRUVIUS approach pursues the vision of model-based development that "Everything is a model", and aims to reach this goal with the concept of Orthographic Software Engineering that the system under development, in all its facets, is represented by a single underlying model, and that automatically generated, user-specific views give developers access to the information in this model.

In this thesis, we have presented a systematic construction method for a modular SUM metamodel, which integrates legacy metamodels non-intrusively, and thus provides compatibility to existing metamodels and standards. To this end, the relation of views and view types to the single underlying model and its metamodel has been formalised, including the description of view and view types scopes and editability. The construction of the modular SUM metamodel is embedded in a view-centric development process, with which existing software development processes can be migrated to a VITRUVIUS-based process, or which can be used for the instantiation of VITRUVIUS-based development projects. The process is founded on the development process and developer role model of OSM and refines the creation of the SUM and its metamodel as well as the description of the OSM-specific developer role *methodologist*.

Metamodel evolution affects every development process that makes use of metamodels and models at some point. The change metamodel that has been presented in this thesis offers a uniform way of representing modifications at the metamodel level as well as at the instance level. This representation is the base of a change impact analysis that can be used to determine the effects of changes to metamodels on existing instances without executing the changes. This is an important contribution to metamodel design and supports metamodel developers in the planning of the releases of new versions of a metamodel. Based on this analysis, a conformance relation between metamodels has been defined in this thesis, which describes the substitutability between different versions of a metamodel or between structurally similar metamodels. The change metamodel is agnostic of whether the changes are elicited in a delta-based or in a state-based way. The state-based conformance checking, which has been presented in this thesis, offers a tool-independent analysis of metamodel changes for determining possible re-use of metamodels.

The flexible view types concept, which is the main contribution of this thesis, has been developed for the purpose of defining custom, user-specific views on heterogeneous models. The approach has been implemented in the textual, declarative *ModelJoin* query language, which offers a compact description method for the rapid definition of flexible view types. In the context of VITRUVIUS, flexible views can be used both by methodologists and users to define view types on the modular SUM metamodel. The ability of *ModelJoin* to integrate data from heterogeneous models into highly customizable view types, which exceed the possibilities of pure projectional model query approaches, allow methodologists to define view types as independent, stable interfaces on heterogeneous model data, and allow developers to define user-specific view types that satisfy information needs that were not foreseen by the methodologist during the creation of the SUM metamodel.

Although the development of a prototype that implements all phases of the VITRUVIUS development process is ongoing work, the metamodel evolution methods as well as the flexible view type definitions with the *ModelJoin* have been implemented and can be used independently of the planned VITRUVIUS prototype. The completeness of the *ModelJoin* language has been evaluated by a reachability analysis for the elements in the Ecore metamodel. While the aptitude of the ModelJoin language for the definition of the projectional and selectional scope of view types has been demonstrated successfully, an extension of the language to support the definition of editability scopes is considered desirable. The VITRUVIUS process as a whole has been evaluated with a scenario from the field of component-based software development, and a scenario from the field of the development of embedded software in the automotive domain. The scenarios have been analysed with the VITRUVIUS development process that has been presented in this thesis. Since the VITRUVIUS protoype does not yet support the implementation of SUM metamodels and the synchronisation policies for their sub-metamodels, the development of the modular SUM metamodel has been described at the conceptual level for these scenarios, while the view type definition has been conducted using the ModelJoin prototype. The evaluation of the scenarios revealed semantic dependencies between the formalisms that had not been specified before, and would have been managed manually, or in a non-uniform way through particular synchronisation mechanisms of specialised tools. Fragmentation and complexity can be reduced best by the introduction of flexible views and the VITRUVIUS approach, while the introduction of controlled redundancy and the reduction of inconsistencies have yet to be evaluated fully once the VITRUVIUS prototype is available.

The VITRUVIUS approach and the flexible view types offer new perspectives for the development of software and the combination of software models with non-software domain models, such as energy topology models, traffic simulations, production plant planning, and other systems. The foundation of model-based development and sophisticated methods for automatic synchronisation and generation of views offer developers of domain-specific software als well as users means to create view types and views rapidly, while reducing the accidental complexity of managing large models and heterogeneous formalisms. Flexible views give users access to consistent, up-to-date, and complete information about the system under consideration, which is tailored to the information needs of different developer roles.

A. ModelJoin Language Definition

```
grammar edu.kit.ipd.sdq.mdsd.ModelJoin with org.eclipse.xtext.common.
    Terminals
import "http://www.eclipse.org/emf/2002/Ecore" as ecore
generate modelJoin "http://www.kit.edu/ipd/sdq/mdsd/ModelJoin"

Grammar:
   (imports+=Import)*
   (target+=Target)
   (joinExpr+=JoinExpr)*;

JoinExpr :
   (NaturalJoinExpr | LeftOuterJoinExpr | ThetaJoinExpr) 'as'
       targetType=CpxID
   ('{'
   (keepAttributesExpr+=KeepAttributesExpr)?
   (keepCalcAttributesExpr+=KeepCalcAttributesExpr)?
   (keepAggregatesExpr+=KeepAggregateExpr)?
   keepExpr+=KeepExpr*
   '}')?
   ;

NaturalJoinExpr:
   'natural' 'join' left=[ecore::EClass|CpxID] 'with' right=[ecore::
       EClass|CpxID]
;

LeftOuterJoinExpr:
```

```
   'left' 'outer' 'join' left=[ecore::EClass|CpxID] 'with' right=[
        ecore::EClass|CpxID]
;

ThetaJoinExpr:
   'theta' 'join' left=[ecore::EClass|CpxID] 'with' right=[ecore::
        EClass|CpxID] 'where' condition=STRING
;

KeepExpr :
      (KeepTypeExpr | KeepOutgoingExpr | KeepIncomingExpr)
      ('{'
      (keepAttributesExpr+=KeepAttributesExpr)?
      (keepCalcAttributesExpr+=KeepCalcAttributesExpr)?
      (keepAggregatesExpr+=KeepAggregateExpr)?
      keepExpr+=KeepExpr*
      '}')?
;

KeepTypeExpr :
   KeepSuperTypeExpr | KeepSubTypeExpr
;

KeepSuperTypeExpr :
   'keep' 'supertype' superType=[ecore::EClass|CpxID]
      ('as' 'type' targetSuperType=CpxID)?
;

KeepSubTypeExpr :
   'keep' 'subtype' subType=[ecore::EClass|CpxID]
      ('as' 'type' targetSubType=CpxID)?
;

KeepOutgoingExpr :
```

```
   'keep' 'outgoing' outgoing=[ecore::EReference|CpxID]
      ('as' 'type' targetOutgoing=CpxID ('as' 'reference'
          targetReference=CpxID)?)?
;

KeepIncomingExpr :
   'keep' 'incoming' incoming=[ecore::EReference|CpxID]
      ('as' 'type' targetIncoming=CpxID ('as' 'reference'
          targetReference=CpxID)?)?
;

KeepAttributesExpr :
   'keep' 'attributes' attribute=[ecore::EAttribute|CpxID] (','
        attributes+=[ecore::EAttribute|CpxID])*
;

KeepAggregateExpr :
   'keep' 'aggregate' aggregate+=KeepAggregate (','aggregate+=
        KeepAggregate)*
;

KeepCalcAttributesExpr :
   'keep' 'calculated' 'attribute' calculateRule=STRING 'as'
        targetAttribute=CpxID
;

KeepAggregate:
   KeepNumericalAggregate | KeepCollectionAggregate
;

KeepNumericalAggregate :
   aggregateKind=NumericalAggregateKind'('value=[ecore::EAttribute|
        CpxID]')'
```

```
      'over' context=[ecore::EReference|CpxID] 'as' targetAttribute=
          CpxID
;

KeepCollectionAggregate :
   aggregateKind=CollectionAggregateKind (
   '('value=[ecore::EAttribute|CpxID]')' 'over' context=[ecore::
        EReference|CpxID]
   | '('value=[ecore::EReference|CpxID]')'
   ) 'as' targetAttribute=CpxID
;

enum NumericalAggregateKind :
   SUM='sum' | AVG='avg' | MIN='min' | MAX='max'
;

enum CollectionAggregateKind :
   SIZE='size'
;

WhereExpr :
   'true'
;

Projection :
      star='*'
   |  id=ID
   |  cId=CpxID
;

Import:
   'import' importURI=STRING
;
```

```
Target:
   'target' targetURI=STRING
;

CpxID : ID ('.' ID)+;

PackageQualifiedID : ID ('::' ID)* '::' (CpxID|ID) ;
```

Listing 16: Definition of the Concrete Syntax of ModelJoin as an Xtext Grammar

B. Change Classification for Metamodel Evolution

#	Name	Atomic/ Complex	Severity	Derivable
Structural Primitives				
1	Create Package	A	NB	✓
2	Delete Package	A	BR	✓
3	Create Class	A	NB	✓
4	Delete Class	A	BR	✓
5	Create Attribute	A		✓
	– mandatory		BN	
	– non-mandatory		NB	
6	Create Reference	A		✓
	– mandatory		BN	
	– non-mandatory		NB	
7	Delete Feature	A	BR	✓
8	Create Oppos. Ref.	C		✓
	– mandatory		BR	
	– non-mandatory		NB	
9	Delete Oppos. Ref.	C	BR	✓
10	Create Data Type	A	NB	✓
11	Delete Data Type	A	BR	✓
12	Create Enum	A	NB	✓
13	Delete Enum	A	BR	✓
14	Create Literal	A	NB	✓

15	Merge Literal	C	BR	✗
Non-Structural Primitives				
1	Rename	A	BR	✗
2	Change Package	C	BR	✓
3	Make Class Abstract	A	BR	✓
4	Drop Class Abstract	A	NB	✓
5	Add Super Type	A		✓
	– mandatory features		BR	
	– no mandatory feat.		NB	
6	Remove Super Type	A	BR	✓
7	Make Attr. Identifier	A	BN	✓
8	Drop Attr. Identifier	A	NB	✓
9	Make Ref. Comp.	A	BR	✓
10	Switch Ref. Comp.	A	BR	✓
11	Make Ref. Opposite	A	NB	✓
12	Drop Ref. Opposite	A	NB	✓
Specialization/Generalization Operators				
1	Generalize Attribute	C	NB	
2	Specialize Attribute	C	BN	
3	Generalize Reference	C	NB	
4	Specialize Reference	C	BN	
5	Specialize Comp. Ref.	C	BN	
6	General. Super Type	C	NB	
7	Specialize Super Type	C	BN	
Inheritance Operators				
1	Pull up Feature	C		✓
	– mandatory			
	– supercl. abstract		NB	
	– supercl. not abstract		BN	

	– non-mandatory		NB	
2	Push down Feature	C	NB	✓
3	Extract Super Class	C	NB	✓
4	Inline Super Class	C		✗
	– abstract		NB	
	– not abstract		BR	
5	Fold Super Class	C	BR	✗
6	Unfold Super Class	C	BR	✗
7	Extract Sub Class	C	BR	✓
8	Inline Sub Class	C	BR	✓
Delegation Operators				
1	Extract Class	C	BR	✓
2	Inline Class	C	BR	✓
3	Fold Class	C	BR	✓
4	Unfold Class	C	BR	✓
5	Move Feat. over Ref.	C	BR	✓
6	Collect Feat. over Ref.	C	BR	✓
Replacement Operators				
1	Subclasses to Enum.	C	BR	✗
2	Enum. to Subclasses	C	BN	✗
3	Reference to Class	C	BR	✗
4	Class to Reference	C	BR	✗
5	Inheritance to Deleg.	C	BR	✓
6	Deleg. to Inheritance	C	BN	✓
7	Reference to Identifier	C	BR	✗
8	Identifier to Reference	C	BR	✗
Merge/Split Operators				
1	Merge Features	C	BR	✗
2	Split Ref. by Type	C	BR	✗

3	Merge Classes	C	BR	✗
4	Split Class	C	BR	✗
5	Merge Enumerations	C	BR	✗

C. Example Metamodels

C.1. PCM Metamodel

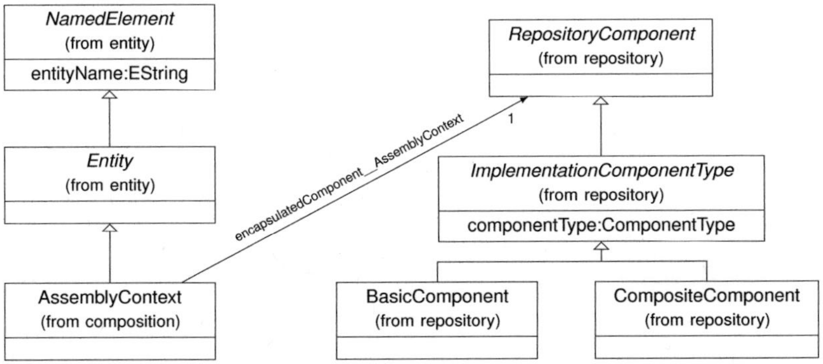

Figure C.1.: Strongly Simplified Extract of the Palladio Component Metamodel (from [29])

C.2. IMDB/Library example

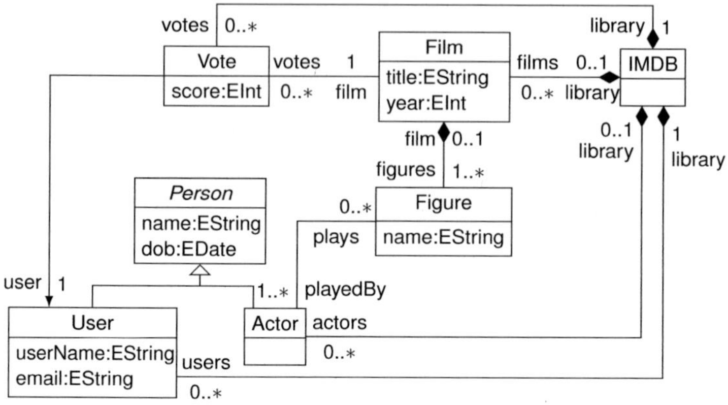

Figure C.2.: IMDB Metamodel

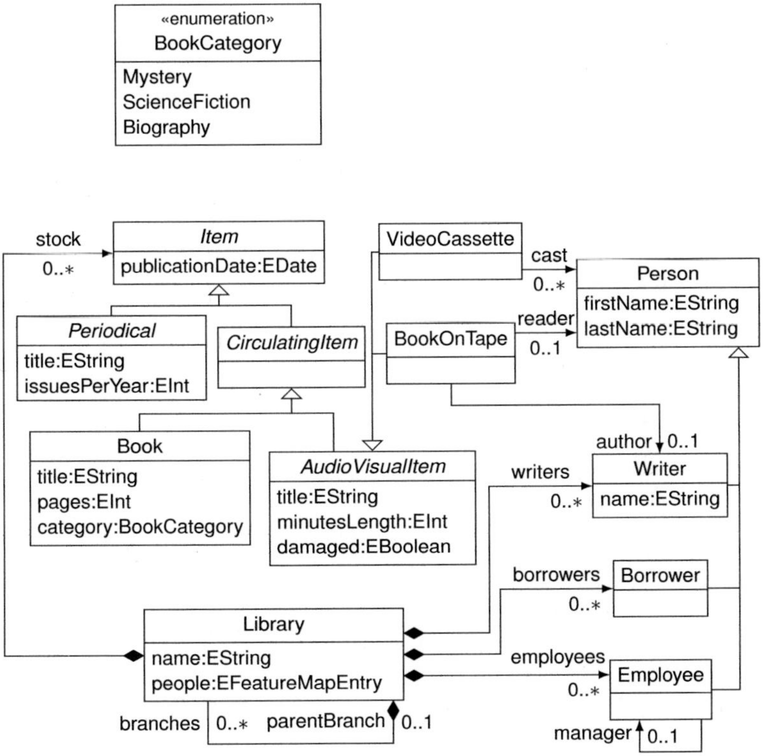

Figure C.3.: Library Metamodel

D. ModelJoin Experiment Task Sheet

D.1. Preparations

- Open an Eclipse Modeling Tools 4.2 with installed PCM 3.4 (available via Eclipse Marketplace) and QVT-O support.
- Import the project provided in the Zip file or check it out from SVN (`https://svnserver.informatik.kit.edu/i43/svn/code/MDSD/trunk/edu.kit.ipd.sdq.mdsd.mj.experiment`) into your workspace.
- Install the Sensor Model plug-in found in the lib folder in the dropins folder of your Eclipse and restart Eclipse.

D.2. Task

Your task is to create an integrated view type (i.e., metamodel) and view on the Sensor Model and the Palladio Component Model. The metamodel of the Sensor Model is depicted in Figure D.1.

In this view type, the measured sensor statistic values, in terms of response time (mean, stddev and variance), are assigned to the corresponding Palladio assembly contexts and components. The view type shall be a partial view type that omits all unnecessary details.

Hint: Since the Sensor Model does not reference the PCM directly, the assignment of `Sensor` elements to PCM model elements has to be made by the `sensorName` attribute, which contains the ID of the PCM element (see the example measurements contained in the Zip file).

D.2.1. Create a new Metamodel

As first step, create a new metamodel that resembles your view type and later on will be the target for your transformation. Therefore, only include those classes, relations and attributes relevant for the task.

D.2.2. Create the Transformation

Create a QVT-O transformation that produces the desired views for the given model and measurement (found in `measurements.xmi`). You can build upon the transformation stub included in the transforms directory. If necessary, adapt your target view type/metamodel to fit your transformation.

D.2.3. Results

Please send the results via mail to Erik Burger or check them into your personal sub-folder at `https://svnserver.informatik.kit.edu/i43/svn/paper/2012/Burger_SoSyM/experiment`

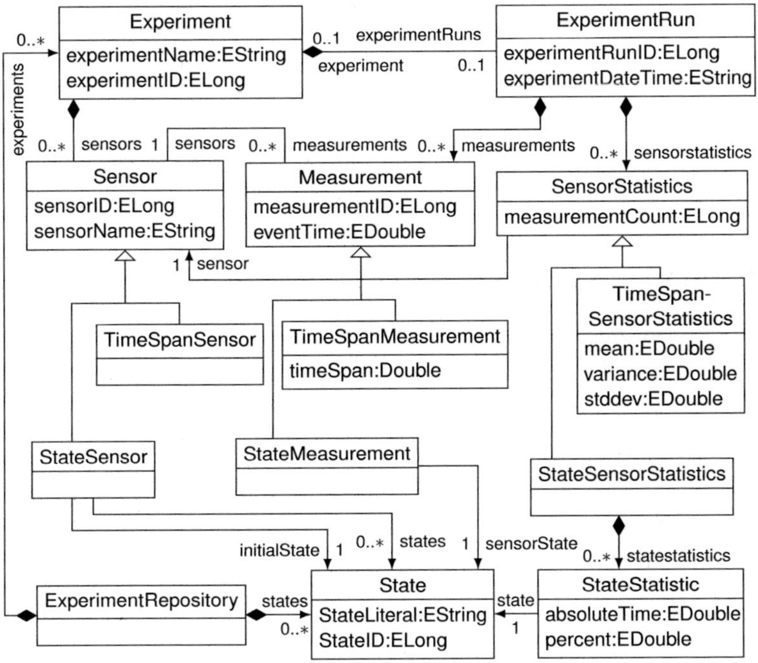

Figure D.1.: The Sensor Model Metamodel

Bibliography

[1] Marcus Alanen and Ivan Porres. "Difference and Union of Models". In: *"UML 2003" – The Unified Modeling Language, Modeling Languages and Applications 6th International Conference, San Francisco, CA, USA, October 20–24, 2003, Proceedings*. Ed. by Perdita Stevens, Jon Whittle and Grady Booch. Vol. 2863. Lecture Notes in Computer Science. Berlin/Heidelberg: Springer Verlag, 2003, pp. 2–17. ISBN: 978-3-540-20243-1.

[2] Michał Antkiewicz, Krzysztof Czarnecki and Matthew Stephan. "Engineering of Framework-Specific Modeling Languages". In: *Software Engineering, IEEE Transactions on* 35.6 (Nov. 2009), pp. 795–824. ISSN: 0098-5589. DOI: 10.1109/TSE.2009.30.

[3] Eric Armengaud, Markus Zoier, Andreas Baumgart, Matthias Biehl, DeJiu Chen, Gerhard Griessnig, Christian Hein, Tom Ritter and Ramin Tavakoli Kolagari. "Model-based Toolchain for the Efficient Development of Safety-Relevant Automotive Embedded Systems". In: *SAE 2011 World Congress & Exhibition*. 2011.

[4] Uwe Aßmann, Steffen Zschaler and Gerd Wagner. "Ontologies, Meta-models, and the Model-Driven Paradigm". In: *Ontologies for Software Engineering and Software Technology*. Ed. by Coral Calero, Francisco Ruiz and Mario Piattini. Springer Berlin Heidelberg, 2006, pp. 249–273. ISBN: 978-3-540-34517-6. DOI: 10.1007/3-540-34518-3_9. URL: http://dx.doi.org/10.1007/3-540-34518-3_9.

[5] Colin Atkinson, Philipp Bostan, Daniel Brenner, Giovanni Falcone, Matthias Gutheil, Oliver Hummel, Monika Juhasz and Dietmar Stoll. "Modeling Components and Component-Based Systems in KobrA". In: *The Common Component Modeling Example*. Ed. by Andreas Rausch, Ralf Reussner, Raffaela Mirandola and František Plášil. Vol. 5153. Lecture Notes in Computer Science. Berlin/Heidelberg: Springer, 2008, pp. 54–84. URL: http://dx.doi.org/10.1007/978-3-540-85289-6_4.

[6] Colin Atkinson, Matthias Gutheil and Bastian Kennel. "A Flexible Infrastructure for Multilevel Language Engineering". In: *Software Engineering, IEEE Transactions on* 35.6 (Nov. 2009), pp. 742–755. ISSN: 0098-5589. DOI: 10.1109/TSE.2009.31.

[7] Colin Atkinson, Dietmar Stoll and Philipp Bostan. "Orthographic Software Modeling: A Practical Approach to View-Based Development". In: *Evaluation of Novel Approaches to Software Engineering*. Ed. by Leszek A. Maciaszek, César González-Pérez and Stefan Jablonski. Vol. 69. Communications in Computer and Information Science. Berlin/Heidelberg: Springer, 2010, pp. 206–219. ISBN: 978-3-642-14819-4.

[8] Franz Baader, Diego Calvanese, Deborah L. McGuinness, Daniele Nardi and Peter F. Patel-Schneider, eds. *The Description Logic Handbook: Theory, Implementation, and Applications*. New York, NY, USA: Cambridge University Press, 2003. ISBN: 0-521-78176-0.

[9] François Bancilhon and Nicolas Spyratos. "Update semantics of relational views". In: *ACM Trans. Database Syst.* 6.4 (Dec. 1981), pp. 557–575. ISSN: 0362-5915. DOI: 10.1145/319628.319634.

[10] Elisa Baniassad and Siobhan Clarke. "Theme: An Approach for Aspect-Oriented Analysis and Design". In: *Proceedings of the 26th International Conference on Software Engineering*. ICSE '04. Washington, DC, USA: IEEE Computer Society, 2004, pp. 158–167.

ISBN: 0-7695-2163-0. URL: http://portal.acm.org/citation.cfm?id=998675.999390.

[11] Victor R. Basili, Gianluigi Caldiera and H. Dieter Rombach. "The Goal Question Metric Approach". In: *Encyclopedia of Software Engineering - 2 Volume Set*. Ed. by John J. Marciniak. John Wiley & Sons, 1994, pp. 528–532.

[12] Steffen Becker, Heiko Koziolek and Ralf Reussner. "Model-based Performance Prediction with the Palladio Component Model". In: *Proceedings of the 6th International Workshop on Software and Performance (WOSP2007)*. ACM Sigsoft, Feb. 2007.

[13] Steffen Becker, Heiko Koziolek and Ralf Reussner. "The Palladio component model for model-driven performance prediction". In: *Journal of Systems and Software* 82 (2009), pp. 3–22. DOI: 10.1016/j.jss.2008.03.066. URL: http://dx.doi.org/10.1016/j.jss.2008.03.066.

[14] Bernhard Beckert, Uwe Keller and Peter H. Schmitt. "Translating the Object Constraint Language into First-order Predicate Logic". In: *In Proceedings, VERIFY, Workshop at Federated Logic Conferences (FLoC*. 2002, pp. 113–123.

[15] Gábor Bergmann, István Ráth, Gergely Varró and Dániel Varró. "Change-driven model transformations". English. In: *Software & Systems Modeling* 11.3 (2012), pp. 431–461. ISSN: 1619-1366. DOI: 10.1007/s10270-011-0197-9. URL: http://dx.doi.org/10.1007/s10270-011-0197-9.

[16] Jean Bézivin. "On the unification power of models". English. In: *Software & Systems Modeling* 4.2 (2005), pp. 171–188. ISSN: 1619-1366. DOI: 10.1007/s10270-005-0079-0. URL: http://dx.doi.org/10.1007/s10270-005-0079-0.

[17] Aaron Bohannon, Benjamin C. Pierce and Jeffrey A. Vaughan. “Relational Lenses: A Language for Updatable Views”. In: *Proceedings of the Twenty-fifth ACM SIGMOD-SIGACT-SIGART Symposium on Principles of Database Systems*. PODS ’06. Chicago, IL, USA: ACM, 2006, pp. 338–347. ISBN: 1-59593-318-2. DOI: 10.1145/1142351.1142399. URL: http://doi.acm.org/10.1145/1142351.1142399.

[18] Grady Booch, James Rumbaugh and Ivar Jacobson. *The Unified Modeling Language User Guide*. 1st ed. Reading, MA: Addison-Wesley, 1998. ISBN: 0-201-57168-4.

[19] Dan Brickley and R.V. Guha, eds. *RDF Schema 1.1*. 25th Feb. 2014. URL: http://www.w3.org/TR/2014/REC-rdf-schema-20140225/.

[20] Saartje Brockmans, Peter Haase, Luciano Serafini and Heiner Stuckenschmidt. “Formal and Conceptual Comparison of Ontology Mapping Languages”. In: *Modular Ontologies*. Ed. by Heiner Stuckenschmidt, Christine Parent and Stefano Spaccapietra. Vol. 5445. Lecture Notes in Computer Science. Springer Berlin Heidelberg, 2009, pp. 267–291. ISBN: 978-3-642-01906-7. DOI: 10.1007/978-3-642-01907-4_13. URL: http://dx.doi.org/10.1007/978-3-642-01907-4_13.

[21] Manfred Broy. “Challenges in Automotive Software Engineering”. In: *Proceedings of the 28th International Conference on Software Engineering*. ICSE ’06. Shanghai, China: ACM, 2006, pp. 33–42. ISBN: 1-59593-375-1. DOI: 10.1145/1134285.1134292. URL: http://doi.acm.org/10.1145/1134285.1134292.

[22] Cédric Brun and Alfonso Pierantonio. “Model Differences in the Eclipse Modelling Framework”. In: *UPGRADE The European Journal for the Informatics Professional* IX.2 (2008), pp. 29–34. URL: http://www.cepis.org/upgrade/files/2008-II-pierantonio.pdf.

[23] Hugo Bruneliere, Jordi Cabot, Frédéric Jouault and Frédéric Madiot. "MoDisco: a generic and extensible framework for model driven reverse engineering". In: *Proceedings of the IEEE/ACM international conference on Automated software engineering*. ASE '10. Antwerp, Belgium: ACM, 2010, pp. 173–174. ISBN: 978-1-4503-0116-9. DOI: 10.1145/1858996.1859032. URL: http://doi.acm.org/10.1145/1858996.1859032.

[24] H. W. Buff. "Why Codd's Rule No. 6 Must be Reformulated". In: *SIGMOD Record* 17.4 (1988), pp. 79–80.

[25] Erik Burger. "Flexible Views for Rapid Model-Driven Development". In: *Proceedings of the 1st Workshop on View-Based, Aspect-Oriented and Orthographic Software Modelling*. VAO '13. Montpellier, France: ACM, 2013, 1:1–1:5. ISBN: 978-1-4503-2070-2. DOI: 10.1145/2489861.2489863. URL: http://doi.acm.org/10.1145/2489861.2489863.

[26] Erik Burger. "Flexible Views for View-Based Model-Driven Development". In: *Proceedings of the 18th international doctoral symposium on Components and architecture*. WCOP '13. Vancouver, British Columbia, Canada: ACM, 2013, pp. 25–30. ISBN: 978-1-4503-2125-9. DOI: 10.1145/2465498.2465501. URL: http://doi.acm.org/10.1145/2465498.2465501.

[27] Erik Burger and Boris Gruschko. "A Change Metamodel for the Evolution of MOF-Based Metamodels". In: *Proceedings of Modellierung 2010*. Ed. by Gregor Engels, Dimitris Karagiannis and Heinrich C. Mayr. Vol. P-161. GI-LNI. Klagenfurt, Austria, 26th Mar. 2010. URL: http://sdqweb.ipd.kit.edu/publications/pdfs/burger2010a.pdf.

[28] Erik Burger, Jörg Henß, Steffen Kruse, Martin Küster, Andreas Rentschler and Lucia Happe. *ModelJoin. A Textual Domain-Specific Language for the Combination of Heterogeneous Models*. Tech. rep.

1. Karlsruhe Institute of Technology, Faculty of Informatics, 2014. URL: http://digbib.ubka.uni-karlsruhe.de/volltexte/1000037908.

[29] Erik Burger, Jörg Henß, Martin Küster, Steffen Kruse and Lucia Happe. "View-Based Model-Driven Software Development with ModelJoin". English. In: *Software and Systems Modeling* 14 (2014). Ed. by Robert France and Bernhard Rumpe, pp. 1–24. ISSN: 1619-1366. DOI: 10.1007/s10270-014-0413-5.

[30] Erik Burger and Aleksandar Toshovski. "Difference-based Conformance Checking for Ecore Metamodels". In: *Proceedings of Modellierung 2014*. Vol. 225. GI-LNI. Vienna, Austria, 21st Mar. 2014. URL: http://sdqweb.ipd.kit.edu/publications/pdfs/burger2014a.pdf.

[31] Andrew Carton, Cormac Driver, Andrew Jackson and Siobhán Clarke. "Model-Driven Theme/UML". In: *Transactions on Aspect-Oriented Software Development VI*. Ed. by Shmuel Katz, Harold Ossher, Robert France and Jean-Marc Jézéquel. Vol. 5560. Lecture Notes in Computer Science. Springer Berlin Heidelberg, 2009, pp. 238–266. ISBN: 978-3-642-03763-4. DOI: 10.1007/978-3-642-03764-1_7. URL: http://dx.doi.org/10.1007/978-3-642-03764-1_7.

[32] Ruzanna Chitchyan, Awais Rashid, Pete Sawyer, Alessandro Garcia, Mónica Pinto Alarcon, Jethro Bakker, Bedir Tekinerdoğan, Siobhán Clarke and Andrew Jackson. *Survey of Analysis and Design Approaches*. Tech. rep. AOSD-Europe, May 2005. URL: http://www.comp.lancs.ac.uk/computing/aod/papers/d11.pdf.

[33] Antonio Cicchetti, Federico Ciccozzi and Thomas Leveque. "A hybrid approach for multi-view modeling". In: *Electronic Communications of the EASST* 50 (2011).

[34] Antonio Cicchetti, Davide Di Ruscio and Alfonso Pierantonio. "A Metamodel Independent Approach to Difference Representation". In: *Journal of Object Technology* 6.9 (Oct. 2007). Ed. by Jean Bézivin and Bertrand Meyer. TOOLS EUROPE 2007 — Objects, Models, Components, Patterns, pp. 165–185. ISSN: 1660-1769. DOI: 10.5381/jot.2007.6.9.a9. URL: http://www.jot.fm/contents/issue_2007_10/paper9.html.

[35] Siobhán Clarke and Elisa Baniassad. *Aspect-Oriented Analysis and Design*. Addison-Wesley Professional, 2005. ISBN: 0321246748.

[36] Siobhán Clarke, William Harrison, Harold Ossher and Peri Tarr. "Subject-oriented design: towards improved alignment of requirements, design, and code". In: *ACM SIGPLAN Notices* 34.10 (Oct. 1999), pp. 325–339. URL: http://www.acm.org/pubs/citations/proceedings/oops/320384/p325-clarke/.

[37] Edgar Frank Codd. *The relational model for database management: version 2*. Boston, MA, USA: Addison-Wesley Longman Publishing Co., Inc., 1990. ISBN: 0-201-14192-2.

[38] Derek Coleman, Patrick Arnold, Stephanie Bodoff, Helena Gilchrist, Fiona Hayes and Paul Jeremaes. *Object-oriented Development: the Fusion method*. Englewood Cliffs, NJ: Prentice Hall, 1994.

[39] Yanja Dajsuren, Mark van den Brand, Alexander Serebrenik and Rudolf Huisman. "Automotive ADLS: A Study on Enforcing Consistency Through Multiple Architectural Levels". In: *Proceedings of the 8th International ACM SIGSOFT Conference on Quality of Software Architectures*. QoSA '12. Bertinoro, Italy: ACM, 2012, pp. 71–80. ISBN: 978-1-4503-1346-9. DOI: 10.1145/2304696.2304710. URL: http://doi.acm.org/10.1145/2304696.2304710.

[40] Umeshwar Dayal and Philip A. Bernstein. "On the Correct Translation of Update Operations on Relational Views". In: *ACM Trans. Database Syst.* 7.3 (Sept. 1982), pp. 381–416. ISSN: 0362-5915.

DOI: 10.1145/319732.319740. URL: http://doi.acm.org/10.1145/319732.319740.

[41] Juan De Lara, Hans Vangheluwe and Manuel Alfonseca. "Meta-modelling and graph grammars for multi-paradigm modelling in AToM3". In: *Software and Systems Modeling* 3.3 (2004), pp. 194–209.

[42] Trip Denton, Edward Jones, Srini Srinivasan, Ken Owens and Richard W. Buskens. "NAOMI – An Experimental Platform for Multi–modeling". In: *Model Driven Engineering Languages and Systems*. Ed. by Krzysztof Czarnecki, Ileana Ober, Jean-Michel Bruel, Axel Uhl and Markus Völter. Vol. 5301. Lecture Notes in Computer Science. Springer Berlin Heidelberg, 2008, pp. 143–157. ISBN: 978-3-540-87874-2. DOI: 10.1007/978-3-540-87875-9_10. URL: http://dx.doi.org/10.1007/978-3-540-87875-9_10.

[43] Zinovy Diskin, Yingfei Xiong, Krzysztof Czarnecki, Hartmut Ehrig, Frank Hermann and Fernando Orejas. "From State- to Delta-Based Bidirectional Model Transformations: the Asymmetric Case". In: *Journal of Object technology* 10 (2011), 6:1–25. DOI: 10.5381/jot.2011.10.1.a6.

[44] Zinovy Diskin, Yingfei Xiong, Krzysztof Czarnecki, Hartmut Ehrig, Frank Hermann and Fernando Orejas. "From State- to Delta-Based Bidirectional Model Transformations: The Symmetric Case". In: *Model Driven Engineering Languages and Systems*. Ed. by Jon Whittle, Tony Clark and Thomas Kühne. Vol. 6981. Lecture Notes in Computer Science. Springer Berlin / Heidelberg, 2011, pp. 304–318. ISBN: 978-3-642-24484-1. DOI: 10.1007/978-3-642-24485-8_22.

[45] Mauro Dragoni, Chiara Francescomarino, Chiara Ghidini, Julia Clemente and Salvador Sánchez Alonso. "Guiding the Evolution of a Multilingual Ontology in a Concrete Setting". In: *The Semantic Web: Semantics and Big Data*. Ed. by Philipp Cimiano, Oscar Corcho,

Valentina Presutti, Laura Hollink and Sebastian Rudolph. Vol. 7882. Lecture Notes in Computer Science. Springer Berlin Heidelberg, 2013, pp. 608–622. ISBN: 978-3-642-38287-1. DOI: 10.1007/978-3-642-38288-8_41. URL: http://dx.doi.org/10.1007/978-3-642-38288-8_41.

[46] *EAST-ADL Domain Model Specification.* Version 2.1.12. EAST-ADL Association. Nov. 2013. URL: http://www.east-adl.info/Specification/V2.1.12/EAST-ADL-Specification_V2.1.12.pdf.

[47] Eclipse Foundation. *Eclipse Modeling Framework Homepage.* http://www.eclipse.org/modeling/emf/. last retrieved 2007-10-24. URL: http://www.eclipse.org/modeling/emf/.

[48] Jean-Marie Favre. "Languages Evolve Too! Changing the Software Time Scale". In: *Proceedings of the Eighth International Workshop on Principles of Software Evolution.* IWPSE '05. Washington, DC, USA: IEEE Computer Society, 2005, pp. 33–44. ISBN: 0-7695-2349-8. DOI: 10.1109/IWPSE.2005.22. URL: http://dx.doi.org/10.1109/IWPSE.2005.22.

[49] Anthony Finkelstein, Jeff Kramer, Bashar Nuseibeh, L. Finkelstein and Michael Goedicke. "Viewpoints: A Framework for Integrating Multiple Perspectives in System Development". In: *International Journal of Software Engineering and Knowledge Engineering* 2.1 (1992), pp. 31–57.

[50] J. Nathan Foster, Michael B. Greenwald, Jonathan T. Moore, Benjamin C. Pierce and Alan Schmitt. "Combinators for bi-directional tree transformations: a linguistic approach to the view update problem". In: *SIGPLAN Not.* 40.1 (Jan. 2005), pp. 233–246. ISSN: 0362-1340. DOI: 10.1145/1047659.1040325.

[51] Martin Fowler, Kent Beck, John Brant, William Opdyke and Don Roberts. *Refactoring: Improving the Design of Existing Code.* Addison-Wesley, Reading, MA, USA, 1999.

[52] Robert France and Bernhard Rumpe. “Does model driven engineering tame complexity?” English. In: *Software & Systems Modeling* 6.1 (2007), pp. 1–2. ISSN: 1619-1366. DOI: 10.1007/s10270-006-0041-9. URL: http://dx.doi.org/10.1007/s10270-006-0041-9.

[53] Holger Giese and Robert Wagner. “Incremental Model Synchronization with Triple Graph Grammars”. In: *Model Driven Engineering Languages and Systems*. Ed. by Oscar Nierstrasz, Jon Whittle, David Harel and Gianna Reggio. Vol. 4199. Lecture Notes in Computer Science. Springer Berlin / Heidelberg, 2006, pp. 543–557. ISBN: 978-3-540-45772-5.

[54] Martin Glinz, Stefan Berner and Stefan Joos. “Object-oriented modeling with Adora”. In: *Information Systems* 27.6 (2002), pp. 425–444. ISSN: 0306-4379. DOI: http://dx.doi.org/10.1016/S0306-4379(02)00015-7. URL: http://www.sciencedirect.com/science/article/pii/S0306437902000157.

[55] Michael Goedicke, Torsten Meyer and Gabriele Taentzer. “ViewPoint-Oriented Software Development by Distributed Graph Transformation: Towards a Basis for Living with Inconsistencies”. In: *Proceedings of the 4th IEEE International Symposium on Requirements Engineering*. RE ’99. Washington, DC, USA: IEEE Computer Society, 1999, pp. 92–99. ISBN: 0-7695-0188-5. URL: http://dl.acm.org/citation.cfm?id=647646.731261.

[56] Thomas Goldschmidt. “View-based textual modelling”. PhD thesis. Karlsruhe, 2011. ISBN: 978-3-86644-642-7. URL: http://digbib.ubka.uni-karlsruhe.de/volltexte/1000022234.

[57] Thomas Goldschmidt, Steffen Becker and Erik Burger. “View-Based Modelling – A Tool-Oriented Analysis”. In: *Proceedings of the Modellierung 2012*. Ed. by Elmar J. Sinz and Andy Schürr. Vol. P-201. GI-Edition – Lecture Notes in Informatics (LNI). Bamberg, Mar. 2012.

[58] Thomas Goldschmidt, Steffen Becker and Axel Uhl. "Incremental Updates for Textual Modeling of Large Scale Models". In: *Proceedings of the 15th IEEE International Conference on Engineering of Complex Computer Systems (ICECCS 2010) - Poster Paper*. IEEE, 2010.

[59] Georg Gottlob, Paolo Paolini and Roberto Zicari. "Properties and Update Semantics of Consistent Views". In: *ACM Trans. Database Syst.* 13.4 (Oct. 1988), pp. 486–524. ISSN: 0362-5915. DOI: 10.1145/49346.50068. URL: http://doi.acm.org/10.1145/49346.50068.

[60] Joel Greenyer, Sebastian Pook and Jan Rieke. "Preventing Information Loss in Incremental Model Synchronization by Reusing Elements". In: *Modelling Foundations and Applications*. Ed. by Robert B. France, Jochen M. Kuester, Behzad Bordbar and Richard F. Paige. Vol. 6698. Lecture Notes in Computer Science. Springer Berlin Heidelberg, 2011, pp. 144–159. ISBN: 978-3-642-21469-1. DOI: 10.1007/978-3-642-21470-7_11. URL: http://dx.doi.org/10.1007/978-3-642-21470-7_11.

[61] W3C SPARQL Working Group, ed. *SPARQL 1.1 Overview*. W3C Recommendation. 21st Mar. 2013. URL: http://www.w3.org/TR/2013/REC-sparql11-overview-20130321/.

[62] Thomas R. Gruber. "A translation approach to portable ontology specifications". In: *Knowledge Acquisition* 5.2 (1993), pp. 199–220. ISSN: 1042-8143. DOI: http://dx.doi.org/10.1006/knac.1993.1008. URL: http://www.sciencedirect.com/science/article/pii/S1042814383710083.

[63] Thomas Haitzer and Uwe Zdun. "Semi-automated architectural abstraction specifications for supporting software evolution". In: (Oct. 2013). URL: http://eprints.cs.univie.ac.at/3862/.

[64] Lucia Happe, Erik Burger, Max Kramer, Andreas Rentschler and Ralf Reussner. "Completion and Extension Techniques for Enterprise Software Performance Engineering". In: *Future Business Software – Current Trends in Business Software Development*. Ed. by Gino Brunetti, Thomas Feld, Joachim Schnitter, Lutz Heuser and Christian Webel. Progress in IS. New York, Heidelberg: Springer International Publishing, 2014. ISBN: 978-3-319-04143-8. DOI: 10.1007/978-3-319-04144-5.

[65] Ábel Hegedüs, Ákos Horváth, István Ráth and Dániel Varró. "Query-Driven Soft Interconnection of EMF Models". In: *Model Driven Engineering Languages and Systems*. Ed. by Robert France, Jürgen Kazmeier, Ruth Breu and Colin Atkinson. Vol. 7590. Lecture Notes in Computer Science. Springer Berlin / Heidelberg, 2012, pp. 134–150. ISBN: 978-3-642-33665-2. URL: http://dx.doi.org/10.1007/978-3-642-33666-9_10.

[66] Florian Heidenreich, Jendrik Johannes, Mirko Seifert and Christian Wende. "Closing the Gap Between Modelling and Java". In: *Software Language Engineering*. Springer, 2010, pp. 374–383.

[67] Christian Hein, Tom Ritter and Michael Wagner. "Model-Driven Tool Integration with ModelBus". In: *Workshop Future Trends of Model-Driven Development*. 2009.

[68] Christian Heinzemann and Steffen Becker. "Executing Reconfigurations in Hierarchical Component Architectures". In: *Proceedings of the 16th International ACM SigSoft Symposium on Component-Based Software Engineering (CBSE)*. ACM, 2013.

[69] Jörg Henss, Philipp Merkle and Ralf H. Reussner. "Poster Abstract: The OMPCM Simulator for Model-Based Software Performance Prediction". In: *Proceedings of the 6th International ICST Conference on Simulation Tools and Techniques*. Cannes, France, 2013.

[70] Markus Herrmannsdörfer. "COPE – A Workbench for the Coupled Evolution of Metamodels and Models". In: *Software Language Engineering*. Ed. by Brian Malloy, Steffen Staab and Mark Brand. Vol. 6563. Lecture Notes in Computer Science. Springer Berlin Heidelberg, 2011, pp. 286–295. ISBN: 978-3-642-19439-9. DOI: 10.1007/978-3-642-19440-5_18. URL: http://dx.doi.org/10.1007/978-3-642-19440-5_18.

[71] Markus Herrmannsdörfer. "Operation-based Versioning of Metamodels with COPE". In: *Proceedings of the 2009 ICSE Workshop on Comparison and Versioning of Software Models*. CVSM '09. Washington, DC, USA: IEEE Computer Society, 2009, pp. 49–54. ISBN: 978-1-4244-3714-6. DOI: 10.1109/CVSM.2009.5071722. URL: http://dx.doi.org/10.1109/CVSM.2009.5071722.

[72] Markus Herrmannsdörfer, Sander D. Vermolen and Guido Wachsmuth. "An extensive catalog of operators for the coupled evolution of metamodels and models". In: *Proceedings of the Third international conference on Software language engineering*. SLE'10. Berlin/Heidelberg: Springer, 2011, pp. 163–182. ISBN: 978-3-642-19439-9. URL: http://www4.in.tum.de/~herrmama/publications/SLE2010_herrmannsdoerfer_catalog_coupled_operators.pdf.

[73] Thomas Hettel. "Model round-trip engineering". PhD thesis. Queensland University of Technology, 2010. URL: http://eprints.qut.edu.au/32082/.

[74] Rich Hilliard. *On Metamodels in 42010*. Feb. 2011. URL: http://www.iso-architecture.org/ieee-1471/docs/Hilliard-On-Metamodels-in-42010.pdf.

[75] Rich Hilliard, Ivano Malavolta, Henry Muccini and Patrizio Pelliccione. "On the Composition and Reuse of Viewpoints across Architecture Frameworks". In: *Joint Working IEEE/IFIP Conference on Software Architecture (WICSA) and European Conference*

on Software Architecture (ECSA). Aug. 2012, pp. 131–140. DOI: 10.1109/WICSA-ECSA.212.21.

[76] "ISO/IEC Standard for Systems and Software Engineering – Recommended Practice for Architectural Description of Software-Intensive Systems". In: *ISO/IEC 42010 IEEE Std 1471-2000 First edition 2007-07-15* (July 2007), pp. c1–24. DOI: 10.1109/IEEESTD.2007.386501.

[77] *ISO/IEC/IEEE Std 42010:2011 – Systems and software engineering – Architecture description*. Los Alamitos,CA: IEEE, 2011.

[78] Rod Johnson, Juergen Hoeller, Alef Arendsen, Thomas Risberg and Dmitriy Kopylenko. *Professional Java Development with the Spring Framework*. Birmingham, UK, UK: Wrox Press Ltd., 2005. ISBN: 0764574833, 9780764574832.

[79] Frédéric Jouault and Ivan Kurtev. "Transforming models with ATL". In: *Satellite Events at the MoDELS 2005 Conference*. Vol. 3844. LNCS. Berlin: Springer Verlag, 2006, pp. 128–138. URL: http://doc.utwente.nl/61719/.

[80] Frederick Phillips Brooks Jr. "No Silver Bullet Essence and Accidents of Software Engineering". In: *Computer* 20.4 (1987), pp. 10–19. ISSN: 0018-9162. DOI: 10.1109/MC.1987.1663532.

[81] *JSR 40: Java^{TM} Metadata Interface(JMI) Specification*. 2002. URL: https://www.jcp.org/en/jsr/detail?id=40.

[82] Gregory Karvounarakis, Sofia Alexaki, Vassilis Christophides, Dimitris Plexousakis and Michel Scholl. "RQL: A Declarative Query Language for RDF". In: *Proceedings of the 11th International Conference on World Wide Web*. WWW '02. Honolulu, Hawaii, USA: ACM, 2002, pp. 592–603. ISBN: 1-58113-449-5. DOI: 10.1145/511446.511524. URL: http://doi.acm.org/10.1145/511446.511524.

[83] Timo Kehrer, Udo Kelter and Gabriele Taentzer. "A rule-based approach to the semantic lifting of model differences in the context of model versioning". In: *Proceedings of the 2011 26th IEEE/ACM International Conference on Automated Software Engineering*. ASE '11. Washington, DC, USA: IEEE Computer Society, 2011, pp. 163–172. ISBN: 978-1-4577-1638-6. DOI: 10.1109/ASE.2011.6100050. URL: http://dx.doi.org/10.1109/ASE.2011.6100050.

[84] Timo Kehrer, Udo Kelter and Gabriele Taentzer. "Consistency-preserving edit scripts in model versioning". In: *Automated Software Engineering (ASE), 2013 IEEE/ACM 28th International Conference on*. Nov. 2013, pp. 191–201. DOI: 10.1109/ASE.2013.6693079.

[85] Evgeny Kharlamov, Dmitriy Zheleznyakov and Diego Calvanese. "Capturing Model-Based Ontology Evolution at the Instance Level: The Case of DL-Lite". In: *J. of Computer and System Sciences* 79.6 (2013), pp. 835–872.

[86] Gregor Kiczales, Erik Hilsdale, Jim Hugunin, Mik Kersten, Jeffrey Palm and William G. Griswold. "An Overview of AspectJ". In: *Proceedings of the 15th European Conference on Object-Oriented Programming*. ECOOP '01. London, UK, UK: Springer-Verlag, 2001, pp. 327–353. ISBN: 3-540-42206-4. URL: http://dl.acm.org/citation.cfm?id=646158.680006.

[87] Gregor Kiczales, John Lamping, Anurag Mendhekar, Chris Maeda, Cristina Videira Lopes, Jean-Marc Loingtier and John Irwin. "Aspect-Oriented Programming". In: *Proceedings of the European Conference on Object-Oriented Programming (ECOOP)*. Finland: Springer-Verlag, Berlin, Germany, June 1997.

[88] Jacques Klein, Franck Fleurey and Jean-Marc Jézéquel. "Transactions on Aspect-oriented Software Development III". In: ed. by Awais Rashid and Mehmet Aksit. Berlin, Heidelberg: Springer-Verlag, 2007. Chap. Weaving Multiple Aspects in Sequence Dia-

grams, pp. 167–199. ISBN: 3-540-75161-0, 978-3-540-75161-8. URL: http://dl.acm.org/citation.cfm?id=1805812.1805819.

[89] Andreas Knöpfel, Bernhard Gröne and Peter Tabeling. *Fundamental Modeling Concepts: Effective Communication of IT Systems*. Wiley, 2006. ISBN: 978-0-470-02710-3.

[90] Dimitrios S. Kolovos, Richard F. Paige and Fiona A.C. Polack. "The Epsilon Transformation Language". In: *Theory and Practice of Model Transformations*. Ed. by Antonio Vallecillo, Jeff Gray and Alfonso Pierantonio. Vol. 5063. Lecture Notes in Computer Science. Springer Berlin Heidelberg, 2008, pp. 46–60. ISBN: 978-3-540-69926-2. DOI: 10.1007/978-3-540-69927-9_4. URL: http://dx.doi.org/10.1007/978-3-540-69927-9_4.

[91] Dimitrios S. Kolovos, Louis M. Rose, Nikolaos Drivalos Matragkas, Richard F. Paige, Fiona A.C. Polack and Kiran J. Fernandes. "Constructing and Navigating Non-invasive Model Decorations". In: *Theory and Practice of Model Transformations*. Ed. by Laurence Tratt and Martin Gogolla. Vol. 6142. Lecture Notes in Computer Science. Springer Berlin Heidelberg, 2010, pp. 138–152. ISBN: 978-3-642-13687-0. DOI: 10.1007/978-3-642-13688-7_10. URL: http://dx.doi.org/10.1007/978-3-642-13688-7_10.

[92] Patrick Könemann. "Capturing the Intention of Model Changes". In: *Model Driven Engineering Languages and Systems*. Ed. by DorinaC. Petriu, Nicolas Rouquette and Øystein Haugen. Vol. 6395. Lecture Notes in Computer Science. Springer Berlin Heidelberg, 2010, pp. 108–122. ISBN: 978-3-642-16128-5. DOI: 10.1007/978-3-642-16129-2_9. URL: http://dx.doi.org/10.1007/978-3-642-16129-2_9.

[93] Heiko Koziolek. "Parameter Dependencies for Reusable Performance Specificationsof Software Components". PhD thesis. University

of Oldenburg, 2008. URL: http://sdqweb.ipd.uka.de/publications/pdfs/koziolek2008g.pdf.

[94] Heiko Koziolek, Steffen Becker and Jens Happe. “Predicting the Performance of Component-based Software Architectures with different Usage Profiles”. In: *Proc. 3rd International Conference on the Quality of Software Architectures (QoSA’07)*. Vol. 4880. Lecture Notes in Computer Science. Springer-Verlag Berlin Heidelberg, July 2007, pp. 145–163. URL: http://sdqweb.ipd.uka.de/publications/pdfs/koziolek2007b.pdf.

[95] Max E. Kramer, Erik Burger and Michael Langhammer. “View-centric engineering with synchronized heterogeneous models”. In: *Proceedings of the 1st Workshop on View-Based, Aspect-Oriented and Orthographic Software Modelling*. VAO ’13. Montpellier, France: ACM, 2013, 5:1–5:6. ISBN: 978-1-4503-2070-2. DOI: 10.1145/2489861.2489864. URL: http://doi.acm.org/10.1145/2489861.2489864.

[96] Max E. Kramer, Zoya Durdik, Michael Hauck, Jörg Henss, Martin Küster, Philipp Merkle and Andreas Rentschler. “Extending the Palladio Component Model using Profiles and Stereotypes”. In: *Palladio Days 2012 Proceedings (appeared as technical report)*. Ed. by Steffen Becker, Jens Happe, Anne Koziolek and Ralf Reussner. Karlsruhe Reports in Informatics ; 2012,21. Karlsruhe: KIT, Faculty of Informatics, 2012, pp. 7–15. URL: http://digbib.ubka.uni-karlsruhe.de/volltexte/documents/2350659.

[97] Philippe Kruchten. *The Rational Unified Process: An Introduction*. 3. ed., 6. pr. Addison-Wesley object technology series. Upper Saddle River, NJ [u.a.]: Addison-Wesley, 2007. ISBN: 0-321-19770-4.

[98] Philippe B. Kruchten. “The 4+1 View Model of Architecture”. In: *Software, IEEE* 12.6 (Nov. 1995), pp. 42–50. ISSN: 0740-7459. DOI: 10.1109/52.469759.

[99] *On the Use of Operators for the Co-Evolution of Metamodels and Transformations*. 2011.

[100] Philip Langer, Tanja Mayerhofer, Manuel Wimmer and Gerti Kappel. "On the Usage of UML: Initial Results of Analyzing Open UML Models". In: *Proceedings of Modellierung 2014*. Vol. 225. GI-LNI. Vienna, Austria, 21st Mar. 2014, pp. 289–304.

[101] Philip Langer, Konrad Wieland, Manuel Wimmer and Jordi Cabot. "EMF Profiles: A Lightweight Extension Approach for EMF Models". In: *Journal of Object Technology* 11.1 (2012), 8:1–29. ISSN: 1660-1769. DOI: 10.5381/jot.2012.11.1.a8.

[102] Philip Langer, Manuel Wimmer, Petra Brosch, Markus Herrmannsdörfer, Martina Seidl, Konrad Wieland and Gerti Kappel. "A posteriori operation detection in evolving software models". In: *Journal of Systems and Software* 86.2 (2013), pp. 551–566. ISSN: 0164-1212. DOI: http://dx.doi.org/10.1016/j.jss.2012.09.037. URL: http://www.sciencedirect.com/science/article/pii/S0164121212002762.

[103] Michael Langhammer. "Co-evolution of component-based architecture-model and object-oriented source code". In: *Proceedings of the 18th international doctoral symposium on Components and architecture*. ACM. 2013, pp. 37–42.

[104] Michael Langhammer, Sebastian Lehrig and Max E. Kramer. "Reuse and configuration for code generating architectural refinement transformations". In: *Proceedings of the 1st Workshop on View-Based, Aspect-Oriented and Orthographic Software Modelling*. VAO '13. Montpellier, France: ACM, 2013, 6:1–6:5. ISBN: 978-1-4503-2070-2. DOI: 10.1145/2489861.2489866. URL: http://doi.acm.org/10.1145/2489861.2489866.

[105] Erhan Leblebici, Anthony Anjorin and Andy Schürr. "Developing eMoflon with eMoflon". In: *ICMT 2014*. Lecture Notes in Computer Science (LNCS). accepted for publication. Springer Verlag. Heidelberg: Springer Verlag, 2014.

[106] Jens Lechtenbörger. "The impact of the constant complement approach towards view updating". In: *Proceedings of the twenty-second ACM SIGMOD-SIGACT-SIGART symposium on Principles of database systems*. PODS '03. New York, NY, USA: ACM, 2003, pp. 49–55. ISBN: 1-58113-670-6. DOI: 10.1145/773153.773159.

[107] Jens Lechtenbörger and Gottfried Vossen. "On the Computation of Relational View Complements". In: *ACM Trans. Database Syst.* 28.2 (June 2003), pp. 175–208. ISSN: 0362-5915. DOI: 10.1145/777943.777946. URL: http://doi.acm.org/10.1145/777943.777946.

[108] Edward A. Lee. "Cyber Physical Systems: Design Challenges". In: *Object Oriented Real-Time Distributed Computing (ISORC), 2008 11th IEEE International Symposium on*. 2008, pp. 363–369. DOI: 10.1109/ISORC.2008.25.

[109] Sebastian Lehrig and Thomas Zolynski. "Performance Prototyping with ProtoCom in a Virtualised Environment: A Case Study". In: *Palladio Days 2011 Proceedings (appeared as technical report)*. Ed. by Steffen Becker, Jens Happe and Ralf Reussner. Karlsruhe Reports in Informatics ; 2011,32. Karlsruhe: KIT, Fakultät für Informatik, 2011, pp. 15–22. URL: http://digbib.ubka.uni-karlsruhe.de/volltexte/1000025188.

[110] Bennett P. Lientz and E. Burton Swanson. *Software Maintenance Management*. Boston, MA, USA: Addison-Wesley Longman Publishing Co., Inc., 1980. ISBN: 0201042053.

[111] Ivano Malavolta, Henry Muccini, Patrizio Pelliccione and Damian A. Tamburri. "Providing Architectural Languages and Tools Interoperability through Model Transformation Technologies". In: *Software*

Engineering, IEEE Transactions on 36.1 (Jan. 2010), pp. 119–140. ISSN: 0098-5589. DOI: 10.1109/TSE.2009.51.

[112] *OMG Model Driven Architecture*. URL: http://www.omg.org/mda/.

[113] Philipp Meier, Samuel Kounev and Heiko Koziolek. "Automated Transformation of Component-Based Software Architecture Models to Queueing Petri Nets". In: *Modeling, Analysis Simulation of Computer and Telecommunication Systems (MASCOTS), 2011 IEEE 19th International Symposium on*. July 2011, pp. 339–348. DOI: 10.1109/MASCOTS.2011.23.

[114] William Mendenhall, Robert J. Beaver and Barbara M. Beaver. *Introduction to Probability and Statistics*. 12th ed. Stamford, CT: Cengage Learning, 2005. ISBN: 9780534418700.

[115] Philipp Merkle and Jörg Henss. "EventSim – An Event-driven Palladio Software Architecture Simulator". In: *Palladio Days 2011 Proceedings (appeared as technical report)*. Ed. by Steffen Becker, Jens Happe and Ralf Reussner. Karlsruhe Reports in Informatics ; 2011,32. Karlsruhe: KIT, Fakultät für Informatik, 2011, pp. 15–22. URL: http://digbib.ubka.uni-karlsruhe.de/volltexte/1000025188.

[116] *Meta Object Facility (MOF) 2.0 Query/View/Transformation Specification*. Object Management Group. January 2011. URL: http://www.omg.org/spec/QVT/1.1/.

[117] *Meta Object Facility (MOF) Core*. Version 2.4.1. Object Management Group. August 2011. URL: http://www.omg.org/spec/MOF/2.4.1/.

[118] Object Management Group (OMG). *MOF 2.0 Core Specification (formal/2006-01-01)*. 2006. URL: http://www.omg.org/cgi-bin/doc?formal/2006-01-01.

[119] Francesco Moscato, Francesco Flammini, G. Di Lorenzo, Valerio Vittorini, Stefano Marrone and Mauro Iacono. "The Software Architecture of the OsMoSys Multisolution Framework". In: *Proceedings of the 2Nd International Conference on Performance Evaluation Methodologies and Tools*. ValueTools '07. Nantes, France: ICST (Institute for Computer Sciences, Social-Informatics and Telecommunications Engineering), 2007, 51:1–51:10. ISBN: 978-963-9799-00-4. URL: http://dl.acm.org/citation.cfm?id=1345263.1345328.

[120] Shin-Cheng Mu, Zhenjiang Hu and Masato Takeichi. "An Injective Language for Reversible Computation". In: *Mathematics of Program Construction*. Ed. by Dexter Kozen. Vol. 3125. Lecture Notes in Computer Science. Springer Berlin Heidelberg, 2004, pp. 289–313. ISBN: 978-3-540-22380-1. DOI: 10.1007/978-3-540-27764-4_16. URL: http://dx.doi.org/10.1007/978-3-540-27764-4_16.

[121] Natalya F. Noy and Mark A. Musen. "Traversing Ontologies to Extract Views". In: *Modular Ontologies*. Ed. by Heiner Stuckenschmidt, Christine Parent and Stefano Spaccapietra. Vol. 5445. Lecture Notes in Computer Science. Springer Berlin Heidelberg, 2009, pp. 245–260. ISBN: 978-3-642-01906-7. DOI: 10.1007/978-3-642-01907-4_11. URL: http://dx.doi.org/10.1007/978-3-642-01907-4_11.

[122] Bashar Nuseibeh, Jeff Kramer and Anthony Finkelstein. "A framework for expressing the relationships between multiple views in requirements specification". In: *Software Engineering, IEEE Transactions on* 20.10 (1994), pp. 760–773. ISSN: 0098-5589. DOI: 10.1109/32.328995.

[123] *OMG Object Constraint Language (OCL)*. Object Management Group. Jan. 2012. URL: http://www.omg.org/spec/OCL/2.3.1/.

[124] *OMG Systems Modeling Language (OMG SysML)*. Version 1.3. Object Management Group. June 2012. URL: http://www.omg.org/spec/SysML/1.3/.

[125] *OMG Unified Modeling Language (UML)*. Object Management Group. Aug. 2011. URL: http://www.omg.org/spec/UML/2.4.1/.

[126] W3C OWL Working Group, ed. *OWL 2 Web Ontology Language: Document Overview*. W3C Recommendation. 11th Dec. 2012. URL: http://www.w3.org/TR/2012/REC-owl2-overview-20121211/.

[127] Christine Parent and Stefano Spaccapietra. "An Overview of Modularity". In: *Modular Ontologies*. Ed. by Heiner Stuckenschmidt, Christine Parent and Stefano Spaccapietra. Vol. 5445. Lecture Notes in Computer Science. Springer Berlin Heidelberg, 2009, pp. 5–23. ISBN: 978-3-642-01906-7. DOI: 10.1007/978-3-642-01907-4_2. URL: http://dx.doi.org/10.1007/978-3-642-01907-4_2.

[128] Jan Polowinski. "Towards RVL: A Declarative Language for Visualizing RDFS/OWL Data". In: *Proceedings of the 3rd International Conference on Web Intelligence, Mining and Semantics*. WIMS '13. Madrid, Spain: ACM, 2013, 38:1–38:11. ISBN: 978-1-4503-1850-1. DOI: 10.1145/2479787.2479825. URL: http://doi.acm.org/10.1145/2479787.2479825.

[129] Jorge Posada, Carlos Toro, Stefan Wundrak and Andre Stork. "Using ontologies and STEP standards for the semantic simplification of CAD models in different engineering domains". In: *Applied Ontology* 1.3 (2006), pp. 263–279. URL: http://iospress.metapress.com/content/1XBR3P1MVJD7NT4P.

[130] Michael J. Pratt. "Introduction to ISO 10303—the STEP Standard for Product Data Exchange". In: *Journal of Computing and Information Science in Engineering* 1.1 (2001), pp. 102–103. ISSN: 1530-9827. DOI: 10.1115/1.1354995.

[131] Janis Putman. *Architecting with RM-ODP*. Upper Saddle River, NJ: Prentice Hall, 2001.

[132] Rajagopal Rajugan, Elizabeth Chang and Tharam S. Dillon. "Ontology Views: A Theoretical Perspective". In: *On the Move to Meaningful Internet Systems 2006: OTM 2006 Workshops*. Ed. by Robert Meersman, Zahir Tari and Pilar Herrero. Vol. 4278. Lecture Notes in Computer Science. Springer Berlin Heidelberg, 2006, pp. 1814–1824. ISBN: 978-3-540-48273-4. DOI: 10.1007/11915072_88. URL: http://dx.doi.org/10.1007/11915072_88.

[133] M.P. Reddy, Bandreddi E. Prasad, P.G. Reddy and Amar Gupta. "A methodology for integration of heterogeneous databases". In: *IEEE Transactions on Knowledge and Data Engineering* 6.6 (Dec. 1994), pp. 920–933. ISSN: 1041-4347. DOI: 10.1109/69.334882.

[134] Ralf Reussner, Steffen Becker, Erik Burger, Jens Happe, Michael Hauck, Anne Koziolek, Heiko Koziolek, Klaus Krogmann and Michael Kuperberg. *The Palladio Component Model*. Tech. rep. Karlsruhe: KIT, Fakultät für Informatik, 2011. URL: http://digbib.ubka.uni-karlsruhe.de/volltexte/1000022503.

[135] Cornelius Rosse and José L.V. Mejino Jr. "The Foundational Model of Anatomy Ontology". In: *Anatomy Ontologies for Bioinformatics*. Ed. by Albert Burger, Duncan Davidson and Richard Baldock. Vol. 6. Computational Biology. Springer London, 2008, pp. 59–117. ISBN: 978-1-84628-884-5. DOI: 10.1007/978-1-84628-885-2_4. URL: http://dx.doi.org/10.1007/978-1-84628-885-2_4.

[136] James Rumbaugh, Michael Blaha, William Premerlani, Frederick Eddy and William Lorenson. *Object-Oriented Modeling and Design*. 1. Englewood Cliffs, NJ: Prentice Hall, Inc., Oct. 1991.

[137] Douglas C. Schmidt. "Guest Editor's Introduction: Model-Driven Engineering". In: *Computer* 39.2 (2006), pp. 25–31. ISSN: 0018-

9162. DOI: http://doi.ieeecomputersociety.org/10.1109/MC.2006.58.

[138] Andy Schürr. "Specification of graph translators with triple graph grammars". In: *Graph-Theoretic Concepts in Computer Science*. Ed. by Ernst W. Mayr, Gunther Schmidt and Gottfried Tinhofer. Vol. 903. Lecture Notes in Computer Science. Springer Berlin Heidelberg, 1995, pp. 151–163. ISBN: 978-3-540-59071-2. DOI: 10.1007/3-540-59071-4_45. URL: http://dx.doi.org/10.1007/3-540-59071-4_45.

[139] Christoph Seidl, Ina Schaefer and Uwe Aßmann. "DeltaEcore – A Model-Based Delta Language Generation Framework". In: *Proceedings of Modellierung 2014*. Vol. 225. GI-LNI. Vienna, Austria, 21st Mar. 2014.

[140] Amit P. Sheth and James A. Larson. "Federated database systems for managing distributed, heterogeneous, and autonomous databases". In: *ACM Comput. Surv.* 22 (3 Sept. 1990), pp. 183–236. ISSN: 0360-0300. DOI: 10.1145/96602.96604.

[141] Andrea Sindico, Marco Di Natale and Gianpiero Panci. "Integrating SysML with Simulink using Open-source Model Transformations." In: *SIMULTECH*. Ed. by Janusz Kacprzyk, Nuno Pina and Joaquim Filipe. SciTePress, 2011, pp. 45–56. ISBN: 978-989-8425-78-2. URL: http://dblp.uni-trier.de/db/conf/simultech/simultech2011.html#SindicoNP11.

[142] Carl-Johan Sjöstedt, Martin Törngren, Jianlin Shi, De-Jiu Chen and Viktor Ahlsten. "Mapping Simulink to UML in the design of embedded systems: Investigating scenarios and transformations". In: *OMER4 Post-proceedings, 2008*. QC 20100810. 2008, pp. 137–160.

[143] Hyun Seung Son, Woo Yeol Kim, Robert Young Chul Kim and Hang-Gi Min. "Metamodel Design for Model Transformation from

Simulink to ECML in Cyber Physical Systems". In: *Computer Applications for Graphics, Grid Computing, and Industrial Environment*. Ed. by Tai-hoon Kim, Hyun-seob Cho, Osvaldo Gervasi and Stephen S. Yau. Vol. 351. Communications in Computer and Information Science. Springer Berlin Heidelberg, 2012, pp. 56–60. ISBN: 978-3-642-35599-8. DOI: 10.1007/978-3-642-35600-1_8. URL: http://dx.doi.org/10.1007/978-3-642-35600-1_8.

[144] Herbert Stachowiak. *Allgemeine Modelltheorie*. Springer Verlag, Wien, 1973. ISBN: 3-211-81106-0.

[145] Jim Steel and Jean-Marc Jézéquel. "On model typing". English. In: *Software & Systems Modeling* 6.4 (2007), pp. 401–413. ISSN: 1619-1366. DOI: 10.1007/s10270-006-0036-6. URL: http://dx.doi.org/10.1007/s10270-006-0036-6.

[146] Perdita Stevens. "Bidirectional model transformations in QVT: semantic issues and open questions". English. In: *Software & Systems Modeling* 9.1 (2010), pp. 7–20. ISSN: 1619-1366. DOI: 10.1007/s10270-008-0109-9. URL: http://dx.doi.org/10.1007/s10270-008-0109-9.

[147] Heiner Stuckenschmidt and Michael Uschold. "Representation of Semantic Mappings." In: *Semantic Interoperability and Integration*. Ed. by Yannis Kalfoglou, W. Marco Schorlemmer, Amit P. Sheth, Steffen Staab and Michael Uschold. Vol. 04391. Dagstuhl Seminar Proceedings. IBFI, Schloss Dagstuhl, Germany, 12th Apr. 2005. URL: http://dblp.uni-trier.de/db/conf/dagstuhl/P4391.html#StuckenschmidtU05.

[148] Gabriele Taentzer, Claudia Ermel, Philip Langer and Manuel Wimmer. "A fundamental approach to model versioning based on graph modifications: from theory to implementation". English. In: *Software and Systems Modeling* 13.1 (2014), pp. 239–272. ISSN: 1619-

1366. DOI: 10.1007/s10270-012-0248-x. URL: http://dx.doi.org/10.1007/s10270-012-0248-x.

[149] Christian Thum, Michael Schwind and Martin Schader. "SLIM—A Lightweight Environment for Synchronous Collaborative Modeling". In: *Model Driven Engineering Languages and Systems*. Ed. by Andy Schürr and Bran Selic. Vol. 5795. Lecture Notes in Computer Science. Berlin/Heidelberg: Springer, 2009, pp. 137–151.

[150] Aleksandar Toshovski. "Wiederverwendung von Metamodellen in ModelJoin-Sichten". MA thesis. Am Fasanengarten 5, 76131 Karlsruhe, Germany: Karlsruhe Institute of Technology (KIT), July 2013. URL: http://sdqweb.ipd.kit.edu/publications/pdfs/toshovski2013a.pdf.

[151] Marcel Verhoef, Thomas Liebich and Robert Amor. "A multi-paradigm mapping method survey". In: *Workshop on Modeling of Buildings through their Life-cycle*. Stanford University, California, USA, 1995, pp. 233–247.

[152] V. Vittorini, M. Iacono, N. Mazzocca and G. Franceschinis. "The OsMoSys approach to multi-formalism modeling of systems". English. In: *Software and Systems Modeling* 3.1 (2004), pp. 68–81. ISSN: 1619-1366. DOI: 10.1007/s10270-003-0039-5. URL: http://dx.doi.org/10.1007/s10270-003-0039-5.

[153] Christian Vogel, Heiko Koziolek, Thomas Goldschmidt and Erik Burger. "Rapid Performance Modeling by Transforming Use Case Maps to Palladio Component Models". In: *Proceedings of the 4th ACM/SPEC International Conference on Performance Engineering*. ICPE '13. Prague, Czech Republic: ACM, 2013, pp. 101–112. ISBN: 978-1-4503-1636-1. DOI: 10.1145/2479871.2479888. URL: http://doi.acm.org/10.1145/2479871.2479888.

[154] Guido Wachsmuth. “Metamodel Adaptation and Model Co-adaptation”. In: *ECOOP 2007 – Object-Oriented Programming*. Ed. by Erik Ernst. Vol. 4609. Lecture Notes in Computer Science. Springer Berlin Heidelberg, 2007, pp. 600–624. ISBN: 978-3-540-73588-5. DOI: 10.1007/978-3-540-73589-2_28. URL: http://dx.doi.org/10.1007/978-3-540-73589-2_28.

[155] Dennis Westermann, Jens Happe and Roozbeh Farahbod. “An Experiment Specification Language for Goal-Driven, Automated Performance Evaluations”. In: *Proc. of the ACM Symposium on Applied Computing, SAC 2013*. 2013, to appear.

[156] Manuel Wimmer, Andrea Schauerhuber, Gerti Kappel, Werner Retschitzegger, Wieland Schwinger and Elizabeth Kapsammer. “A survey on UML-based aspect-oriented design modeling”. In: *ACM Comput. Surv.* 43 (4 Oct. 2011), 28:1–28:33. ISSN: 0360-0300. DOI: 10.1145/1978802.1978807.

[157] A.T. Wood-Harper, Lyn Antill and D.E. Avison. *Information systems definition: the multiview approach*. Computer science texts. Blackwell Scientific, 1985.

[158] Object Management Group (OMG). *Meta Object Facility (MOF) 2.0 XMI Mapping Specification, v2.1 (formal/05-09-01)*. 2006. URL: http://www.omg.org/cgi-bin/apps/doc?formal/05-09-01.pdf.

[159] Fouad Zablith, Grigoris Antoniou, Mathieu d’Aquin, Giorgos Flouris, Haridimos Kondylakis, Enrico Motta, Dimitris Plexousakis and Marta Sabou. “Ontology evolution: a process-centric survey”. In: *The Knowledge Engineering Review* FirstView (May 2014), pp. 1–31. ISSN: 1469-8005. DOI: 10.1017/S0269888913000349. URL: http://journals.cambridge.org/article_S0269888913000349.

[160] Rixin Zhang and Ajay Krishnan. “Using Delta Model for Collaborative Work of Industrial Large-Scaled E/E Architecture Models”. In: *Model Driven Engineering Languages and Systems*. Ed. by Jon

Whittle, Tony Clark and Thomas Kühne. Vol. 6981. Lecture Notes in Computer Science. Springer Berlin / Heidelberg, 2011, pp. 714–728. ISBN: 978-3-642-24484-1. DOI: 10.1007/978-3-642-24485-8_52.

The Karlsruhe Series on Software Design and Quality

Edited by Prof. Dr. Ralf Reussner // ISSN 1867-0067

Band 1 **Steffen Becker**
Coupled Model Transformations for QoS Enabled Component-Based Software Design. 2008
ISBN 978-3-86644-271-9

Band 2 **Heiko Koziolek**
Parameter Dependencies for Reusable Performance Specifications of Software Components. 2008
ISBN 978-3-86644-272-6

Band 3 **Jens Happe**
Predicting Software Performance in Symmetric Multi-core and Multiprocessor Environments. 2009
ISBN 978-3-86644-381-5

Band 4 **Klaus Krogmann**
Reconstruction of Software Component Architectures and Behaviour Models using Static and Dynamic Analysis. 2012
ISBN 978-3-86644-804-9

Band 5 **Michael Kuperberg**
Quantifying and Predicting the Influence of Execution Platform on Software Component Performance. 2010
ISBN 978-3-86644-741-7

Band 6 **Thomas Goldschmidt**
View-Based Textual Modelling. 2011
ISBN 978-3-86644-642-7

Die Bände sind unter www.ksp.kit.edu als PDF frei verfügbar oder als Druckausgabe bestellbar.

The Karlsruhe Series on Software Design and Quality

Edited by Prof. Dr. Ralf Reussner // ISSN 1867-0067

Band 7 **Anne Koziolek**
Automated Improvement of Software Architecture Models for Performance and Other Quality Attributes. 2013
ISBN 978-3-86644-973-2

Band 8 **Lucia Happe**
Configurable Software Performance Completions through Higher-Order Model Transformations. 2013
ISBN 978-3-86644-990-9

Band 9 **Franz Brosch**
Integrated Software Architecture-Based Reliability Prediction for IT Systems. 2012
ISBN 978-3-86644-859-9

Band 10 **Christoph Rathfelder**
Modelling Event-Based Interactions in Component-Based Architectures for Quantitative System Evaluation. 2013
ISBN 978-3-86644-969-5

Band 11 **Henning Groenda**
Certifying Software Component Performance Specifications. 2013
ISBN 978-3-7315-0080-3

Band 12 **Dennis Westermann**
Deriving Goal-oriented Performance Models by Systematic Experimentation. 2014
ISBN 978-3-7315-0165-7

Die Bände sind unter www.ksp.kit.edu als PDF frei verfügbar oder als Druckausgabe bestellbar.

The Karlsruhe Series on Software Design and Quality

Edited by Prof. Dr. Ralf Reussner // ISSN 1867-0067

Band 13 **Michael Hauck**
Automated Experiments for Deriving Performance-relevant Properties of Software Execution Environments. 2014
ISBN 978-3-7315-0138-1

Band 14 **Zoya Durdik**
Architectural Design Decision Documentation through Reuse of Design Patterns. 2014
ISBN 978-3-7315-0292-0

Band 15 **Erik Burger**
Flexible Views for View-based Model-driven Development. 2014
ISBN 978-3-7315-0276-0

Die Bände sind unter www.ksp.kit.edu als PDF frei verfügbar oder als Druckausgabe bestellbar.